Antony Hopkins, composer and conductor, was born in 1921 and educated at Berkhampstead School and the Royal College of Music. He soon became known as a composer of incidental music for the radio, and has since written numerous scores for the BBC, chamber operas, and music for plays, films and ballets. He is a former Professor of the Royal College of Music and Gresham Professor of Music, City University, London. He is a regular broadcaster, perhaps most famous for his series called *Talking About Music*.

His other books include *Music All Around Me* and *Lucy and Peterkin*. This book was previously published in three volumes as *Talking About Symphonies*, *Talking About Concertos* and *Talking About Sonatas*.

ANTONY HOPKINS

# TALKING ABOUT MUSIC

Symphonies, Concertos and Sonatas

illustrated by John Barkwith

Pan Books London and Sydney

First published in Great Britain by
Heinemann Educational Books Ltd in three volumes:
*Talking about Symphonies* (1961), *Talking about Concertos* (1964)
and *Talking about Sonatas* (1971)
This one-volume edition published 1977 by Pan Books Ltd,
Cavaye Place, London SW10 9PG
© Anthony Hopkins 1961, 1964, 1971
ISBN 0 330 24824 3
Printed in Great Britain by
Richard Clay (The Chaucer Press) Ltd, Bungay, Suffolk

to Roger Fiske, Walter Todds
and the late Arthur Langford

PART 2

# Talking about Concertos

# PART 3

# Talking about Sonatas

NOTE It is impossible in writing a book of this nature to gauge accurately just how much the reader already knows. If I have, at times, wasted space on fairly elementary matters like key relationships, I ask the knowledgeable reader to be indulgent; if at other times I have assumed too much, I would remind the less-informed that there are many excellent books on the rudiments of music which will clear up any obscurities. A.H.

PART I

# TALKING ABOUT SYMPHONIES

## CHAPTER I

# KNOWING THE FORM

To hear music is a pleasant relaxation; to listen to it properly demands one's full attention. It is a communication between minds, and nobody can expect fully to enjoy listening to any large-scale work, be it a symphony, a sonata or a concerto, unless he has at least a basic knowledge of form and its relevance to musical thought.

Such music is conceived by the composer in an almost entirely intellectual way; it is neither 'mood' music nor 'programme' music. One might say that the first movement of a symphony, in particular, is to music what the thesis or monograph is to literature; in it the composer selects certain musical materials, usually of a concise nature, and explores their potentialities to the limit; they can be developed both physically and emotionally—physically by extending their length, changing their rhythmic shape or by any one of a number of techniques, emotionally by altering the mood which they originally suggested. Perhaps the hardest thing for the untrained ear to grasp is what might be termed the architectural aspects of a major composition. (Musicologists have coined the word 'architectonic' to describe these, but this strikes me as being technical jargon of a rather forbidding kind.) The reason for the uninitiated listener's difficulty is quite easy to trace; it is a matter of recognition and memory, of being able to store music in the mind and instantly to recognize derivations and extensions.

To a composer it is vital that you should be able to compare what happens on page one of a symphony with some later moment, say page forty-one. At this point he may make some miraculous twist, turning the music in a totally unexpected direction, thereby revealing some new and unsuspected facet. If the listener is merely conscious of the immediate sounds that are audible at any given moment, he will miss the whole purpose of such a passage; he might just as well listen to a nocturne or a waltz, a type of music which is only concerned with establishing a mood. Such pieces are the equivalent of the short poem or literary vignette; the whole intention of a symphony is to explore the innermost possibilities of its material, and to make its themes grow and proliferate. What such 'development' means we can investigate in greater detail at a later time;[1] for the moment, let us have a quick look at the basic form which embraces most symphonies. The textbooks call it Sonata Form, though it is common to many types of composition, including sonatas, trios, quartets, symphonies and, in a somewhat modified guise, concertos.

If you take a tune like 'The Bluebells of Scotland' you will find that it consists of a first phrase, which is immediately repeated, then a rather different melodic shape, followed by a final repetition of the opening. Not to get too technical about it, you could describe it as A A B A. Now this extremely simple and fundamental musical shape is so profoundly satisfying in its logic and symmetry that it is capable of very considerable elaboration. It is in fact the foundation on which sonata form has been built; one does not have to be a mathematician to be able to see a parallel between these two formulae.

| (i) | A | A | B | A |
|-----|---|---|---|---|
| (ii) | Exposition | Exposition repeated | Development | Exposition repeated again |

The reason for the repetitions of the first section, or *exposition* we shall see in a moment; meantime, a third technical term must be learnt and that is the *recapitulation*, which is what musicians call the fourth section of the formula above instead of the rather clumsy 'exposition repeated again' which I have used. In fact, even to suggest that this fourth section is a mere repetition is dangerous; one of the biggest misunderstandings of the dramatic potentialities of the sonata springs from this too easy generalization. But then the textbook definition of sonata form can scarcely be said to be illuminating; too often, the most exciting and fruitful shape that composers have ever devised is reduced to this chillingly academic verbiage.

[1] See pp. 8-11.

Sonata-form, which is normally applicable to first movements only, consists of three main sections, the Exposition, Development, and Recapitulation; the Exposition begins with the first subject in the tonic key which is joined by a modulatory bridge passage to the contrasting second subject, which may usually be expected to appear in the dominant; this section is rounded off with a codetta which finalizes the newly established key, and by tradition the whole exposition is repeated. In the Development section which follows, the composer amplifies, extends, and explores the potentialities of the material presented in the Exposition; the Recapitulation re-states the material in its original form, but with a modified and non-modulatory bridge passage so that the second subject is now in the tonic, thus confirming the tonality of the movement.

How infinitely unlovable such definitions make music sound! It is like a botanist who reduces flowers to stamens and pistils but cannot appreciate the beauty of a bed of roses. What is worse is the inflexibility of such a formula; few sonatas would fit into this rigid mould, for curiously enough, it is impossible to say with any certainty how this extraordinarily fruitful form actually materialized. There was no composers' conference at Margate in 1773 at which sonata form was finally ratified; like Topsy in *Uncle Tom's Cabin*, it just grew, and its consequent freedom from academic restraint is one of its greatest glories.

The fairest comparison I can think of is to regard the first movement of a sonata as one would regard a house. We all understand the function of a house, and we appreciate the infinite variety that this generic term can encompass. There are small houses and great houses, houses with two rooms or a hundred rooms, one floor or six; so do sonatas and symphonies vary, and to compare an early Haydn symphony with Sibelius's seventh, or a Scarlatti sonata with Liszt's great piano sonata in B minor is like comparing an attractive cottage to Blenheim Palace. To pursue this comparison in greater detail will shed a good deal of light on the forbidding definition of sonata form which is printed above. Let us start with a basic house—what a county council would be entirely justified in calling a 'dwelling-unit'.

*Fig. 1*

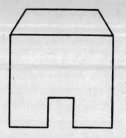

As you see, it has a front door, and a number of sonatas and symphonies also have front doors; the first page of the Pathétique Sonata of Beethoven is nothing but an imposing entrance, as are the slow introductions to his first and second symphonies. A composer may or may not have such an introduction at will; it is a matter for his personal taste entirely. As a general rule, however, the earlier symphonies are more likely to have a slow introduction, since the symphony was originally derived from the orchestral suite; such suites tended to begin with grave and solemn dances, and reserved the quicker movements like the gigue (or jig) to the end. The parallel between this and the joyful finale of a symphony is too obvious to need underlining. Having examined the front door, having experienced the introduction to the movement proper, let us continue our exploration of this particular house.

When you go inside a house, all sorts of architectural possibilities are available; you may find a hall, with several doors opening off it into different rooms; or you may find one immense room with a staircase leading directly from it. The same thing applies to the sonata or symphony; it can have one, two, three or more contrasting ideas, or one big theme, or a mixture of large-scale melody and small concentrated patterns. The so-called 'first subject' is seldom one tune; it usually consists of a group of themes, often brief in themselves but adding up to a total conception of unity, just as the downstairs part of a house is a unit, even though it may have several rooms. In order to go upstairs and find those rooms that are designed for the other functions of living we must use the staircase, and this in musical terms is known as the bridge passage. It leads us from one mood to another, from one set of themes to another; even more important, it leads us from one 'key' to another. Just what this means we shall see later on (pages 12–16), but for the moment let us continue our exploration of the house.

Once upstairs, we find contrasting rooms, and again they may be any shape, size or number; we called the downstairs part the first subject, and as you might expect, the upstairs part represents the second subject. Of the two, this is the more likely to be a lyrical sustained melody, since its emotional function is usually to be a foil to the first subject material, which, in order to arrest our attention, naturally tends to be positive and rhythmically alive. To round off our house we have an attic—not the most exciting room in the building, and musically this is represented by what is called a 'codetta'.[1] Those repeated Amens which so often end a classical movement are a typical example. Our completed house looks like this:

*Fig. 2*

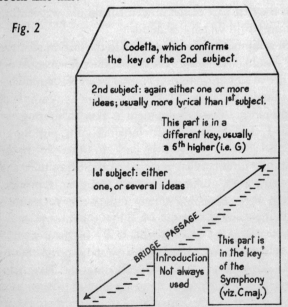

Codetta, which confirms the key of the 2nd subject.

2nd subject: again either one or more ideas; usually more lyrical than 1st subject.

This part is in a different key, usually a 5th higher (i.e. G)

1st subject: either one, or several ideas

BRIDGE PASSAGE

Introduction Not always used

This part is in the 'key' of the Symphony (viz. C maj.)

---

[1] A substantial example is called a 'coda', of which 'codetta' is merely a diminutive.

Once we have fully explored this set-up, our composer, like an over-eager host, says, 'I wonder, would you mind if we just went over it all again?' On the face of it, this would seem an unreasonable demand; why should we listen again to music we have only just heard? This is where we come to grips with the architectural aspect of music I have already mentioned. It is absolutely essential to our understanding of the symphony, sonata or quartet we are listening to that we should be able to store in our memories the exact proportions and relationships of the material the composer has presented to us. Keeping to the simile of the house, we must know where every bit of furniture is, the size of the rooms, the colour of the wall-papers, the pattern of the curtains; otherwise we shall never appreciate the significance of what is still to come. Of course nowadays we feel that we are so familiar with the classical repertoire that we tend to omit this custom of repeating the exposition, thereby doing neither our comprehension nor the work any great service. Only when we are truly sure of our knowledge of the first part of the movement should we venture into the exciting world which lies ahead.

The term Development, which is applied to the section we have now reached, should be self-explanatory; but since few people are capable of actually thinking in terms of music it remains somewhat vague in most listeners' minds. If I were to continue my simile of the house, I should say that development is akin to shifting the furniture around, redecorating the downstairs rooms, putting up new curtains, and adding a wing at the back. In other words, the composer takes the now familiar material of the exposition, and looks at it in a new light, pushing it around, changing its proportions, extending here, chopping there, until we have learnt a whole world of new truths about it. I feel that the most practical way I can show you what development really means is to take something that is familiar to you, and subject it to the sort of treatment it might receive from a classical composer. Here then is the immortal Daisy, still withholding her answer to the classic question.[1]

---

[1] Music quoted by kind permission of Francis, Day & Hunter Ltd.

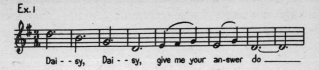

Ex.1

Dai - - sy, Dai - - sy, give me your an-swer do _____

Now the first four bars immediately suggest a sequence that would enable the composer to shift through various keys. (Again I should like to remind you that I shall be dealing with 'keys' and 'tonality' at the end of this chapter.) Without altering the original shape, one could do something on these lines:

Ex.2

Allegro con fuoco

(Dai-sy, Dai-sy)

(Daisy double speed)

etc.

Material like this, built on what is called the common chord—the notes a bugle plays—are the stock-in-trade of every classical composer. Daisy can be married to the tragic events of a Beethoven symphony without too much trouble.

Ex.3

Dai - - sy

Dai - - sy

etc.

A more serene treatment such as might appeal to Brahms would
be found in this rather denser texture:

Now so far I have only suggested ways of treating the first
limb of the tune; what about the second part, the 'Give me your
answer, do' bit? Taking just this much of the phrase,

it is a very simple matter to contrive something on these lines:

Or if you need something with more strength, what about this?

You will notice that both these last examples incorporate elements of the 'Daisy, Daisy' idea as well. This then is what is meant
by the term Development, and it should be remembered that the
examples I have given here are only a few of literally hundreds of
possibilities that spring to a composer's mind when confronted
with a combination of notes of this kind.

Returning to the subject of sonata form, from which this brief
bicycle trip stemmed, we come now to the Recapitulation, which
is perhaps the most misunderstood section of all. Many a thesis on
the subject tends to imply that the Recapitulation is no more than
a slavish reprise of the first few pages in which executants and
audience alike can go to sleep without risk of missing anything of
importance. Nothing could be further from the truth. Many a
quickly made friendship has been reconsidered in the light of subsequent knowledge: the whole essence of sonata form as a drama
is that the composer presents us with certain material in the
Exposition; in the Development we get to know a great deal
about it that we never dreamed of; in the Recapitulation we
reassess the material *in the light of the experience gained*. I cannot
overemphasize the importance of that statement. Once we have
experienced the Development, once we have learnt the hidden
secrets of the characters involved, once we have seen these relationships altered, we can never feel the same about them. In a play, we
meet the characters in the first act; as it progresses, our feelings
towards them change; new layers of character are revealed, showing heroism or weakness, treachery or loyalty. Now we know
them as whole people, and by the time they take the curtain-call

our conception of them can well have altered enormously. The same thing applies in music. A theme is like a living thing; one may find it difficult to feel affection for a tiny stunted clump of green in a flower-bed, but once it has grown into a great shrub covered with flowers one's feelings change to a glowing pride. The first two bars of Beethoven's Fifth Symphony are unremarkable enough; it is when we see what he makes of them that we salute a masterpiece.

One major structural alteration in the Recapitulation is perhaps worth mentioning at this stage, and that is the modification of the bridge passage. In order that he may avoid getting into a vicious circle of modulation, the composer has to make the second subject stay in the same 'key' as the first; consequently the staircase gets rebuilt, to turn back on itself.

Fig. 3

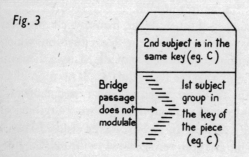

Few recapitulations are ever exact in proportions; most have several moments of surprise, often involving new 'development'.

We come now to this vital question of 'key' or 'tonality'. When we learn that a symphony is in D major or B flat minor it has more significance than a mere label, for to a composer 'key' is one of the most important elements in music—so much so that it takes on an almost mystical quality. Nobody can say exactly why keys possess the attributes they seem to have, but the most likely reason stems from the early days when music was written in keys with only one or two sharps or flats. Before the invention of what is known as 'Equal Temperament',[1] it was impossible to

[1] A method of tuning a keyboard so that it is imperceptibly out of tune, which makes the conflict between sharps and flats tolerable.

tune a keyboard instrument so that it could play in all keys and still be in tune; so the inaccessible keys acquired a quality of remoteness; they were lands into which a composer ventured at his peril. Ever since, the keys with a number of sharps and flats in their signature have possessed a slightly exotic quality; the simple keys are more 'everyday'. There is, however, more to it than that, and if you will bear with me a little longer we can investigate this mystery more fully. Again I should like to use the house as a simile, but this time there are twelve of them, built in a circle, like

*Fig. 4*

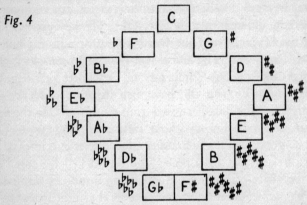

a newly planned housing estate. Each house has a resident, named as you will see in the illustration, and the houses to the right represent what are called the 'sharp' keys (♯), those on the left the 'flat' (♭). You will see that C has no sharps or flats; in other words, it is entirely on the white notes of the piano. G has one sharp which means that it has one note different from C; E has four sharps, which means that four of its notes are different from the scale of C. The same principle applies on the flat side. B flat has two flats, i.e. two notes in its scale are different from the scale of C. The bottom house is a semi-detached residence inhabited by two identical twins, G flat and F sharp. On the piano they are the same note, but written differently. It is easy to see why their scales are identical, since by now, in our journey 'away' from C, we find that these two keys have six notes different from C major, and as there are only seven notes in a scale, the mere fact of six being changed from the original departure-point will not allow for any alternatives.

In a classical sonata, or for that matter in most suites and many other forms of music, the first subject will be in a particular key and the next important theme, call it the second subject or what you will, will be in the house next-door in a clockwise direction. If a Bach allemande begins in B♭, half-way through it will arrive at F; if a Mozart sonata has the first subject in A, the second will be in E. This relationship is one of the great unwritten laws of music; the keys are closely related because, as you can see, there is only one note different in their two scales. The key you start in is called the 'Tonic', from the word Tone; the adjacent one is called the 'Dominant'. The house next-door in an *anti*-clockwise direction is called the Sub-dominant, and these three keys (e.g. C, F, and G, or A♭, E♭, and D♭) have such an interdependence on one another that the music can pass from the key of C to the key of G, or from C to F, almost without the listener being aware of it.

So far so good; where the housing estate comes into its own as a means of clarifying this aspect of music is when we come to analyse the effect of a distant modulation—a journey *across* the estate. The moment that a composer moves the music from say C major to G♭ major, he has stepped into a wildly remote land; in his terms it is a major talking-point—as though the village gossips were to say, 'What *was* Mr C doing visiting Miss D Flat's house at that time of night?' You can appreciate the impact of this by playing 'The Bluebells of Scotland' in the modified version below.

Ex.8

The ear at once tells you that something disastrous has hap-pened; the earth has given way beneath your feet, and for the moment what you might call your 'tonal orientation' has been vastly disturbed.

You can understand then that this business of modulation, of moving into remote keys, is an important weapon in the composer's armoury; the most dramatic moment in a symphony or sonata is not necessarily the loudest; often it is a hushed chord emerging from a silence, but a chord in a key remote from the original starting-point.[1]

Two aspects of tonality remain, and then we can feel equipped to tackle a symphony intelligently. The first concerns what are known as 'minor' keys. Turn back to Fig. 4, and you will find that the relationship is easier to follow. If a piece is in C minor, it means that the resident of the house marked C is irresistibly drawn towards the house marked E♭; he becomes so obsessed with it that he begins to lose the essential qualities of 'C-ness'. A minor key always means that the house three doors away in an *anti-clockwise* direction casts a great shadow over the original. G minor is G clouded or obsessed by the essential elements of B♭; B minor is B influenced by D. D♭ minor is a difficult one. Count three along in an anti-clockwise direction, counting the G♭/F♯ house as one; you will arrive at E, which is a 'sharp' key. A composer will always think of D♭ minor as C♯ minor for this reason; D♭ and C♯ are only two names for the same note on the piano; Ex. 9 shows

Ex.9

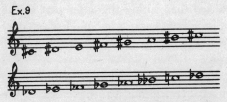

[1] Modulation can also give a quite tangible effect of 'journeying' in music; turn back to Ex. 2 and you will find that the apparent visual symmetry of the right-hand part is made not only tolerable but positively exciting by its movement from one 'key' to another. The first bar is in G major; in the next bar, the G♯ switches us towards A minor (bar 3). The G♯ in the bass in bar 2 strikes a responsive echo in bar 4 with the note A♭. This is the same note on the keyboard, and it is here used rather like a pun, a note with two meanings; as G♯ it took us to A minor; as A♭ it takes us to F minor (bar 4) and then through A♭ to D♭ major (bars 5–7). If you follow this journey round the 'housing estate' in Fig. 1, you will see that it takes us diametrically across. The progression is G→C (=A minor)→A♭ (=F minor)→D♭. The next paragraph explains 'minor' keys.

two versions of the scale of C♯ minor, one written in flats and one in sharps. You will see at once why the sharps are easier to read and to write.

One useful aspect of the minor keys is that they enable a composer to journey to remote keys more smoothly. For instance, if Mozart begins a tune in F major, and then changes it to F minor, which is a smooth and acceptable change, he has thereby shifted the music three steps towards the 'darker' keys of D♭ or G♭. He is that much farther away from home.[1]

The use of the word 'darker' brings me to the last point about tonality. We have already seen how the keys with a large number of sharps or flats came to have an exotic quality (see p. 13). The undeniable fact emerges that certain keys have emotional connotations in composers' minds; this is so profoundly a part of a musician's instinct that it even makes a difference when we come to the apparently similar keys of G♭ and F♯. Ask a concert pianist to try 'thinking' the last section of César Franck's Symphonic Variations in G flat major instead of F sharp, and he will think you are mad: it just wouldn't seem right. Yet the actual notes the hands play would be the same: only the thought behind them would alter. Fig 5 gives an indication of the sort of mood we can legitimately expect to associate with the cycle of keys.

Naturally there is no absolute hard-and-fast rule about this; also it must be realized that during the latter part of the nineteenth century these distinctions became less and less apparent; the whole key system was beginning to break down, and the so-called 'chromatic' music of Liszt and Wagner moved so rapidly from key to key that there was no longer any significance in modulation as such. The logical conclusion was the 'atonal' music of Schön-berg and his disciples which jettisoned the key system entirely.

Now it would seem that I have spent an inordinate amount of time discussing first movement structure; surely the other movements deserve equal consideration? Curiously enough they do not;

[1] It is worth mentioning that E♭ major is called the 'relative major' of C minor. In a symphony in a minor key the second subject will usually be in the relative major rather than the dominant; a symphony in C major would have the second subject in G; a symphony in C minor would have the second subject in E♭.

*Fig. 5*

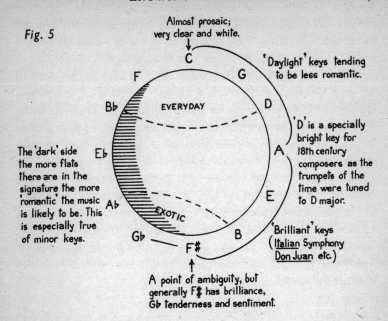

Almost prosaic;
very clear and white.
↓
C

'Daylight' keys tending
to be less romantic.

F        G

Bb        EVERYDAY        D

'D' is a specially
bright key for
18th century
composers as the
trumpets of the
time were tuned
to D major.

The 'dark' side
the more flats
there are in the
signature the more
'romantic' the music
is likely to be. This
is especially true
of minor keys.

Eb        A

Ab        E

EXOTIC

Gb        B

F#

'Brilliant' keys
(Italian Symphony
Don Juan etc.)

↑
A point of ambiguity, but
generally F# has brilliance,
Gb tenderness and sentiment.

in nearly every case it is the first movement which is the hard intellectual core of a symphony. The other movements have a more purely entertaining function. The way that Beethoven adapted the Minuet-and-Trio to his own purposes, thereby creating the new form of the Scherzo, is too well known to need any laborious description here; slow movements are normally easy to listen to, being more openly melodic than any other part of a symphony; the finale may be in sonata form, or it can be a rondo, or variations. Normally it is happy or triumphant in mood, since the composer is human enough to wish to excite his audience into an enthusiastic reception of his work.

To sum up, listening to a symphony means concentration; it means storing up in your memory each musical event in turn, for it is necessary to appreciate change and growth as they occur; form is significant, deviation from form even more so. Composers delight in laying traps for the unwary listener; often Beethoven or Mozart will present us with three similar phrases; just as you feel you can confidently predict what will happen next, they will whip the ground from beneath your feet by twisting the music in an unexpected direction. Also important, but so far unmentioned, is a sense of period. Harmonies that might pass unnoticed in a Schubert score may well be revolutionary in Mozart; we need to try and approach each work with an awareness of its pristine qualities—after all, everything was 'modern' once. There are some kinds of music, 'entertainment' music, which are not so demanding; but a symphony is the equivalent of a philosophical treatise, however seductive its sounds may be. I do not expect to read Ian Fleming and Bertrand Russell with an exactly similar approach; obviously one demands far greater concentration than the other. When you hear a symphony by a great composer you are listening to the thoughts of a major intellect speaking to you in a highly specialized language. Do not be so beguiled by the sound of his voice that you pay no heed to the words he is uttering; do not confuse the sound of music with its sense.

## CHAPTER II

# HAYDN
## Symphony No. 86 in D (*c.* 1786)

1. Adagio leading to Allegro Spiritoso. 2. Capriccio (Largo). 3. Menuetto (Allegretto). 4. Finale (Allegro con spirito).

Orchestra: 1 flute; 2 oboes; 2 bassoons; 2 horns; 2 trumpets; 2 timpani; normal complement of strings.

This symphony is one of a set of six written for a concert-giving organization in Paris, *Les Concerts de la Loge Olympique*. Robbins Landon, the foremost authority on Haydn, classifies it as one of the finest symphonies Haydn ever wrote.

I T WAS REALLY HAYDN who was most responsible for lifting the status of the symphony from a glorified suite to a work of real stature. Evidence of its derivation is still clear in the titles which he attached to some of the movements in this work, but no one can doubt from the very first page that this symphony is a composition of real significance. Admittedly there are occasional patches of the rustic rum-tum-tum that is liable to crop up when Haydn is in one of his less sophisticated moods; but they are more than counterbalanced by some of his finest and most imaginative passages, scattered freely throughout the score.

He begins with a solemn adagio to get the audience into a suitably serious frame of mind;[1] but here is no conventional blare of horn, trumpet, and kettledrum, but an introduction scored with the utmost delicacy. At first glance it would appear to be a conventional opening, merely establishing the tonality of D major, as a card-player might say which suit was trumps. But then as we look closer at the score we find some very subtle touches; the tune is

[1] A perfect example of a 'front-door'; see p. 6.

on the first violins and two oboes. Marked at the unexpectedly
low volume of *piano*, it is accompanied by plucked chords on the
lower strings, alternating with quaver rests. It is one of the maxims
of teaching composition that one should 'let the air in'; to have
everyone playing all the time produces a porridge-like consistency,
and Haydn here lightens the texture of the music, thereby allowing the tune to come through clearly without needing to be *forte*.
Not until the eighth bar do we really sense the weight of the full
orchestra, and the dignity and grandeur of this moment is enhanced by the transparency of what has gone before. First the
violins then the lower strings have sweeping scales that cut across
the sustained harmonies supporting them on wind and brass; these
are no empty convention, but grand heraldic gestures, like great
banners dipping in salute.

The introduction lasts some twenty-one bars of slow 3/4 time—
a little over a minute; finally the music comes to rest on three clear
chords of A major, the dominant of D. The stage has now been
set for the first movement proper, and at this point Haydn could
choose several alternatives; the most likely course would be to have
a sudden strong allegro, clearly based on D major harmony—
something like this perhaps:

Ex.10

Another possibility would be a quiet bustle of excitement such
as we find at the start of the overture to *The Marriage of Figaro*. The
one thing we can be almost certain of is that the new theme will
be unequivocally in the key of D major. However, Haydn, in
common with many another great composer, depends upon us
expecting this, and it delights him to foil our expectations by giving
us something completely unforeseen instead. Having paved the

way most carefully for a D major entrance, probably of some pomp and majesty when we remember those 'banners', he now gives us a handsome surprise in the shape of a quiet, frivolous theme whose harmony utterly contradicts D major, since its bass note is actually D sharp.

A comparison of Exx. 10 and 11 will clearly show the difference between orthodoxy and genius; the first is predictable and un-inspired, the second shows the hand of a master.

To a knowledgeable listener, this will have been a considerable shock, and Haydn is now quick to show that all is forgiven and that he means no real harm; effortlessly he steps back into D major (see Ex. 11, bar 4), as though never for a moment had he contemplated doing anything else. The rest of the orchestra seem profoundly relieved to find order thus restored, and they all come bouncing in with a very rustic delight in a passage which shows little of the subtlety which preceded it. For twenty-seven bars they chug on merrily with a good deal of sound and fury signifying not very much. The section ends with a typical cadence rounding things off.

At this point we have every justification for imagining that the second subject is about to appear; all the signs are there—we've reached the dominant key of A, we've had what sounded like a rather blustering bridge-passage, and this single repeated E and its attendant diminuendo suggest some new event. Again I will underline the wit of Haydn's music by suggesting a less inspired alternative.

Ex. 13

That is attractive enough, but again its compliance with the 'rules', however imaginary they may be, deprives it of spice. Haydn prefers something infinitely more unexpected; without a note of warning, he whips us back to the opening idea again, and just as before, it is once more in a contradictory key.

Ex. 14

By doing this, Haydn defers the arrival of the second subject so as to heighten its effectiveness when it ultimately arrives. When it does appear, it proves to be a graceful dance-like affair, with each phrase preceded by a little hopping up-beat.

Ex. 15

The graceful mood doesn't last long, however, and the codetta or tail-piece is very stormy before the main exposition ends.

Many Haydn works have a relatively short development section, but in this case there is an elaborate and dramatic development which concerns itself with most of the important material from the exposition. Initially, it concentrates on the 'surprise' idea

in Ex. 11, but just as the music is becoming positively spiritual
with a mysterious cadence in C sharp major,

Ex.16

the rustic rum–tum–tum theme comes bounding back again. This
effectively rules the roost until Haydn comes to a charming
example of the sort of double bluff one often finds in classical
music. You will remember how he avoided the predictable in
Ex. 14; how just as you were expecting the second subject he shot
back to the opening theme? What then would you anticipate at
this apparently similar moment?

Ex.17        *(cf. Ex.14 bar 2)*

With complete confidence you could assert that at this point
you are prepared to hear the first theme again, exactly as you do
in bars 3 and 4 of Ex. 14. Haydn knows this as well as you do, so
with enchanting waywardness he once again foils expectation and
does what he *ought* to have done originally—he leads into the
second subject.

Ex.18

One can almost hear him say, 'Fooled again!' It is points like
these that so perfectly illustrate the importance of memory and
comparison in listening to a work of this nature. More than half
the joy of listening to this symphony lies in an appreciation of
Haydn's dexterity in avoiding the obvious. Despite the seemingly
conventional idiom of the music, so easily dismissed as the routine
formality of eighteenth-century composition, every page is full of
subtle and highly personal touches; but they need a cultivated ear

to spot them, and since they are nearly always concerned with comparing this phrase with that, they need also the ability to review the whole movement as one span.

This is less likely to be true of the later movements. Nearly always the first movement of a symphony contains the toughest fibre; it is not too fanciful to suggest that at this period the symphony was expected to represent the whole of man. The first movement is his intellect, the second his sensuality, the third his manners, and the finale his sense of fun. Thus one finds development of small thematic units in the opening movement, the sensuous beauty of extended melody in the second, the formal grace of the minuet in the third, and a gay or even boisterous rondo to round off the picture. It is for this reason that analytical essays such as these tend to spend far longer on first movements than on any others—they are so much more complex.

In this symphony the second movement is marked Largo and Capriccio, two apparently contradictory terms, since to be capricious very slowly would savour of a paradox. In fact, nothing very capricious happens; the term is merely Haydn's justification for the overt emotionalism of the movement. Such is its freedom of key and melody, such its tenderness and passion, that he must have felt that sensuousness of this order might seem out of place in a serious work. Right from the start he has one of those heart-turning phrases which have a profoundly emotional effect by dint of their very simplicity. To an ear dulled by a surfeit of Tchaikovsky and Chopin, these harmonies may seem nothing special; once again it takes a subtle response to modulation and dissonance to fully appreciate Haydn's skill. He begins in un-ashamed G major:

Ex.19

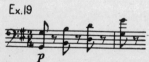

but then in the second bar, he suddenly passes a shadow over the phrase, only to release the tension a moment later.

Ex.20

The asterisk marks the tension-point, the twist of the knife in the wound; without this it would be colourless; with it, it is infinitely touching. Again the scoring is miraculous, allowing the sustained lines to stand out clearly against the detached chords beneath.

Soon the mood changes to that of a formal dance, replete with the elaborate gestures of the period, simple in outline but complex in detail. However, do not be deceived by the apparent effortlessness of all this. There are big happenings ahead, and some very startling surprises to catch the indolent listener napping. Here is an example; at this point Haydn seems to be heading for a nice sit-down in D major, but as you see he averts this by a sudden and unexpected chord of B flat.

This is after all a fairly stock interrupted cadence, and we can survive worse shocks than that. It is enough though just to disturb our equilibrium, and now, while we are still off balance, Haydn really rocks us with an alarming shift of tonality and mood. The atmosphere becomes electric with drama, just as the calm of a summer evening can suddenly be dispelled by thunder.

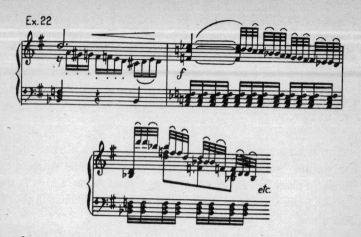

The prettiness and elegance of the preceding passages are only skin-deep; here is the stuff of tragedy and high drama. Like a clap of thunder, though, it is soon over; passages like this justify the name Capriccio for this movement. There are several such outbursts, but for the most part it is gentle and tender; some passages are as romantic as it is possible for a composer of this period to be. Look out for one section where the singing bass line of violas and 'cellos is accompanied by delicate little clashes in the violins above and sighs of passion from the oboe. Once again, though, there is a very ungentle outburst immediately afterwards, as if to show that mere sentiment is not enough. Perhaps these storms are only lovers' quarrels and not to be taken too seriously; the main thing to realize is that this movement shows Haydn at his most inspired; small wonder that it was received with enthusiasm by the Paris audiences of the time.

More unexpected are the treasures to be found in the next movement. The Menuet and Trio are so frequently a little four-square for present-day taste; it almost seems as though the confinement of a strict dance-form might have restricted the composers' imagination. In this instance, Haydn starts out formally enough with a dance rhythm calculated to set even the Duke of York's foot tapping—to whom, by the way, the work has sometimes (erroneously) alleged to have been dedicated. Nothing could be clearer than the initial rhythmic patterns of this movement; the experienced listener, familiar with Haydn's guile, will expect a trap. Sure enough, he has some more surprises for us. Just a little way into the second main stanza the rhythm suddenly seems to hesitate as though the players had lost all confidence.

Ex. 23

This subtle interruption of the symmetrical patterns just makes all the difference; no sooner has he broken the chain than he embarks on a shatteringly beautiful sequence in which he piles one delicate clash upon another; surely these are the pains of love of which the poets of the time made so much.

Ex. 24

Few composers have such a blend of sophistication and innocence in their music as Haydn; after the delicate subtlety of Ex. 24, the trio seems like music for peasants. It is straight dance-music, not all that different from what one might hear today in the Tyrol played on the accordion by a self-taught musician. Haydn never lost touch with the simple flavour of folk-music, and to find exquisitely wrought counterpoint side by side with rustic dances is quite the normal thing in his compositions. It is a sad commentary on the self-consciousness of contemporary music that such simplicity is no longer acceptable.

The last movement is like a children's game, gay and full of sparkling mischief. Again one cannot fail to be impressed by the delicacy of touch; Haydn deploys his comparatively slender resources with immense skill and economy. Remember that the horns and trumpets of the time were very limited in range and facility, so his occasional insistence on repeated notes is understandable. As always with such a composer one is constantly aware of the way in which a straightforward idea is given distinction. Here is a sequence which is merely a long ascending scale of two octaves; but how cleverly its simple bone-structure is disguised.

Ex. 25

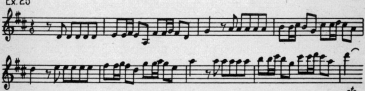

The second subject looks forward to the frivolity of Rossini; both Haydn and Mozart frequently use material which would readily transplant into an operatic score. Above all, the sheer high spirits of this movement leave the most lasting impression. It is all very well to call him Papa Haydn, but there was certainly a lot of the child still in him when he wrote music like this; it's young and fresh and tireless. Unlike some of the self-searching works of the nineteenth century, this was written for your enjoyment and delight. There is no room for sorrow, anguish, and introspection here; even the stormy moments in the Largo soon resolve into sunshine. Small wonder that he lived to a nice healthy old age when he had a spirit as eternally youthful as is revealed in this delectable score.

## CHAPTER III

# MOZART

## Symphony in D (K.504), The 'Prague' (1786)

1. Adagio, leading to Allegro. 2. Andante. 3. Finale: Presto.

Orchestra: 2 flutes; 2 oboes; 2 bassoons; 2 horns; 2 trumpets;
2 timpani; normal complement of strings.

Completed on 6 December 1786 and presumably intended for a
first performance in Prague on the occasion of his subsequent
visit there in January of the following year. Both this and the
preceding Haydn symphony bear testimony to the remarkable
interchange of music between capital cities at a time when
travelling was a matter of great discomfort; thus we find Haydn
writing for Paris, Mozart for Prague.

So MAGNIFICENT is the final great trilogy of symphonies[1] that
Mozart wrote in six unbelievable weeks in 1788 that we tend
to forget quite how perfect some of the earlier symphonies are. In
the so-called 'Prague' symphony we find a splendid example of
Mozart's mature orchestral writing; composed only five years
before his death, it shows him as a master of every emotion and
a matchless craftsman. It is neither as tragic as the fortieth
symphony in G minor, nor as staggering in its intellectual
mastery as the 'Jupiter'; it occupies a happy position between
the two in which grace and beauty are married to a faultless
technique.

Prague seems to have been a singularly fortunate city for
Mozart; works which the fickle Viennese had failed to appreciate
were received with rapture when transferred to the rival capital,
and the huge success of *The Marriage of Figaro* in Prague must have
encouraged Mozart, in sheer gratitude, to give particular attention

---

[1] The symphonies No. 39 in E♭, No. 40 in G minor, and No. 41 in C (the 'Jupiter').

to a symphony destined to have its first performance there.[1] Before making any attempt to analyse this symphony it would be a worth while step to discuss the art of listening as it affects this composer, whose music gives me personally the greatest pleasure of all.

Listening to Mozart is rather like walking along a hedgerow that is absolutely ablaze with wild flowers; you get several impressions, of which the most superficial is that this is just a hedge and as such hardly merits your notice. In this category come the people who regard Mozart as a light appetizer before getting down to a main meal of Beethoven, Brahms, and Tchaikovsky. Next you have the person who realizes that there are a lot of flowers about, but of a rather common kind; he is the one who dismisses Mozart as 'pretty', and regards the delicate eighteenth-century conventions of rococo decoration as merely trivial. Lastly you have the enthusiast who takes the trouble to examine each flower, observing the miraculous detail, savouring every aspect of its simple perfection.

In fact, there was never a composer so subtle in harmony, so elegant in thought as Mozart, and if we are to appreciate every nuance that is to be found in his scores, then we have got to be infinitely more responsive to detail than we are when we listen to a nineteenth-century work; for while the emotional content may be every bit as deeply felt as it is in Tchaikovsky's music, it will be expressed with far greater reticence. If I may digress for a moment into the pages of the 'Jupiter' symphony it will be possible to demonstrate the relationship between harmony and emotion fairly clearly. The third and fourth bars of the 'Jupiter' read as follows:

Ex.26   Allegro vivace

To an ear jaded by late nineteenth-century harmony these chords may seem ordinary enough, but in Mozart's time these

[1] On 17 January 1787.

sweet dissonances unquestionably had a highly emotional flavour. Play them slowly, and linger on the first and third beats of the bar; savour the interval of a seventh between D and C in the first chord, the even sharper clash in the second full harmony when the melody-note of D is sounded against the C and E beneath—in effect, three adjacent notes sounding simultaneously. The important thing to realize about these harmonies is that composers of a later age had to resort to more extreme chords to achieve the same emotional result. A classic example of the more expressive type of Romantic harmony is to be found in the opening bars of Wagner's *Tristan*.

Ex.27

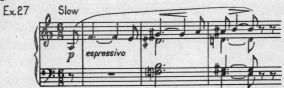

Different though they may be, the function of the chords in this and the preceding example is the same. In both cases the harmonies are points of emotional tension which is then relaxed, like hands clasped in the traditional (and universal) expression of grief.

Play these two examples at the same slow tempo and it is not difficult to see a similarity of effect; if Wagner's harmonic palette is richer, more 'advanced' than Mozart's, it is simply because the whole history of music shows a gradual extension of harmonic resources, a process of adding notes to previously existing chords, of thickening textures, even of extending the compass of the instruments themselves. Such a process was artistically essential since each composer of significance has the capacity to 'patent', as it were, certain sounds. When Beethoven began his fourth piano concerto with the chord of G major spaced in this particular way,

Ex.28

he created a sound which could never be used again without instantly suggesting the opening of this concerto. It is an exclusive 'Beethoven' model, not to be copied. Anyone coming after him had to find a new way of spacing out that harmony, a way which would establish it as being in turn 'his'. Thus we find Stravinsky taking exactly the same components that Beethoven used, i.e. the notes G, B, and D, but reassembling them to produce a totally different sonority.

Ex.29
Slow

Now it so happened that Mozart arrived at a period in history when the type of harmony which we are accustomed to hearing in the great bulk of the normal concert repertoire was comparatively new and virginal. Just as the twentieth-century composer uses a different harmonic idiom from that of the nineteenth, so did Mozart use a type of harmony, and in particular a *texture* that had first begun to be formulated by Bach's sons. Listen to the music of J. C. Bach[1] and you can hear where Mozart learnt his style, a style which broke away completely from that established by the great John Sebastian. However, apart from Haydn, nobody of sufficient stature had yet appeared to develop these new resources of harmony and texture in anything like the same way that Mozart was able to; consequently he could achieve the maximum effect with the minimum effort.

It is vital that we should realize this, that we should reacquire the 'taste' of a Mozart harmony; for while the underlying emotion in his music is frequently 'romantic' in the deepest sense of the

[1] John Christian Bach (1735–82). J. S. Bach's youngest son; spent some time in London and greatly influenced the young Mozart when the Mozart family came to London in 1764.

word, he invariably expresses himself with infinitely greater economy and restraint than the post-Beethoven composer. In the first four bars of the 'Jupiter' symphony, Mozart expresses an alternation of heroism and tenderness; the heroism is not more heroic, nor the tenderness more tender if they happen in later years to be expressed in phrases twice as long on an orchestra double the size. All that happens is that the expression of the emotions concerned becomes that much more obvious. Mozart's music may display a world in miniature, but it is not a miniature world.

With these considerations in mind, our understanding of the 'Prague' symphony is likely to be enhanced; like the Haydn symphony discussed in the previous chapter (which was in all likelihood written in the same year), this work begins with a slow introduction. The tempo is the sole thing they have in common, however, for Haydn goes from lyricism to grandeur where Mozart goes from an imposing start to a tune of extreme pathos. Notice how in nearly every classical symphony the composer is at pains to establish a completely sure sense of tonality in the listener right from the start. Over and over again we find first themes or introductions based on a 'common chord' motif or repeated assertions of the tonic or keynote. Here Mozart reiterates the note D no fewer than five times, underlining it with an imposing triplet figure which almost suggests military pomp and splendour.

Ex.30

Most unexpectedly, the response to this arresting but immensely confident opening is a sequence of highly emotional chords, grouped in pairs like falling sighs, and leading in their turn to a haunting phrase on the first violins, accompanied by sympathetic chords on the lower strings. Nowhere else in the thirty-six bars of this profound introduction does the confident feeling of the opening reappear; the mood remains intensely emotional, racked with spasms of deep anguish in related minor keys, and with striking alternations between ominous brass and pleading strings. When one considers that trumpets and drums alike are confined to a choice of two notes (D and A) throughout the stormy second half of this introduction, one can only be amazed at the simplicity with which Mozart achieves his effects.

Once we reach the allegro, thereby entering the first movement proper, we find Mozart in a characteristically restless mood. The violins fidget at the keynote, in uneasy syncopations that are only slightly relieved when they ultimately flower into a little wisp of melody.

(As a touching variation of this try playing A♯ for A♮ in bars 2–4 in the left hand, a subtle harmonic twist Mozart introduces later.)

This same figure (Ex. 31, bars 5–6) is soon extended, while above it Mozart introduces new material; he frequently uses links of this nature, looking back over his shoulder at something that has gone before and using it as a counter-melody to some new idea. Regarding bars 5–6 of the preceding example as stage one, we can trace this rhythmic pattern through stage two:

Ex.32

until in stage three, some pages later, we find traces of both these ideas, now further illuminated by a wonderfully lyrical counterpoint in the second violins. Notice here how the sustained line will glow through the texture of the music, simply by virtue of being surrounded with staccato phrases.

Ex.33

Not only is the serene beauty of the second violin line a marvellous foil to the more agile parts surrounding it, it also manages to give an extraordinary poignancy to what otherwise might seem a rather busy little passage, for with the utmost skill Mozart arranges a dissonance (and consequently an emotional tension) on each first beat. Isolate the chords marked with an asterisk and you will see what I mean.

Another enchanting example of this 'brought forward' technique appears when we come to the second subject. At a first glance this would seem to be a rather trivial tune.

Such simplicity is misleading, for Mozart merely regards the

Ex.34

melody so far as a starting-point. The first modification we find is when he puts it into the minor,[1] underlining its longer notes with sad little echoes on the bassoons; the magical surprise comes at the restoration of the major key which quickly ensues, for now, while bassoons take over the original melody, the violins produce an enchanting new counter-theme, so beguiling in shape that it could well be regarded as the true second subject.

In the development section of this symphony, Mozart amuses himself by adding a new element in which various pairs of instruments play prettily with daisy-chains of scales, continually overlapping and unwinding.

He then proceeds to work this against much of the material that we have had so far, more particularly the bustling little theme in bars 5–6 of Ex. 31. It is easy for a reasonably equipped theoretician to be a trifle condescending about a passage like the preceding example; after all, it represents a fairly orthodox trick of counter-point. What is an especial delight in Mozart's music, though, is to see the way he transmutes these textbook tags into pure poetry. Many a worthy but uninspired organist would be capable of producing the type of imitation that is quoted above; only a genius of Mozart's calibre could take this same material and

[1] Thereby producing a close resemblance to the finale of Beethoven's Pianoforte Sonata, Op. 31, No. 2.

change its very essence to something as full of pathos as this.

Ex.37

In the face of harmonies like these, anyone who cannot bring himself to admit the essential Romanticism of Mozart's music is being wilfully blind. This study has not set out to be a bar-by-bar analysis of the first movement; the person who requires that might just as well buy a score and do it for himself. What I hope it has done is to pinpoint some of the reasons that cause me to be so enthusiastic about this and many other symphonies by Mozart. Counting the introduction, the movement is 302 bars long, or thirty-one pages of miniature score. Within this comparatively short span are contained passages as stormy as Beethoven, as lyrical as Schubert, as gay as Rossini, as emotional as Liszt or Wagner; all these are expressed in an idiom so elegant in style, so utterly distinguished in thought, so without ostentation or emotional self-indulgence that the mind of the understanding listener will never tire of the infinite variety concealed beneath its delectable surface.

Somewhat unusually for a symphony of this period, the 'Prague' has only three movements, a scheme which might be due to some special planning on Mozart's part, but which more probably was occasioned by the rapid approach of his visit to Prague, and his consequent eagerness to finish the symphony at all costs, even if he had to dispense with the conventional Menuet and Trio. Certainly there is no evidence of hurry in the slow movement itself; it is unusually rich in decoration and harmony, recalling the mood of some of the more contemplative arias in the operas. As always, his deployment of the orchestra is astonishingly colourful when one considers how relatively new the art of orchestration was. This may seem a rather provocative statement, but a dispassionate consideration of Bach's use of the orchestra in the Brandenburg Concertos or the Suites makes one realize that he could be quite indiscriminate in the way he transferred music from one instrument to another. Oboe parts and string parts were completely interchangeable; and the grand old man of Leipzig was quite happy to have his entire band playing complex counterpoint for half a dozen pages on end. The result is sometimes a somewhat indigestible porridge of semiquavers which intertwine with a relentlessness that defies even the most well-intentioned performers. Look at bars 30–61 of the first Brandenburg Concerto and you will see an example of the sort of passage I mean. This is not to say that Bach was not capable of imaginative colouring when he put his mind to it; nevertheless, orchestration was not a primary consideration for him.

Mozart's use of soft holding-notes on horns or wind produces a lovely blend of sound, and his melodic line is constantly changing in colour, from violins to flute, flute to oboe, then to bassoon or 'cellos. On occasion he will use the strings in unison against sustained harmony in the wind and brass; but whereas earlier composers would most probably have conceived such a combination as being suitable for loud passages only, Mozart uses it for quiet mystery and a complete change of texture. Admittedly Haydn too was extraordinarily inventive in his orchestration at times, but he had the benefit of a permanent orchestra to experiment with; much that Haydn must have learned from experience Mozart seems to have divined by instinct.

The slow movement of the 'Prague', an Andante in 6/8 time, starts with an interesting example of a subtle balance between what are called diatonic and chromatic notes. (Diatonic notes are those which 'belong' to a particular scale, chromatic notes are outsiders, and have the exotic quality which one always attributes to foreigners. In the scale of C, the white notes on the keyboard are the diatonic, the black notes are chromatic. The diatonic notes are associated with simplicity and the direct statement; the chromatic with more highly coloured matters, whether they be pathetic or stormy.) Mozart begins this movement with an extremely simple-looking pastoral phrase, which, for its first two bars, preserves an unsullied aspect of G major; he then introduces a welter of chromatic notes, thereby adding an element of decorative sophistication which brings the music back from the country into the concert-hall. The deceptive simplicity of much of this music should not hoodwink us into believing that Mozart was simple; there is not a bar in which his conscious, if effortless, technique is not apparent. The placing of each modulation, the balance between stillness and movement, the calculated increase of emotion brought about by decoration, the uncanny selection of harmonies that just evade the obvious—all these are the hall-marks of a superlative craftsman. A detailed analysis would be boring; get hold of a score, and study it with a resolute determination to take nothing for granted.

The finale shows Mozart in an unusual mood, nearer to Beethoven's boisterousness than his fastidious taste normally allowed him to go. It begins with the type of eager bustle that we find so often in the operas.

Ex. 38

This phrase, with its innocent eagerness, he soon tries to blast off the face of the earth with a series of gigantic blows. Savage though these sound, I cannot believe they are really meant to be taken seriously. It is the ferocious roar of a child wearing a mask, quite different from the alternations of *ff* and *p* that we find in Beethoven's Fifth Symphony. Only at one point does Mozart seem to become caught up in a real paroxysm of anger, and at that moment we find something uncannily near to Beethoven at his most awe-inspiring. The difference between the simulation of anger and the real thing is quite easy to spot. When we hear one sustained chord at a time in brass and wind lasting for four bars, then we are witnessing sheer braggadocio; when on the other hand we find that same chord repeated, worried at like this,

I think we can safely assume that the frivolity of much of the move-ment has been for the moment put aside. Alfred Einstein goes so far as to say that this movement, despite all its appearance of cheerfulness, leaves 'a wound in the soul'; in it, 'beauty is wedded to death'.[1] At the risk of seeming to contradict one of the world's great authorities on Mozart, I would suggest that that is an over-statement as far as this particular movement is concerned. There are many works of Mozart in which I feel that the phrase 'tears behind the smile' describes the emotion conveyed by the music. In this symphony, however, I feel that he went deep enough in the first movement; surely the finale is a joyful offering to the people of Prague, a people who welcomed him in their midst and who loved him and his music. With his thoughts winging towards them and the excitement of a production of *Don Giovanni* ahead

[1] Alfred Einstein: *Mozart: his character and work*: Cassell, 1946.

of him, I have the impression that this finale at least can be taken too seriously. In its one passage of genuine terror the music would seem to have got a little out of hand; but all is quickly forgiven and one carries away the memory of a sunlit work, full of a radiance that is hard to equal.

## CHAPTER IV

# BEETHOVEN

## Symphony No. 3 in E♭ (Op. 55), The 'Eroica'

1. Allegro con brio. 2. Marcia funebre; Adagio assai. 3. Scherzo and Trio; Allegro vivace. 4. Finale; Allegro molto—Poco andante, con espressione—Presto (Variations).

Orchestra: 2 flutes; 2 oboes; 2 clarinets; 2 bassoons, 3 horns; 2 trumpets; 2 timpani; normal complement of strings—by now more than either Haydn or Mozart would have had.

Started in the summer of 1803, finished by the spring of the following year; second only to his Ninth Symphony in dimensions and substantially bigger in scope than anything written before it. This was probably the first time three horns had been used in the orchestra; note also the now standard acceptance of clarinets—instruments that were only invented in Mozart's time, and consequently only used by him in five of his forty-one symphonies.

S O MUCH HAS ALREADY been written about Beethoven and his music that it seems almost presumptuous to add anything else to the pile; the fact remains, however, that there are always new listeners to be catered for, not to mention the many thousands of music-lovers who, while they may be familiar with the sound of the Beethoven symphonies, have still never read any of the books by Grove, Tovey, Dickinson, Riezler, Schauffler, Evans, and the many other writers who together have contributed the 200 treatises, analyses, biographies, character studies, and essays that are listed in Grove's Dictionary alone. If, then, some of the material in this essay is already known to you, have consideration for those for whom even the background of this famous symphony may still be only vaguely realized.

It is difficult when we think about Beethoven's music not to be influenced by the extraordinary facts of his life. If a Hollywood film producer had invented a story in which a man who was to be generally regarded as the world's greatest composer was made stone deaf for half his creative life, not only the critics but also the general public would have thought it pretty far-fetched. A dumb poet would be a little more probable, a blind artist a little less. A deaf composer is a mockery of the gods—an object of pity if his talent is small, but a tragedy on a Grecian scale when he is one of the greatest creators of all time. Yet this deafness undoubtedly gives us a clue to many of the more baffling problems that his music presents; can we be surprised that the terrible birth-pangs which his compositions had to survive made his music unlike anyone else's?

Despite the hopelessness of his situation, Beethoven never gave up trying to have a physical contact with music. Even though he could no longer hear a note, he used to supervise rehearsals of his works, watching like a hawk, relating the movements of the players to the imagined sounds in his head. A violinist called Böhm, the leader of a quartet who used to play Beethoven's later compositions (in spite of considerable hostility from the public), tells us of a rehearsal of the E♭ quartet, Op. 127. The work had been played once at a concert but was regarded as a meaningless fiasco, so the players went to Beethoven for coaching. Böhm had an idea that Beethoven's directions at the end of the work were wrong. The composer had put *Meno vivace*—less quickly—and Böhm felt that this slowing up of the music weakened its effect. He told the other members of the quartet to stick to the same tempo, and see what Beethoven said. Imagine the barely furnished room, cluttered with heaps of music and manuscript paper; in the middle, the four musicians playing, and in a corner the squat broad figure of the composer. His face is scarred with smallpox, his clothes are shabby beyond belief, his hair unkempt; but the eyes, deepset beneath bushy eyebrows, are staring at the performers with intense concentration. Every movement of their hands and fingers is related in his mind to the music he has written but never heard. In Böhm's own words: 'Beethoven, crouched in a corner, heard nothing, but watched with strained attention. After the last stroke of the bows, he said laconically, "Let it remain so", went to the desks and crossed out the *Meno vivace* in the four parts.'

This story, which is undoubtedly authentic, gives us some idea of the sort of concentration Beethoven must have had. Think of watching a film without a sound-track, a film of a string-quartet, and having to work out from the movements of the players exactly what and how they are playing, and you will get an impression of what he must have endured. What torture it must have been for this man to watch this dream-like performance of music he had never heard, nor ever would hear. It was not until 1822 that the final impact of total deafness struck him brutally at a rehearsal of *Fidelio* which he was bravely attempting to conduct. It was impossible to work under him, and finally his friend Schindler handed him a note, saying, 'I beg you not to go on; will explain at home.' Like a knife, the message cut through Beethoven's dreams and he rushed from the theatre, to collapse in tears of bitterest anguish at his house. In his later works the bearing of such a monstrous burden seemed to give him a super-natural strength, an ability to explore the profoundest depths of human suffering, yet still to attain a divine peace.

At the time of the 'Eroica' Symphony, the picture was not quite so black. His deafness had begun, but was still not total; he had won through the first spiritual struggle which the onset of his disease had brought in its train. The first agony of mind, which is so heartbreakingly conveyed in the famous *Heiligenstadt Testament* of October 1802, had been overcome. He was reconciled to his fate, and the sunlit gaiety of the Second Symphony, written when he was in the depths of despair, had proved to be a remedy more potent than anything medical science had to offer. With extra-ordinary resolution he planned, as he put it, to start upon 'a new road'; he remembered a commission given some four years previously, when the French ambassador in Vienna, General Bernadotte, had suggested that he might compose a symphony in honour of Napoleon. At the time Beethoven looked on the French leader as a saviour of his people; all his revolutionary instincts spoke in sympathy with the struggle the French had had to shake off the aristocratic tyranny they had endured too long. By the spring of 1804 the new symphony was finished, and one day Beethoven's disciple Ries saw a fair copy of the score lying on the master's piano. The title-page simply contained two names: at the top, 'Buonaparte'; at the bottom, 'Luigi[1] van Beethoven'. Here then was the tribute from one great man to another, a tribute unadorned by flowery speeches that might smack of insincerity. Only a few days later the idol proved to have feet of clay; on 18 May of that year Napoleon assumed the title of Emperor; when Beethoven heard the news he flew into a rage. 'After all, then,' he cried, 'he is nothing but an ordinary mortal! He will trample the rights of man underfoot, and become a greater tyrant than anyone.' Stamping across the room, he seized the score and tore the title-page in half. This tattered relic still exists and bears silent witness to the truth of the story. In the end, the work appeared as a 'Heroic symphony, composed to preserve the memory of a great man,[2] and dedicated to his Serene Highness Prince Lobkowitz'—one of Beethoven's patrons. It is one of the ironies of fate that the symphony that was designed to celebrate the end of much that the aristocracy stood for should ultimately be dedicated to a prince, even if he was a beneficent patron of the arts.

The first movement begins with two great chords of E♭ major. Beethoven's first sketches for the symphony show an interesting variation; his original idea was that these two chords should be based on dominant harmony; what is more, they were unevenly spaced.

Ex.40

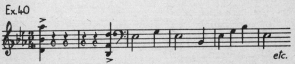

etc.

[1] A curious eccentricity on Beethoven's part since he normally signed himself Ludwig.
[2] *Composta per festeggiare il Sovvenire di un grand'Uomo.*

Apparently he then became worried by the gap between the first and second chords, and experimented with the possibility of filling it with some vaguely suggested notes.

Fortunately this unconvincing alternative was scrapped, and the infinitely stronger opening that we now know was finally devised. The brief introduction over, we hear the principal theme of the movement on the 'cellos. Like most classical symphonic material it is based on a common chord. Mozart at the age of twelve had hit on a remarkably similar theme at the start of his little opera *Bastien and Bastienne*. To compare them is an apt demonstration of the difference between charm and strength. Mozart, thirty-five years earlier, had written this:

All is tranquil and serene; the even measures of dance music suggest elegant behaviour in aristocratic circles. Compare the Beethoven to that, and what a storm is there, with the sudden twist to the foreign note of C♯, and the agitation of the syncopated G's in the violins above.

Here, then, are two conflicting ideas; the assurance of E♭ major once established is then undermined by the dissenting C♯; at once the violins reflect the uneasiness which this unexpected note inevitably brings. The almost pastoral mood of the opening is deceptive; it is as though the sculptor were caressing the stone with his hands before striking the first hammer-blows which will hew it into shape. By the twenty-fifth bar we find strongly accented chords breaking across the beat—

until finally the first theme returns in triumph.

It is already idle to speculate on any episode in Napoleon's career which these violent changes of mood might represent. The stimulus to Beethoven's imagination was no more than a 'trigger' action; once the musical material entered his head he would have been unlikely to have had thoughts for any external sequence of events. Commentators of the time produced fantastic theories about the work, such as the seriously made suggestion that Napoleon's army had arrived in Egypt by the time the Development had been reached since one of its episodes was a theme of 'decidedly Oriental colouring'. If the violent cross-accentuation of the preceding example indicates a battle it is indeed a brief one, since in a matter of twenty bars the mood relents and we discover a charming section in which each of the woodwind in turn plays a little three-note phrase, like children passing a toy from hand to hand to be admired.

This of course is a quickened-up version of bars 4-5 of Ex. 43. But we must not pay too much attention to detailed phrases in this score, fascinating though their relationships may be. It is a huge canvas on a generous scale, and one of its most remarkable features is the way in which Beethoven changes its mood with the utmost frequency and yet welds the whole vast movement together completely satisfactorily. In the next hundred bars or so we find a great variety of new ideas. In addition to the three-note phrase above, there is this rising scale on clarinets,

which is mirrored in descending bassoons; this is followed by a far more athletic phrase for the strings,

and by way of further contrast a positively Mendelssohnian little theme

which might be labelled the 'true' second subject were it not for the fact that Beethoven never uses it again till the Recapitulation. Varied though these fragments may seem detached from their context in this way, the fact remains that in the course of the movement they appear to follow on one after the other in a marvellously natural and spontaneous way. Remember, though, that nothing like this had ever been done before under the title of Symphony, and it is particularly suitable that this revolution in symphonic form should have been written to celebrate the most famous son of a revolution.

The Development begins mysteriously with ghostly echoes of the rhythm of the opening theme; however, far and away the most useful idea is the athletic rhythm of Ex. 47. This Beethoven uses as a unifying force; up to now, he hasn't revealed to us that it will fit against the 'cellos' opening phrase. The more excitable rhythm has an inflammatory effect, and the pastoral mood of the first few notes is transformed into a veritable tempest.

Ex.49

Intermittently the sheer volume of sound created here is reduced to a sudden *piano*, but at such moments the music is still too disturbed to subside entirely and little flickers of restlessness persist in the second violins. One of the most remarkable passages in the movement comes a little later on; its revolutionary aspect is enhanced by a nice piece of symbolism. Beethoven starts what appears to be a fugue, albeit an agitated and fiery one.

Ex.50

Within thirteen bars of its inception this ordered counterpoint is engulfed in a storm of passion. It is as though all shackles with the past were being violently broken; 'modern' chords shatter the ancient traditions of fugue. Like a Samson shaking the very foundations of harmony, Beethoven wrestles with the music in a passage such as had never been heard before. Dissonances of extraordinary violence pound across the natural feel of the rhythm, and for more than thirty bars the framework of the music seems to be battered out of shape. Finally, all passion spent, a forlorn little tune emerges in the remote key of E minor, a tune which in my opinion seldom seems to be interpreted with quite the feeling of exhaustion which its position implies.

This is the innocent wisp of melody which suggested the Ancient Nile to a mid-nineteenth-century critic!

The other really outstanding moment in this wonderful movement comes just before the return home to the Recapitulation. For some time we have had the impression that something is in the air; the music seems almost overcome by a feeling of inertia, and then, tentative and distant, the horns breathe the first four notes of the opening theme. This is the famous 'wrong-note' entry that caused so much comment when it was first heard. The actual notes are these:

It is pathetic to see how petty minds have tried to 'correct' Beethoven's wonderfully picturesque touch. At the level of a first-year harmony student, one could say that the chord above the horn entry doesn't 'fit'; but why a man of Wagner's stature should have suggested that Beethoven had really intended the second violins to have G instead of A♭ in those two vital bars is beyond me. Other nineteenth-century authorities thought the horn part was intended to be in the tenor clef, which would make it read B♭DB♭F. Both emendations seem incredibly narrow-minded. Even the devoted disciple Ries suggested at the first rehearsal of the work that 'the damned horn-player' had come in wrong. Beethoven's only reply was to aim a terrific clout at him, which fortunately missed. Once it is divorced from considerations of textbook harmony, what a wonderful effect this moment is; the gradual reduction of the orchestral texture to a whisper, then faint and evocative the distant horn-call which is instantly received with a great shout of acclamation by the rest of the orchestra. Here, one might say, is a moment that does savour of 'programme' music, as though a great concourse of people awaited the arrival of their hero, and at the distant sound of his fanfare, shouted aloud.

In triumph the original theme returns, but with a marvellously subtle change which seems to symbolize an easing of its inner conflict. The C♯ in bars 5–6 of Ex. 43 no longer turns back on itself to D but drops to C♮ in a moment that suggests the sort of modulation that Schubert made so much his own. Compare Exx. 43 and 53 closely in terms of *sound* and you will appreciate the emotional change which this seemingly simple modification brings about.

continuing in
F major

Always up to now the curious C♯ has suggested that the music was going to modulate, though quite in what direction it was difficult to see; each time, Beethoven has sternly drawn it back towards the home key of E♮ major. This time he allows it to have its head and the feeling of release is almost physical.

The Recapitulation is by no means exact; page after page reveals new touches to the attentive ear, until the movement ends with a coda[1] of quite extraordinary richness—so much so that it seems almost like a new development section. Very often the demarcation of the coda or codetta from its preceding music seems a matter of purely theoretical interest; here Beethoven gives us an absolutely unmistakable sign that something of the greatest significance is still in store. Quite quietly the music comes to rest in the tonic key of E♮ major. Then suddenly out of the blue comes an immense chord of D♭, a tone lower, and still a shock even to ears that have experienced Bartók and Stravinsky. In 1805 it must have seemed an earthquake.

Ex. 54

The dramatic effect is twofold, for not only are the swift and unprepared changes of key from E♮ to D♭ and then to C major immensely exciting, but their shock value is enhanced by sudden alternations of *p*, *f*, *p*, and *ff*. Just as the audience is recovering its breath, Beethoven sheds a totally unexpected light on the opening theme by matching it to a positively skittish counter-melody.

This in turn leads to further new developments. Only by real

[1] See footnote, p. 7.

Ex.55

familiarity can one begin to appreciate the magnificent architecture of this great musical structure. It is an idealized conception of an anarchic society, where law, order, and unity are imposed from within, and not by the imposition of petty regulations from outside. To try to relate its purely musical form to worldly events is not merely imperceptive; it is an act of wilful misunderstanding; no events of ordinary life could change from one mood to another with such startling rapidity without making us all end up in the madhouse. Yet such changes are perfectly rational in music since music obeys other laws, laws that can bring acceptance of what might seem inexplicable in any other terms.

The second movement is a funeral march, but quite what Beethoven's motives were for electing to write one here I do not know. At a guess, I should say that it is merely a concession to the 'heroic' calibre of the music, in that heroes tend to be buried in pomp and ceremony; it would be unwise to assume that Beethoven was tactlessly anticipating Napoleon's funeral. There is even quite good evidence that the music was projected a couple of years earlier as a tribute to the English general, Sir Ralph Abercrombie, killed at the Battle of Alexandria in 1801. Composers are great opportunists, and it seems most likely that the incomplete march started on this earlier occasion gave Beethoven some material that came nicely to hand when he wanted it. So much for any relationship to a hard-and-fast programme.

Technically, one of the most interesting things in this movement is Beethoven's avoidance of drums at the beginning. With all their associations with military pomp, few composers could have resisted using them; instead he contents himself with low rumbles on the double basses, who here, most unusually for the period, have a separate part from the 'cellos. Stripped of decorations, the first phrase of the funeral melody consists of the notes GCE♭C, which, for what it's worth, spell out the principal theme of the first movement in the minor and backwards. This seems to me to be no more than a happy coincidence calculated to excite the musicological mind. So many classical themes are built on the common chord that it would not be difficult to show a thematic relationship between works separated from each other by generations.

The immense span of the phrases in this movement and its slow tempo mean that it is exceptionally long—too long for some, like the man in the gallery at the first performance whom Czerny heard moaning, 'I'd give a kreuzer if only it'd stop.' For those who are prepared to adjust themselves to its measured tread there are ample rewards, and a great deal more variety than one at first realizes. Periodically the feeling of unalloyed grief is softened by episodes like the one in C major in which the woodwind instruments commune together over a gentle murmuring of triplets from the strings.

Structurally this is rather similar to the beautiful A major clarinet tune in the middle of the slow movement of the Seventh Symphony,[1] and such contrasts are like the warming rays of the sun on a grey afternoon. Overall, the march leaves an impression of profound grief, and again I would emphasize the stark impossibility of devising a programme of Napoleonic episodes which would fit both the death-like finality of this movement and the immensely gay and vital scherzo which now follows. A much

[1] See p. 65.

more convincing and indeed brilliant elucidation of the 'programme' of the symphony has been suggested by J. W. N. Sullivan in his penetrating study of Beethoven's spiritual development.[1] He sees the 'Eroica' as a 'transcription of personal experience'. The first movement shows Beethoven's courage and defiance of fate; the second, the deep despair which his deafness had brought on, and to which I have already referred; the Scherzo celebrates the tremendous uprising of creative energy which the composer had experienced as he emerged from his own private hell, and of which the brilliant Second Symphony is a vivid reminder. In the finale, the choice of variation form symbolizes the range of achievement which is now open to the 'Promethean' energy of the reawakened spirit. This analysis seems to me both psychologically sound and musically convincing; it changes the 'programme' of the symphony to the musical exposition of general states of mind—which is precisely the sort of thing which music can do successfully. When it comes to illustrating actual events it is far less happy, unless a written catalogue of what it is supposed to be representing is supplied. We accept an atmospheric image of the sea in Debussy's *La Mer*; we can appreciate the difference between the Swan and the Asses in *The Carnival of the Animals*; but the intelligent mind revolts at the thought of the first movement of the 'Eroica' representing Napoleonic squadrons of cavalry; Beethoven's only attempt at such pictorialism, in the 'Battle' symphony, was a foregone disaster.

A scherzo such as we now find was a form virtually invented by Beethoven, of which this is the first outstanding example. Admittedly the corresponding movement in the second symphony has many points of originality, and speaks to us in an idiom that goes beyond the resources of Mozart or Haydn. Remarkable though it is, it still remains light-weight; in comparison, the 440 bars of the 'Eroica' scherzo seem to establish a new conception of the permissible scale for such a movement. The classic Menuet and Trio from which the scherzo form was

[1] J. W. N. Sullivan: *Beethoven*: William Brown and Co., 1927.

derived has now receded so far into the background that it is completely forgotten.

The movement begins with a quiet and excited bustle on the strings out of which emerges a tune of infectious gaiety played by the first violins doubled at the upper octave by a solo oboe. Despite the fact that the piece is in E♭ major, this vital theme appears in B♭, an unexpected twist which obviously caused Beethoven considerable head-scratching, since his first sketches all indicate that the melody should be in the tonic key of E♭. It is interesting to compare his first version with the one we now know. Here is the preliminary sketch:

Ex.57

and it breaks off there.

The presence of an A♮ in the third full bar shows that his mind was already veering towards the dominant key of B♭, since A♮ is the essential modulating note that will take us from E♭ major to B♭ major. Where this sketch shows a weakness, which Beethoven subsequently rectified, is in its initial departure on a journey which is too soon contradicted by a return home. If you play the example above and then immediately compare it with the final version below, you will realize the superiority of Beethoven's revision, since once it has set out towards B♭ major it avoids the tame return to E♭ and states the tune clearly in the new key regardless of academic sanction.

Ex.58

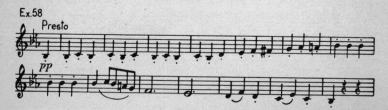

This wisp of melody flits bat-like through the score; the volume remains at a low level in spite of the gaiety of the music.

At one point, Beethoven twists the tail of the principal theme by detaching the last four bars of the example above and playing tag with them through the orchestra.

At last, with a great thump of timpani and a blare of brass, the whole band come sweeping in with the main theme—the justification for this joyful noise being that it is the first time that the theme has appeared in the home key of E♭. Over and over again one finds comparable passages in classical music which merely underline the importance of the key system; a tonality lost leads to passages of vagueness and mystery, a tonality rediscovered is greeted with acclamation and triumph. Had Beethoven retained his first sketch for this movement (see Ex. 57) he would have deprived himself of the musical justification for this exciting climax. The effect of jubilation is all the greater in that the orchestra appear to be tumbling over themselves with excitement—so much so that the theme overlaps itself, like voices babbling in a crowd.

Momentarily, the strings stand clear from the ruck, and a new

theme marked by strong off-beat accents impresses itself on our
memories.

Much has been made of the possible relationship between this
and the initial theme of the first movement,[1] but I feel it is unlikely to be anything more than a subconscious reflection. When
Beethoven does use cyclic unity of this kind, as for instance he
does when he makes the scherzo theme of the Fifth Symphony
reappear in the finale, he generally makes his intentions pretty
clear. If you consider the state of a composer's mind when
creating a work on this scale, it is only natural that all sorts of
related themes should be swirling about in his brain at one and
the same time. So tempestuous a movement as the first allegro of
this symphony must have given him many a sleepless night, and
its patterns would have sunk so deeply into his subconscious that
it is small wonder if they have influenced subsequent passages.
Commentators who greet the theme above as a deliberate reference to the first movement conveniently ignore the striking
difference it makes when Beethoven subsequently changes its
rhythm to duple time—an ingenious way of making an apparent
*accelerando*.

It would seem to be far more likely that Beethoven was consciously trying to *avoid* any suggestion of the first movement, since
he rejected a theme for the Trio which does certainly have both
melodic and rhythmic similarities. Of the four or five sketches he
made for the middle section of this great scherzo, the first bears
a strong resemblance to the 'cello tune from the opening allegro.

[1] See p. 46, Ex. 43.

Ex.63

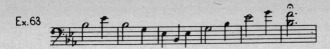

Even allowing for the fact that the choice of notes here is to a certain extent dictated by what was comfortable for a horn to play, the first two bars of this example do seem to be suspiciously close to the first bars of the opening theme. Surely then Beethoven's total rejection of this idea indicates his distaste for such a relationship. Instead, we find the three horns embarking on a theme which is still built on the 'common chord' of E♭ major out of practical necessity,[1] but which goes out of its way to avoid any suggestion of earlier material.

Ex.64

Where this Trio is remarkable is in the increasingly poetic element which it introduces; it is the epitome of that peculiarly German romanticism which we find so often in the music of Schumann and Wagner, and this is perhaps its first expression.

The *pp* start of the movement makes the return to the opening material a comparatively simple matter; a last sigh from the horns recedes into a twilight stillness, and then once again the strings (but this time reduced in numbers by the elimination of second violins and violas) bring us back to the bustle and gaiety with which the movement had begun.

Ever since the first performance of the 'Eroica', the Finale has been the movement most open to criticism. In part, this may have been due to the overall dimensions of the work, which far exceed those of any earlier symphony; performances were even given omitting the Scherzo and Finale, and a characteristic example of

[1] The horn in Beethoven's time had no valves, and in consequence could only play the 'harmonic series'; for further explanation see any musical dictionary.

critical acumen was displayed in a London magazine called the *Harmonicon*, which in its April issue of 1829 said that 'if this symphony is not by some means abridged, it will soon fall into disuse'. In fact, it is difficult to visualize any alternative form for this finale, except possibly a fugue. Drama and fantasy have had their say in the first movement, grief and pathos in the second, gaiety and high spirits in the third; the one notable omission has been what might be termed the 'craft' element in composition. Obviously, enormous skill has been displayed throughout, but not of the conscious kind that the writing of a fugue or set of variations involves. In the event, Beethoven decided to elaborate a theme which must have been an especial favourite, since he had already used it in his 'Prometheus' ballet-music, and also as the basis for the Op. 35 piano variations. It is just possible that there may have been some subtle connection in his mind between the 'heroic' aspect of Napoleon and the legendary figure of Prometheus, though I tend to believe that by the time he reached this movement, thoughts of Napoleon had become a very minor consideration, so deeply would he have been involved in a purely musical conception.

He begins with a torrent of semiquavers which may well have been in the back of Tchaikovsky's mind when he came to write the finale of his Fourth Symphony; but whereas Tchaikovsky's passage suggests a Bacchanale, this obviously presages something of a highly serious nature. An impressive pause leads us to a quiet and positively skeletonic statement of the 'Prometheus' theme on *pizzicato* strings.

Ex. 65

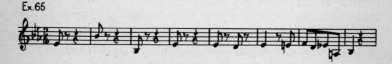

To describe this as the 'Prometheus' theme is misleading—as misleading as Beethoven is (deliberately) in suggesting that we are now hearing a tune on which variations are to be built.

What he has done is the equivalent of starting a set of variations on 'God Save the King' with *pizzicato* 'cellos and basses doing this:

Ex. 66

In other words, what we have heard is not a theme, but the *bass* of a theme, and its elevation to the status of a melody is typical of Beethoven's dry humour.[1] Strings and woodwind proceed to play Grandmother's Footsteps with this undistinguished-looking fragment; there is a silence of three beats, and then an apparently inexplicable outburst of three explosive B flats on full wind, brass, and timpani. Another silence, and then a quiet sustained B♭, as if these rowdy intruders were apologizing for their bad manners. However, after four more bars of decorum, the heckling begins again; this time even the strings are infected, and the same explosions occur, together with a similar apology.

On the face of it, this is sheer madness on Beethoven's part. It is, of course, an elaborate trick; a fair comparison would be the schoolboy joke relating to this picture:

The viewer is supposed to make several fruitless guesses as to the subject, whereupon the artist, falling about with mirth, reveals that it is a giraffe walking past a window. Judging from his music, this would have convulsed Beethoven; for in just the same way, what he has done here is to give us a suggestion of an outline without any of the vital details. He prolongs the suspense still further by embarking on two quite orthodox variations on what we have heard so far; we are even ready to believe that this

[1] It is curious that none of our more 'psychological' critics has suggested that this promotion of a simple bass line to melodic status *might* be a symbolic representation of the improved lot of the post-Revolutionary French worker. . . .

skeleton of a theme is the real thing, and that the B♮ outbursts are mere eccentricity. Then comes the revelation; at last we see that the picture wasn't a complete picture at all, but only a part of it. The presumptuous bass takes its proper place, like a servant that has been caught trying on his master's clothes; for the first time we hear the true melody which had been in Beethoven's mind the whole time. Put *with* the bass, like this, all becomes clear, and the loud B flats followed by the 'apology' fall into perspective.

So breathtaking a revelation is naturally greeted with a good deal of excitement by the orchestra, and there is a fair amount of running hither and thither before the music settles down to a serious discussion of the now fully comprehended material. Since the practical jokes are over, and a serious fugue is about to be launched, the key very properly turns to the more severe climate of C minor. Thus modified, the 'bass' which has so misled us takes on new stature, and we at once respond to the change of mood.

Ex.68

This is worked out in ever-increasing complexity and animation, until the 'Prometheus' melody unexpectedly reappears in the wildly remote key of B minor. This in turn is varied in the woodwind, while the first violins have a scampering phrase that suggests the sort of frenzied activity which we associate today with 'novelty' pieces with names like 'Toboggan-run' or 'Holiday on Wheels'. It would be wearisome to chronicle each appearance of the theme from now on; suffice it to say that either the 'bass' or the 'melody' of the theme is never far away. The main scheme of things is a skilful alternation of fugal sections with more openly dramatic chordal writing. By avoiding committing himself to a strict fugue Beethoven has the best of both worlds; he can demonstrate his craftsmanship in some pages while being free to indulge in dramatics when he wishes.

Perhaps the greatest surprise still to come is the central change of tempo, which is prepared as though it were a cadenza in a concerto. In a way, it *is* a cadenza—a cadenza for composer, for now Beethoven seems to embark on a glorious improvisation, in which the 'Prometheus' melody assumes new beauty by being slowed to an Andante. Cadenza-like, this section surveys the material of the movement and treats it with a new freedom; the rigours of counterpoint are forgotten in passages of great harmonic richness. At last the music settles on to a long-reiterated G in the 'cellos, over which curiously alternating harmonies chatter quietly in woodwind and strings; and then, like a sudden door thrown open letting in a blast of cold air, the same cascade of notes with which the movement had begun sweeps us back into a final tumultuous Presto.

So enormous an advance over its predecessors does this work reveal in idiom, in technique, and in the whole conception of what music was capable of expressing, that we cannot be surprised that it caused perplexity and hostility in many listeners before it finally established itself as one of the great landmarks of music. After its first performance it was described in the *Allgemeine Musikalische Zeitung* as

> a lengthy, wild and bold fantasy, most difficult to perform. While there is no lack of strikingly beautiful sections in which one can discern the energy and talent of the composer, the work often strays into utter irregularity . . . there is too much that is shrill and bizarre . . . one almost entirely loses any sense of coherence.

Other critics took Beethoven to task for not continuing the style of his early works. One criticism strikes a very familiar note: it expresses a fear lest music should become so complex that it will become the exclusive preserve of the expert, and that the ordinary listener will leave the concert-hall depressed by incoherent and overblown ideas as well as by the perpetual noise of the full orchestra.[1] How many times through the centuries have these words been spoken about 'contemporary' music?

[1] See Max Graf: *Composer and Critic*: Chapman & Hall 1947.

## CHAPTER V

# BEETHOVEN

## Symphony No. 7 in A major, Op. 92 (1812)

1. Poco sostenuto, leading to Vivace. 2. Allegretto. 3. Scherzo; presto. 4. Finale; allegro con brio.

Orchestra: 2 flutes; 2 oboes; 2 clarinets; 2 bassoons; 2 horns; 2 trumpets; 2 timpani; normal complement of strings.

Notice the return to only two horns, compared with the three in the 'Eroica'. Normally, Beethoven is quite content with two; the Third (3) and Ninth (4) symphonies are the sole examples of his demanding more. There is a gap of over three years between this symphony and its predecessor, No. 6 (Op. 68). There is no particular reason for this except that he had a slight tendency to write works in pairs; thus we find symphonies No. 5 and 6 are Op. 67 and Op. 68. So great an effort of concentration on the largest orchestral form probably made him turn to other fields until the next impulse, which produced No. 7 (Op. 92) and No. 8 (Op. 93).

IN HIS SEVENTH SYMPHONY Beethoven returns to the old classical device of a slow introduction; he had already used this in his First, Second, and Fourth Symphonies, and in a way it is a little surprising to find what would appear to be a retrograde step as late as Op. 92. A comparison with these earlier works is revealing, however, since it shows us how his sense of architectural scale was developing. In the First Symphony the slow introduction is a scant twelve bars; in the Second, we find this nearly trebled to thirty-three bars; the proportions of the Fourth are much the same—thirty-eight bars, but by the time we reach the Seventh Symphony, the introduction takes on the importance of an annexe rather than an entrance since it is no less than sixty-two bars long. When you consider that the entire slow movement of the 'Pathétique' Sonata is a mere seventy-three bars of Adagio 2/4, and that here we have sixty-two bars of 4/4 (twice the length of bar, even if at a slightly quicker tempo), you begin to realize quite how Beethoven's conception of the overall proportions of a movement had changed.

There are many points of originality in this opening. The one that attracts immediate attention is the scoring of the first few bars. Beethoven begins with a full chord, using the entire orchestra including a forte stroke on the drum. Out of this there emerges the only sustained note, on a single oboe—a dramatic contrast indeed. Every 'odd' bar on the first page has a similar explosive chord, but all the way through they are joined to each other by slender strands of woodwind, as though great pillars had decorative ropes connecting them. In each gap we find more voices progressively joining in; the first link is for solo oboe, the next for oboe and clarinet; then four instruments take up the refrain—flute, oboe, clarinet, and horn, so that one has a wonderful sense of some musical ritual in which the instruments take their places according to an ancient preordained pattern. This is true architecture in terms of sound, since it can easily be indicated in visual symbols.

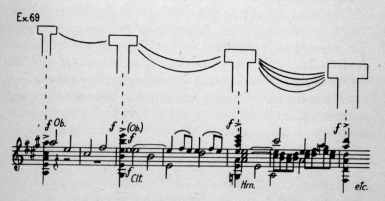

Ex.69

Beethoven may have felt that there was a danger that these long arches of sound might be too great in their span for easy comprehension; so, still keeping the same majestic pace, he now helps us across the chasms by quicker moving notes which carry the ear from point to point with greater ease. Once he has accustomed us to this new development, he returns to the first idea; but this time, what had been a mere sketch has the details filled in. We still find the same steps from pillar to pillar; there is a tremendous difference in the effect, though, for around these striding notes there bustles a multitude of semiquavers. A glance at bars 15–22 of the score will show at once what I mean.

Unexpectedly, the music suddenly begins to quieten; the scales disperse into thin air and the woodwind introduce a theme which suggests a march, but again a march of a curiously ritual quality, as though it belonged to a temple rather than a parade-ground. Its feeling of remoteness is intensified by the tonality of C major in which we now find ourselves. This is foreign territory indeed, and part of our interest must be in waiting to see how Beethoven is going to get back. In a 'thriller', one is kept in a state of suspense wondering how the hero is going to get out of a tight situation; this might be termed a celestial equivalent, since the musician will not only have realized the strange world that the music has entered, but will also be absorbed in observing its return to the familiar pastures of A major.

The strings take up the march theme in their turn, while oboe and bassoon keep nagging away at a G natural—which only serves to underline our remoteness from the home key, since the most essential note to establish the key of A major is a G sharp. Then, with increasing excitement, Beethoven seems to see the way back. Here is a simplified skeleton which shows the various stepping-stones that he uses.

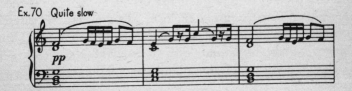

Ex. 70  Quite slow

Ex. 70 *cont.*

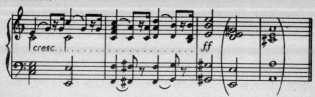

Once again it seems a suitable moment to stress the point already made on p. 63; the crescendo here springs not from any desire on Beethoven's part to illustrate some external excitement; it arises purely because the home key of A major has at last been sighted. The last two chords of Ex. 70 show how he has the tonality of A in his grasp; indeed, a lesser composer would probably have been quite content to have accepted the ending I have suggested in brackets, albeit somewhat decorated. Where Beethoven reveals a master-stroke of genius is that with his goal so nearly reached, and with the knowledgeable listener about to sit back and relax, he pushes on recklessly and launches out into even more obscure keys. Instinct and training tell us that an arrival at this chord of the dominant must be the ultimate solution; by postponing it still further, Beethoven is like an author who rescues his hero from one predicament, only to pitch him into another. The laws of musical symmetry and tonal relationships are such that we can say that if a classical symphony has a slow intro-duction in a particular key, the chances are 99 in 100 that the main part of the movement will be in the same key. Every deviation from that key has the effect of putting off our arrival at what we can be virtually certain is our final destination.

Brushing aside the obvious, Beethoven drags us on by means of the same giant pillars with which we are already familiar. The quiet march theme returns again, this time in F major;[1] a compar-able crescendo to the one quoted in Ex. 70, but with an element of increased tension, finally explodes into a gigantic E natural. For the second time we are in sight of the homeland. There ensues a passage which only goes to emphasize the rightness of

[1] It is worth checking the relative 'distances' of these keys on the housing estate plan on p. 13.

treating music as a language with its own rules, rather than as a mere translation of non-musical events into sound. I have laid enormous emphasis on keys in this analysis; how else can we explain the passage that now confronts us, in which Beethoven repeats the note E over seventy times in ten bars? At this point, he is playing with us. Already he has snatched us away from our ultimate goal of A major; now he keeps us in suspense a new way. 'Are you quite certain we've really made it this time?' he seems to say; and he goes on harping on this one note, teasing us with it, until at last he relents and goes skipping off into one of the happiest themes he ever thought of.

Nothing could more graphically illustrate the increased pleasure that an understanding of musical structure brings than this introduction. On the face of it, these fifteen pages of score are not particularly exciting; the music is slow, but without the compensation of any especially beautiful melody; it has a number of scales traipsing up and down, and several passages where Beethoven flogs one note to death. It would be easy to dismiss it as boring, and to the untrained ear it may well be so. To a musician, as I have tried to show you, it is a whole series of carefully planned moves towards or away from an ultimate destination. Far from merely juggling with tunes and colours and chords, the composer is combining an architect's vision with the campaigning sense of a general,[1] plus, at one point, a conjuror's deception. You can compare music with many other things, but in the long run it boils down to something which cannot be expressed except by the notes themselves. To interpret it entirely in emotional terms, as so many genuine lovers of music tend to do, is to reduce it to the level of a drug. Loud, quick music stimulates; quiet, slow music relaxes. If this were the whole story, what a petty art it would be; such aspects are only the superficialities, as inadequate as it would be to describe a sunset as 'red', or Michelangelo's David as 'a stone man'. Every sound induces an emotional response, even the distant hoot of a train whistle or the cosy clink

[1] Beethoven once said, 'If I knew as much about war as I do about music I could defeat Napoleon himself.'

of a teacup. In music, powerful though the emotional stimulus may be, it is often only a side-effect; the essential difference between so-called Classical and Romantic music lies in the change of balance between form and emotion. Classical music generates emotion from the abstract contemplation and manipulation of form; Romantic music is an expression of personal emotions translated into sound. The misunderstanding arises when people try to interpret music in the wrong terms by expecting to find similar beauties in a Bach fugue and a Chopin nocturne. Both are beautiful but in a totally different way, just as Shakespeare differs from Browning, or Corot from Franz Hals. What we have to learn is sufficient understanding of style and idiom to be able to appreciate the many worlds of music, and not to attempt to force it into our own narrow conception of what is beautiful or proper.

Once Beethoven is launched into the main part of the movement it is all fairly plain sailing. The music is for the most part extrovert and full of good humour. The principal theme is first presented on woodwind, which gives it a suitably pastoral flavour.

Ex.71

The strings seem to take a little while to cotton on to this new mood, and several times they question the woodwind with this interrogatory phrase:

Ex.72

Ultimately they gain confidence, and join in with an enthusiastic rush of semiquavers while 'cellos and basses drum approvingly below.

Particular mention should be made of the variation of tone in this score; seldom before has Beethoven combined such happiness of mood with such violent and arresting changes from loud to soft. The dangers of an excess of rum-ti-tum which sometimes become so apparent in this type of bucolic music are skilfully avoided by the use of unpredictable dynamic marks.[1]

The second subject group is reached with the minimum of formality, and proves to be mainly concerned with two ideas, of which the first is of an unselfconscious singing quality that we normally might only expect to find in Schubert.

Ex.73

The second of these two elements preserves something of the rhythmic character of the first subject, but also introduces a brief but lyrical phrase on the strings by way of contrast.

Ex.74

The end of the exposition and its subsequent join into the development section show us a lovely example of Beethoven's humour at its most slapstick. The closing bars of the exposition consist of a rising scale played as though the strings all had their gloves on, alternating with explosive off-beat E's from the wood-wind and brass, who, to use an Americanism in its literal sense, can't seem to get 'with it'.

Ex.75

[1] The technical term for *f*, *p*, *ff*, *mf*, etc.

This total lack of symphonic decorum prompts the two bars of stunned silence before the double bar. Assuming that we have done the repeat of the exposition, we now find the orchestra ploughing blindly on, only to come to an abrupt halt.

Ex. 76

This second silence provokes the question, 'And where do you think we're going to now?' Observe that this apparent violence is not to be taken seriously; this is the roar of father pretending to be a lion, not the storm and anguish we find in the Fifth or Ninth symphonies. As though entering into the spirit of the game, the violins ever so tentatively suggest that since the whole thing seems to have broken down completely, the only thing to do is to go back to something familiar and start again. Gradually the other sections of the orchestra join in, although still in a very subdued mood after the 'disgrace' of the preceding two examples.

The danger of using a simile such as comparing music to father pretending to be a lion is that it plants an inflexible picture in people's minds. While I am convinced that at that particular moment Beethoven was suggesting a mood of boisterous knockabout humour which can be compared to such domestic larks, music is such a fantastic and unique world that it can translate us from this mood to another infinitely remote in a matter of seconds. It may be all right to see father on his hands and knees wearing the rug at one point, but it is absolutely fatal to look for him anywhere else in the movement. We must always be ready for some purely musical miracle that will lift us back into a more ethereal world. Here, for instance, is Beethoven charging happily along in E major:

Ex. 77

Having arrived triumphantly on this final E, and with such assurance that we feel we are bound to stay there for several pages, he whips round and shoots us into the totally unexpected key of C♯ major.

Ex. 78

The sudden quietness of the sustained wind chord at the end is magical. Now it is just possible that a lesser composer might have got this far, and were he to have done so, we could predict that having reached this new tonal centre of D♭ major (or C♯—they are interchangeable), he would stay in it for at least a while. Beethoven is more subtle; he has yet another switch that catches us right off our guard. At the very instant that the woodwind confirm that departure from E major, just as we get our breath back from the shock, he gives the harmony still another twist and goes to an even more remote key. Go straight from the preceding example into this one and you will see what a striking change this new departure is.

Ex. 79

* Passages like this appear to have had a particularly strong influence on Schumann.

This heart-stopping moment has the same sort of perfection as an impossible return in a tennis-match, or an effortless leg-glide from a ball you were sure had the batsman beaten. Since it is music, however, it is transient beauty made permanent.

One more delightful trap is worth mentioning before we leave this exhilarating movement. It concerns the blustering scale which ends the exposition (p. 71, Ex. 75). Some thirty-five pages later this same scale reappears in identical form, except that it is now in A instead of E. In every respect, the layout is exactly similar —the same fumble-fingered splodges on the strings, the same off-beat squeals from the woodwind, even down to the same two-bar silence. With the memory of the previous version in our minds, we sit there confidently expecting four more bomps and then a silence, out of which will emerge the violins *pp*. Once again Beethoven proves himself a master of the prepared surprise; instead of the awaited four loud notes he gives us one tentative and apologetic little peep from the strings, followed by an equally unnerved squeak from the wind. After a further silence, it is the 'cellos who this time restore order; we in the audience have been bamboozled on every point, and it is game, set, and match to Beethoven.

The second movement was an instant success. Whereas some critics were baffled by the first and last movements,[1] everyone loved the simplicity of the Allegretto. So much so that it was often taken out of its context and played in place of the slow movement of the Second Symphony, which was considered rather long and dreary. The composer's scheme in this movement is to present a tune that is more a sequence of chords than a melody, and then to enrich it by adding a warm and melting counter-tune. Too long to give in full in an essay such as this, I merely quote a few bars, with the counter-melody above:

[1] In Leipzig they said it could only have been composed when Beethoven was either ill or drunk, and Weber said the composer must now be ripe for the madhouse.

Ex. 80

By writing the melody of the third and seventh bars in the way he has, Beethoven has provided conductors and orchestral players with enough food for argument to keep them happy for years. Should the rhythm be played ♫♪ ♫♪, and if so why didn't he write it like that? Or did he want the first two notes to be sneaked in at the end of the previous bar? Or should they be quicker than written: ♫♪ . ♫♪ ? For what it's worth, my own contribution to the debate would be this.

The Elizabethan name for an ornament was a 'relish'; nothing could more aptly convey the true function of ornamentation in music. It is a means of bestowing a special favour on the following note, of picking it out from its neighbours. By electing to write these two notes in an obsolescent form of notation, Beethoven was indicating not *when* they should be played but *how* they should be played—with a special affection, leading to an intensified pathos on the D. Since he was harking back to the period of his youth at this point by reviving a custom that was falling into disuse, it would seem most likely that the notes should be played with and not before the beat, as his father must have told him many a time in the unhappy music-lessons of his boyhood.

The movement is pervaded throughout by the solemn rhythmic pattern we find in each pair of bars in Ex. 80. Its constant reiteration has a hypnotic effect, but in itself this rhythm is without tenderness or compassion. Only when it is illuminated by the

counter-melody does it show any warmth. It is *Fidelio* all over
again, with the prisoners trudging hopelessly around the prison-
yard, only to find their misery evaporating beneath the healing
rays of the sun. Indeed in this movement the sun does shine with the
radiantly beautiful clarinet tune which appears half-way through.

With an accompaniment of gently murmuring triplets from
the first violins we hardly notice the persistent trudge of the 𝄐 𝄐
rhythm which still continues beneath. Beautiful though it is, this
melody does not succeed in dispelling the prevailing gloom, and
after a mere thirty-seven bars it is displaced by stern triplets which
cut descending swathes through the orchestra and herald the
return of the original material. This is treated in a slightly more
elaborate manner, including a ghostly little fugue; the sun comes
out once more in a brief memory of the clarinet tune before the
movement sinks once again into darkness. It ends as it had begun,
with a bleak A minor chord on the woodwind—two covers that
enclose this sad and brooding chapter.

It is easy to see why this movement has always been so popular;
its outlines are clear, its rhythm constant, its whole progress as
orderly as you could wish. The caprice and bluster of the first
movement have been replaced by the stylized pathos of a Greek
chorus, and this oasis of melancholy stillness, for all its sadness, was
welcomed by the puzzled audiences of the day.

The unpredictable Beethoven returns in the Scherzo, which is
full of practical jokes and a bustling animation which must have
seemed very regrettable to the older people in the concert-hall in
Vienna in 1814 when it was first performed. As the London
magazine *Harmonicon* said in July 1825, 'Beethoven's Seventh

Symphony is a composition in which the author has indulged in a great deal of disagreeable eccentricity. . . . We cannot discover any design in it, neither can we trace any connection in its parts. Altogether, it seems to have been intended as a kind of enigma —we had almost said a hoax.'[1]

When one listens to this splendid Scherzo with its extraordinary gaiety and vitality, it is almost incredible that any presumably intelligent connoisseur of music employed by a magazine devoted to musical topics should be able to deliver himself of such misguided rubbish. It is as well to remember, though, how unprepared the less perceptive members of a Beethoven audience were for the unconventionality of his music; where such reactions are still of value is in preventing us from becoming blasé about these compositions today. I would infinitely rather that someone was shocked by Beethoven's music than bored; at least to be shocked shows an awareness of the harmonic daring and formal enterprise that are to be found on nearly every page. Only by realizing the existence of such daring can we obtain the full savour of the excitement that is implicit in this score.

Once again, much of the drama is bound up in this question of tonality. The movement starts in a blustering and impatient mood, as though Beethoven were seizing the arpeggio of F major by the scruff of its neck.

Ex.82
Presto

In literally two seconds—which means in the next bar—and before the startled listeners have recovered from this aggressive battery, the mood changes to a nimble-footed dance. 'On the plains, fairy trains were a-treading measures,' says the madrigal; but Beethoven keeps not the dancers but the audience on the hop, for no sooner have we accustomed ourselves to this change of

[1] Quoted in Nicolas Slonimsky's brilliant and entertaining book, *Lexicon of Musical Invective*: Coleman-Ross: New York, 1953.

mood than he whips us into A major and causes the former bluster
to return. The statutory repeat of the first twenty-four bars only
serves to underline the conflict between these two opposing keys
of F and A, since the return to the beginning involves an abrupt
change from A major back to F major without any intervening
step. The second time round, we find the opening rhythm (shown
in the example above) being passed angrily from hand to hand in
the orchestra, like one of those party games where you have to
get rid of some object before the music stops.

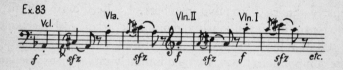

The next section is a typical example of how a classical composer plays with tonality. He has now firmly committed himself
to the sharp keys, and for a moment or two the woodwind chatter
away quite happily. Suddenly aware of how far they are away
from home, the strings, like anxious children, begin to wonder
how they can ever get back—home being F major. After all, here
they are in a key which contradicts the very essence of F, since the
F is sharpened.

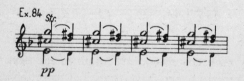

It is the wiser heads in the orchestra who suggest a solution,
although they don't seem any too sure of it; tentatively the lower
instruments—bassoons, horn, 'cellos, and basses—suggest wiping
out this difficult 'sharp' element altogether.

Ex.85

As you can see, there isn't even time for these lower voices to echo the four-times-repeated pattern previously established by the violins before the whole orchestra come in with an enthusiastic shout of 'That's it!' However, it isn't 'it'—not yet, that is to say; but it is a step in the right direction since it has at least got rid of the 'sharp' element. Beethoven now repeats this whole process, thus bringing him through C to B♮ major. Notice the instinctive sense of balance a composer of this period has; so far, the music has veered between F major and the sharp keys to the right of it on the 'housing estate'.[1] Now he compensates for that by a swing to the left; only by introducing more 'flat-ness' into the harmonic scheme can he finally restore the music convincingly to its original key.

The central Trio is exceptionally long, and seems a breath of calm after the explosive vitality that has preceded it. It is based on an old Pilgrims' Hymn which Beethoven came across and happily plundered. As if to emphasize that the hide-and-seek with tonality is over, the violins sustain an almost continuous A, while beneath, the woodwind gently sing their soothing phrases in D major. This reveals an interesting point about the conflicting tonalities of the movement. The note A is in fact a central pivot, and this whole Scherzo is concerned with three harmonizations of A.

Ex.86

[1] See p. 13, Fig. 4.

This means that the first part of the Scherzo is a ding-dong struggle between 1 and 2, while the Trio is a period of respite on 3.

A rough idea of just how far the form of the Scherzo had progressed in importance in Beethoven's hands can be gained by comparing this symphony with the Second. In the earlier work, the Scherzo consists of seven pages of score, of which the first five are repeated, making twelve in all. In the Seventh Symphony, the Scherzo is fifty-seven pages long; what is more significant, the tempo varies noticeably from section to section, and not only in the usual central Trio. The plan is much more complex, since we now find scherzo-trio-scherzo-trio-scherzo, while on the final page there is a last four-bar remembrance of the Trio before the full orchestra impatiently cut in and bring the movement to an abrupt end.

It is curious that we tend to think of this symphony as a rather pastoral, almost light-weight affair when it is not only one of the largest in scale, but also the most extrovert in its boisterous good spirits. The finale bursts at the seams with good humour; Wagner described it as the 'Apotheosis of the Dance', but this is misleading in so far as it suggests the refinement of the ballet rather than the improvised steps of a group of slightly tipsy peasants at a country inn. Unquestionably there is urban music and rural music, two main streams that it is not too far-fetched to suggest stem from the opposing figures of Mozart and Haydn. Mozart has the polish and the sophistication, Haydn the direct and friendly manner. Mozart never gives you the man-to-man dig in the ribs that Haydn will, and of the two composers, Haydn was the more potent an influence on Beethoven. Such an influence is particularly vivid in this movement, with its driving rhythm and robust humour.

As is quite often the case, the Finale is in fairly normal sonata form, but with an enormously extended coda, which as an epilogue balances the lengthy prologue with which the work had begun. The start, needless to say, is yet another joke; Beethoven begins with an extremely positive assertion of E major tonality, only to modify it a couple of beats later, as if a speaker were to say, 'Ladies and gentle-creatures. . . .' Here is no gentleness, though, but a play on harmonies as my suggested address is a play on words.

Ex.87

If you try the experiment of staying in E major for a little longer on the lines suggested below, and then return to the symphony, you will regain the sensation of slight dislocation which Beethoven intended you to experience in the third bar.

Ex.88

A harmony teacher will probably dismiss this argument as nonsense, pointing out that the opening chord is not E major at all, but the dominant of A. I have learnt not to quarrel with theoreticians since the law is always on their side; my reply to the academic approach is to paraphrase the missionary's classic riposte: 'You continue to look at Beethoven your way and I will continue to look at him in his.' Not for a moment would I deny that the opening chord is the dominant; the point at issue is that Beethoven clearly wants you to be gulled into believing that it is the tonic —or to be less technical, E major.

The first subject material is divided into two basic ideas, one of which keeps chasing its tail:

Ex. 89

while the other is made of solid stuff.

Ex. 90

The second subject flirts incessantly with C♯ minor, but seldom commits itself to actually settling there; again the Schumannesque quality of the dotted rhythms is noticeable. Such is the driving force of the music, however, that there is little time to absorb detailed impressions, and Beethoven hurries us on with scant regard for subtlety. Worth noticing is a sudden patch of quiet writing in which he skilfully extends the last bar of Ex. 89, passing the little rising sixth through the whole range of the strings.

Ex. 91

This quieter section is only a brief respite, and in less than a minute we are pitched back into the full hurly-burly of the opening material.

The coda is characterized by a curious marching bass which anticipates the type of figure we might expect to find in a symphony by Sibelius. High sustained chords in the woodwind impose some cohesion on the breathless snatches of semiquavers which scud through the violins and violas, while below, 'cellos and basses grind uneasily like the tremor of an earthquake.

Gradually over this disturbed bass line there accumulates an increasing intensity of sound, building remorselessly until in blazing triumph the opening material of the movement returns. For Beethoven to use the *fff* sign is rare indeed and one of its few appearances is in these closing pages. Rare also are any opinions he ever gave about his own music, but of this work he makes brief mention in two of his letters. In both he refers to it as 'one of my best works'. What more is there to add?

## CHAPTER VI

# BERLIOZ

## Symphonie Fantastique, Op. 14 (1830)

Sub-title: 'An episode in the life of an artist.' Berlioz himself supplied the extensive programme note quoted below:[1]

PROGRAMME OF THE SYMPHONY

A young musician of unhealthily sensitive nature and endowed with vivid imagination has poisoned himself with opium in a paroxysm of love-sick despair. The narcotic dose he had taken was too weak to cause death, but it has thrown him into a long sleep accompanied by the most extraordinary visions. In this condition his sensations, his feelings, and memories find utterance in his sick brain in the form of musical imagery. Even the beloved one takes the form of melody in his mind, like a fixed idea which is ever returning and which he hears everywhere.

FIRST MOVEMENT: Visions and Passions (*Largo—piu mosso— allegro agitato e appassionato assai—religiosamente*)

At first he thinks of the uneasy and nervous condition of his mind, of sombre longings, of depression and joyous elation without any recognizable cause, which he experienced before the beloved one had appeared to him. Then he remembers the ardent love with which she suddenly inspired him; he thinks of his almost insane anxiety of mind, of his raging jealousy, of his reawakening love, of his religious consolation.

SECOND MOVEMENT: A ball (*Valse; allegro non troppo*)

In a ballroom, amidst the confusion of a brilliant festival, he finds the loved one again.

THIRD MOVEMENT: In the country (*Adagio*)

It is a summer evening. He is in the country musing when he

---

[1] English translation by Harry Brett; taken from the full orchestral score published by Breitkopf and Härtel, copyright 1900.

hears two shepherd-lads who play the *ranz des vaches* (the tune used by the Swiss to call their flocks together) in alternation. This shepherd duet, the locality, the soft whisperings of the trees stirred by the zephyr-wind, some prospects of hope recently made known to him, all these sensations unite to impart a long unknown repose to his heart and to lend a smiling colour to his imagination. And then she appears once more. His heart stops beating; painful forebodings fill his soul. 'Should she prove false to him?' One of the shepherds resumes the melody, but the other answers him no more. . . . Sunset . . . distant rolling of thunder . . . loneliness . . . silence.

FOURTH MOVEMENT: The procession to the stake (*Allegretto non troppo*)

He dreams that he had murdered his beloved, that he has been condemned to death and is being led to the stake. A march that is alternately sombre and wild, brilliant and solemn, accompanies the procession. . . . The tumultuous outbursts are followed without modulation by measured steps. At last the fixed idea returns; for a moment a last thought of love is revived—which is cut short by the death-blow.

FIFTH MOVEMENT: The witches' sabbath (*Larghetto; allegro*)

He dreams that he is present at a witches' dance, surrounded by horrible spirits, amidst sorcerers and monsters in many fearful forms, who have come to assist at his funeral. Strange sounds, groans, shrill laughter, distant yells, which other cries seem to answer. The beloved melody is heard again, but it has its noble and shy character no longer; it has become a vulgar, trivial, and grotesque kind of dance. SHE it is who comes to attend the witches' meeting. Friendly howls and shouts greet her arrival. . . She joins the infernal orgy . . . bells toll for the dead . . . a burlesque parody of the *Dies Irae* . . . the witches' round dance . . . the dance and the *Dies Irae* are heard at the same time.

Orchestra: 2 flutes; 2 oboes; 2 clarinets; 4 bassoons; 4 horns; 2 harps; 2 cornets; 2 trumpets; 3 trombones; 2 tubas; 5 or 6 percussion; strings, divided into nine parts in the finale, and having the double basses divided into four in the fourth movement.

The first movement is scored for a basic classical orchestra—double woodwind, four horns, two trumpets, timpani, and strings. The only unorthodox addition is a pair of cornets. The two harps are added in the second movement only. In the Adagio, the second oboe plays a cor anglais; the heavy extra brass and percussion are kept in reserve for the last two movements. The symphony was first performed in 1830 in Paris; Berlioz revised it somewhat the following year and the work as we know it now was given on 9 December 1832, two days before the composer's twenty-ninth birthday. Originally the symphony was intended to introduce a stage performance of a 'lyric mono-drama' entitled *Lélio*, now forgotten.

PERHAPS THE MOST REMARKABLE thing about this literally fantastic symphony is the date of its composition. At the time, Schubert had been dead a scant eighteen months; Mendelssohn was a youth of twenty-one, though an immensely talented one; Schumann was just beginning to compose; Wagner was only seventeen years old. This bare recital of facts may serve to bring home quite how astoundingly original this somewhat despised masterpiece is. It may have faults of taste and construction; it may on occasion seem naïve or overblown; but whatever its weaknesses it remains a landmark in musical history, affirming the liberation of music that Beethoven had initiated, and proclaiming the new era of Romanticism, in which extravagant expression, literary images, and personal feelings were to engulf the formality of the classical age. Up to now, the conception of a symphony had been almost entirely governed by what one might term architectural considerations. Even the slow movement of Beethoven's 'Pastoral' Symphony is not tied to any specific plot; Beethoven himself warned us that we should regard the symphony more as an impression of the countryside than as an actual painting.[1] As opposed to this, Berlioz's approach was revolutionary; he had clearly identified himself with the hero of De Quincey's *Confessions of an Opium-eater*, which he had recently discovered in a rather unreliable translation by Alfred de Musset. Interwoven with this

[1] 'Mehr Ausdruck der Empfindung als Mahlerei.'

romantic if unhealthy fantasy were all the torments of his love for Harriet Smithson, the Irish actress with whom he was infatuated, and whom he was later to marry disastrously. All the lurid details of this affair can be read in Berlioz's autobiography—one of the greatest and most revealing, not to say entertaining, life-stories ever written. There is no more vivid picture of artistic life in Paris in the mid-nineteenth century.[1]

No emotion in Berlioz's life could ever be simple or straight-forward, and his feelings for his Irish lady-love waxed and waned in a disturbingly inconsistent manner. In February 1830, while he was still working on the symphony, he wrote to a friend about his beloved. 'She is still in London,' he said, 'and yet I seem to feel her near me. All my former feelings for her are aroused, and combine to tear me to pieces; I hear my heart beat, and its pulsa-tions shake me as though they were the strokes of the piston-rod of a steam-engine.' (Not the most romantic of similes perhaps, but at least it had the merit of being up-to-date, since Stevenson's Rocket had first startled the world in the previous year.) One finds it hard to take such a passion seriously, however vehement Berlioz's words may have been, since at the time he had never even spoken to the fair Harriet, and his love was therefore exactly comparable to the crush a contemporary adolescent might have for a famous film-star. Only a few months after he had written the letter quoted above, disillusionment set in; for some reason never really elucidated, he conceived feelings of hatred and disgust for the unfortunate Miss Smithson, and this very work which had been planned as a tribute to her was to become a musical diatribe. In his original sketch of the programme for this symphony he described the last movement as 'a vision of a night of revelry'. There was no mention of witches; only when his love turned sour was the intended gaiety changed to a scene of horror.

It is possible that one reason for Berlioz's insistence on a literary 'programme' for the *Symphonie Fantastique* was that in his relative immaturity he did not feel confident enough to handle the

[1] *Memoirs of Hector Berlioz* edited by Ernest Newman: Tudor Publishing Co., New York, 1932.

variations of tempo in which he delights in the first movement without some extra-musical justification. Beethoven had frequently changed the tempo in his later works; instances such as the last quartets or the Op. 109 piano sonata spring to mind. Whereas Beethoven obviously regarded such changes as a logical musical development, Berlioz may well have wanted to justify them by some literary parallel. What is completely his own is something that I can only describe as a purely physical rejoicing in sound for sound's sake. This revelling in sonority was a totally new experience in music, all the more remarkable in a composer as sketchily trained as Berlioz appears to have been.

In his elaborate programme note, Berlioz makes frequent mention of the fixed idea (*idée fixe*), or 'beloved' theme; this is a lengthy musical phrase which is destined to appear in all five movements. It is first suggested in the third bar, when, after a brief woodwind introduction, the strings have a series of intensely emotional phrases of which the first is the most important.

Ex. 93

*(Cf. the passage marked* **⁕——⁕** *in Ex. 94)*

For the moment, however, we are not to know this; it is enough to follow these languishing phrases, marvellously scored as they are. Suddenly and surprisingly, the dark mood of this opening is dissipated by gay fluttering figures on strings and woodwind. We realize at once that we are in the presence of a master of the orchestra. The mood continues to vacillate until the music seems to be caught in some epileptic seizure; as though our opium addict were gasping for breath, we find these extraordinary markings on the score: | *mf dim.* $>$ *pp* $<$ *cresc.* | *ff ppp* —this in a span of only two bars. The music quickens to a tempo four times as fast in which, once established, the motto theme or *idée fixe* makes its first complete appearance. It is sufficiently important to quote in full.

By any standards this is an astonishing piece of music. One could easily criticize the tune itself for being too sequential, but criticism pales before the blazing intensity of its phrases, emphasized as they are by the extraordinary stabbing accents, the wild crescendi and diminuendi, and most of all, the thumping heartbeats beneath the spare and sinewy line of the melody. While it is not inconceivable that Wagner or Schumann might have written a theme on these lines, no one but Berlioz could have treated it in this way. Not until Stravinsky or Britten did anyone dare to orchestrate so uncompromisingly or to use rhythms as abrupt and independent as the ones we find in this accompaniment. No living soul could have taught Berlioz such orchestration or such harmony, and this whole score shows a revolution in musical texture just as remarkable as the one that Beethoven had accomplished in form. His adoration for Beethoven and Gluck ensured that much of his music was a continuation of a tradition; despite his astonishing originality, he had no real wish to break the links with all that he valued from the past. He is like a gigantic stepping-stone, by whose means we can bridge the immense gulf between the classical and modern periods; his flair was for invention, though, and the occasions when he does try to employ classical devices such as the fugue are usually the least satisfactory moments.

In itself the development of this lengthy theme is unremarkable as pure composition; it is the details that are exciting. Once the *idée fixe* has been fully stated, as in Ex. 94, the music goes tearing off into tempestuous blasts of sound, again alternating with strange pleading phrases on the woodwind. Fragments of the motto theme rush past, but there is little time to be aware of anything except the breathless pace of the music.

At the start of the development section proper—in so far as it is not fairly futile to force this work into the corset of normal symphonic form—'cellos and basses occupy themselves with the first few bars of the motto theme.

Ex. 95

All thoughts of this material are soon forgotten, however, in a passage which is a quite incredible anticipation of a technique we associate most readily with Sibelius. The strings rise and fall in wild chromatic eddies above which we hear the banshee cries of the woodwind, like lost spirits driven before the whirlwind. This terrifying passage explodes in a final dissonance, which is followed by three bars of total silence, out of which emerges a single *pp* horn note. Above this, the original theme reappears, taking the limelight pretty extensively for the next few pages of the score. Only a detailed study of these pages will show quite how original Berlioz's conception is; compare any of them at random with one of the Beethoven symphonies and you will notice at once the far greater use of dynamics, the louds and softs, the accents, changes of tempo, and so on. These are the superficial differences; look then at the individual parts—the way he divides 'cellos from double basses, divides the basses themselves; observe the detailed instructions to the percussion players. 'The first quaver of each half-bar to be played with two drum-sticks; the other five quavers with the right-hand drum-stick.' (Fourth movement.) These are the sort of instructions we find in works by Bartók or Villa-Lobos, not in composers of the eighteen-thirties. Other passages show an uncanny prediction of twentieth-century intervals. Play this sequence of notes slowly and ask any musical friend what date he would estimate them to have been composed.

Ex.96

The likelihood of a right answer is exceedingly remote; they occur in the last movement of this work.

Detailed thematic analysis of the type that is so fruitful in a Beethoven symphony is of little value here; Berlioz's development of themes is easily grasped. What is infinitely more important is to be able to appreciate what I might term the 'flavour' of the music; to be able to see in detail just how remarkable it is. From a spiritual standpoint the closing bars of the first movement are childish in their delineation of religious consolation. A few Amen-like chords on the orchestra do not begin to approach the profound depths that we find so often in Beethoven, Bach, and Mozart. To take Berlioz's programme at its face-value would be disastrous; it is thrilling enough to find a young man of twenty-seven daring so much. Let us not look for miracles by expecting him to match the fearlessness of his invention with the maturity of an older head.

The second movement begins with atmospheric rustlings which are particularly notable for the originality of the harp writing, an instrument which, without making any exhaustive research on the subject, I should say was appearing for the first time in a sym-phony. In due course an elegant waltz tune emerges, scored with characteristic delicacy. As a nice instance of Berlioz's delight in orchestral subtleties, look at what he can do with the 'pom-ching-ching' background that inevitably appears in every waltz. As a change from the eternal first beat on 'cellos and basses and the two subsequent beats on violas, second violins, and/or horns, he colours each quaver beat with a different section of the orchestra.

Ex.97 *(Str.)* *(W.W&* *Hrns.)* *p* *(2 Hrps.)*

Meantime, the waltz tune weaves its way with the utmost clarity through this charmingly varied texture.

Suddenly a cold shiver seems to strike the onlookers, and over a quiet but excited *tremolando* in the strings the *idée fixe* is heard again, clearly recognizable, even if somewhat more suave than it has previously been.

Ex.98

*etc.*

A marvellous touch here is the immediate quickening of the pulse that Berlioz conveys when this theme now appears. Beneath the unruffled surface of the melody, which in its woodwind coloration seems as disdainful as a *Vogue* model, 'cellos and basses are given strange off-beat pulsations, perfectly transcribing the muted hammering in the unseen lover's ear as his blood quickens at the sight of his beloved.

Ex.99

*pp*                                                                    *etc.*

In a moment we hear the waltz rhythm pick up, unperturbed by this little drama; the motto theme continues on its elegant way and passes from sight. Only near the end of the movement does it return; perhaps the young man sees his love climbing into her carriage; something certainly happens to disturb him, for this second apparition is greeted by a stormy outburst from the full orchestra. Unregarded in his isolation, he is quickly engulfed in a swirling cavalcade of dancers, and the movement ends in brilliance and gaiety.

The third movement begins with a pastoral dialogue between cor anglais and oboe. Berlioz's romantic imagination had been fired by the sound of Swiss peasants calling the cattle off the mountainside with some sort of pipe or horn. Typically he arranges for the oboe to play behind the stage, so as to give an effect of distance. To start with, these two instruments are un-accompanied, but after several interchanges, the softest possible tremor on violas and 'cellos begins, like a raincloud casting a dark

streak across a pale summer sky. The mood is not unlike Words-
worth—a somewhat idyllic conception of country life, but
evocative for all that.

Violins and flute now introduce a new idea, one of Berlioz's
curiously spare melodies. In his individual way he lets the tune
speak for itself, stripped bare of all but the simplest harmonic
suggestions,[1] so that when at last other instruments do appear one
has a wonderful feeling of added richness. Much of this recalls the
slow movement of Beethoven's 'Pastoral' Symphony, whose influence even goes so far as to suggest actual rhythmic patterns to
Berlioz's ear. Over and over again the woodwind reiterate this
figure, 𝄽, which is surely the cry of the quail in Beethoven's
score. But while there are several such superficial resemblances,
the orchestral texture is entirely different. Beethoven would never
lay out a melody in the stark way that Berlioz does; nor did he
ever devise a rhythm quite so intricate as the one we find a few
pages further on at the next appearance of the motto theme.
Again the tune is allotted to the woodwind, and the similarity of
tonal colour to the ballroom version is obviously intended; but
where before the reaction of 'cellos and basses was a quiet agitation
(see Ex. 99 on p. 93), here there is a passionate outburst of
frustrated emotion. Was there ever a more violent protestation
of love than this?

Ex. 100

Small wonder that one of the critics of the day attacked Berlioz
for wanting to invent new rhythms, as though composers had no
right to do such a thing. The orchestral players of his time must
indeed have scratched their heads over this newfangled stuff.
Imagine the sensation, then, at the first rehearsal when Berlioz

[1] His detractors would say 'because he couldn't harmonize it', but I feel this to be a
narrow-minded judgement.

called for no fewer than four drummers simultaneously at the end of this movement. It is one of the greatest examples of virtuosity in orchestration and every serious student of music should examine the last twenty-five bars of this Adagio with some care. Berlioz reintroduces the cor anglais melody with which he had begun; but now, between each of its phrases, he inserts the most extraordinary effects of distant thunder, scored in such a way that at times four timpani are being played together, making chords of drums. I quote two bars to show the kind of texture he creates.

Ex. 101

Drums 1&2

Drums 3&4

No words of mine can describe the effect of this brilliantly calculated sound; in less skilful hands this coda could easily have been corny in the extreme. After all, a shepherd's pipe alternating with a few distant rumbles of thunder is not the most original of conceptions, and especially to our ears today, it savours too much of the sentimentality of a Victorian engraving. However, Berlioz handles his unusual orchestral palette with uncanny sensitivity, and the soft grumble of deep-voiced timpani is awe-inspiring in its majesty.

These same drums make a fascinating link into the next movement, a strand of colour that binds them together. This is probably fortuitous, though, since this famous 'March to the Stake' is taken from an earlier opera of Berlioz, *Les Francs-Juges*. If the scoring is preserved from the previous version it is even more remarkable, since it means that these extraordinary new sounds were conceived in his early twenties. The march begins with two timpani in G and Bb, *pizzicato* double basses divided into a four-part chord of G minor, and low grunts on horns and bassoons that seem to belong more to the pages of Stravinsky's *Firebird* than to a work written a mere three years after Beethoven's death—indeed quite possibly while Beethoven was still alive, if the scoring remains intact from the earlier version. Gradually the sound accumulates, by the addition of instruments rather than by a crescendo, as though more and more people were falling in behind the tumbril; then, after a sudden explosion of sound, 'cellos and basses declaim a curiously shaped theme based on a descending scale.

Ex. 102

This is repeated many times with varying counterpoints, one of which is its own self in inversion, i.e. a similar scale in contrary motion. Suddenly the dark menace of the first few pages is swept away in a triumphant march scored for full wind and brass. One can only assume that Berlioz sees himself as the victim, and imagines that the mob is on his side; thus the procession to his doom becomes a path of glory. Although there is a tremendous weight of sound here Berlioz does not abuse it, and there are moments of striking contrast. One passage in particular shows an astonishing ear for colour, breaking up the scale theme quoted above into kaleidoscopic fragments.

Ex. 103

In the very next bar he builds up the sound from a wispy *p* to an electrifying *f* by again using four timpani in G, B♭, D, and F in succession. A little later on, we find the much-discussed opposition of the chords of D flat major and G minor, a harmonic conflict so unusual that the players of the time all questioned it: Berlioz obligingly puts a footnote at the bottom of the score assuring us that it is not a mistake.

Right at the end of the movement we find the most dramatic touch of all; we are to assume that our hero has now reached the scaffold. The procession halts, and for a fleeting moment we hear a single clarinet playing the motto theme—a last thought of the beloved. An immense chord cuts it off in mid-phrase, and with a dull *pizzicato* thud the dismembered head bounces into the basket. A shattering roll of drums and sixteen chords of G major finish the movement in a mood of relentless savagery. About sixty-five years later Strauss used an identical technique in *Till Eulenspiegel*; once more one is made to realize that Berlioz anticipated practically every orchestral trick of the second half of the nineteenth century. From this point of view the Finale is perhaps the most remarkable movement of all, as we shall now see.

In the Witches' Sabbath we find spectacular orchestral invention and bad music in roughly equal proportions; it is worth remembering that Moussorgsky's *Night on a Bare Mountain* with which this movement could most easily be compared was written thirty-seven years later. *The Sorcerer's Apprentice* of Dukas with which it also has some points of resemblance was even further away —sixty-seven years. There was literally nothing even remotely like this to have influenced Berlioz; in the portrayal of the macabre and the supernatural he started from scratch, and for all its faults as a composition, this movement must remain a *tour de force* of orchestral colouring. The whole symphony could be called the *Rite of Spring* of the nineteenth century.

The finale begins with a high shimmer of violins and violas, divided into eight parts, with savage growls in 'cellos and double basses, reinforced by a pair of timpani. Spiky semiquavers drift down like dead leaves or a spatter of raindrops, and then 'cellos and basses have an extraordinary bar of ominous rumbling in which they are both divided, while sharp-edged strings pluck out a fanfare above. Distant horn-calls, bat-like screeches—all the romantic trappings of Thomas Lovell Beddoes are to be found here. The literary world was suddenly fascinated by phantasmagoria. Edgar Allan Poe was just beginning to write, and nine years before the *Symphonie Fantastique*, the youthful Beddoes had written a perfect anticipation of its mood:

> . . . It was dark and cold;
> A putrid steam rose from the clammy mould;
> The moon darts through a crevice: at his lips
> He sees a scull's mouth yawn, which thickly drips
> With nauseous moisture; upward to his thigh
> He stood in bones and dust of bodies dead;
> And part was newly melting, part was dry,
> And part, with recent slaughter, glaring red.[1]

Curiously enough, Berlioz describes a scene not unlike this in his memoirs, when, in his early days as a medical student, he was taken to a positive charnel-house of a dissecting room. Its effect on his highly sensitive mind can be imagined.

It is in such a macabre setting then that we now discover the motto theme once more; but no longer does it sustain the mood of aloof beauty which had distinguished it in the second and third movements. Shrill and grotesque on the high E flat clarinet, the theme cavorts like the third witch in *Macbeth*.

Ex.104
Allegro

*etc.*

---

[1] Thomas Lovell Beddoes: *The Improvisatore*: stanza XXIII.

Soon this version is taken up by the whole pack of woodwind; strings and brass add to the tumult. Suddenly the music climbs down to an almost inaudible low C; in a tense hush, near to silence, we hear the distant clang of two bells. There is a flicker of reaction in the waiting throng, instantly quelled by an abrupt and commanding gesture. Again the bells ring out, again there is a similar reaction. The scene is painted so vividly that one can visualize every detail. The ritual begins, as two tubas and four bassoons in unison chant the *Dies Irae*, a traditional melody dating back to medieval times.

With what appears to be complete independence the two bells continue to chime at irregular intervals while the *Dies Irae* theme is diminished, first into dotted crochets and then into a hopping 6/8 rhythm:

The bleak angularity of some of the scoring here conveys a unique quality of sound, and its 'modernity' is remarkable. It seems a pity that Berlioz is suddenly seized with academic aspirations and launches forth into a fugue, of all things. He justifies it by describing it as the 'Witches' Round Dance', and indeed one can imagine them joining in group by group. The slight impression of a sort of Sir Roger de Coverley's Coven is dispelled by a series of jagged Amens that cut across the dance in a positively jazz-like rhythm:

Ex. 107

These chords are taken up with increasing enthusiasm till they pervade practically the whole orchestra. As in the first movement, the listener gains a tremendous impression of pace, a word that I use as distinct from tempo. The *Dies Irae* theme returns as the music dies down to a low grumble, then a further crescendo leads to what Berlioz obviously regarded as the climax of the symphony. In tones of Jack Hornerish pride he indicates on the score that the *Dies Irae* and the Witches Round Dance are here combined; and indeed they are married with little difficulty. As a feat of composition it is scarcely in the same category as the finale of the 'Jupiter' Symphony, but to a composer as insecure in technique as Berlioz it must have seemed a joyful discovery. As soon as he can forget about such academic props the flame of genius flares up again, and he produces some electrifying sounds. Especially worth mentioning is the extraordinary gasping effect he achieves by dynamics as eccentric as these:

$$\left| \begin{array}{cc} \overset{>}{\phantom{.}} & \overset{>}{\phantom{.}} \\ \end{array} \right| \begin{array}{cc} \overset{>}{\phantom{.}} & \overset{>}{\phantom{.}} \\ \end{array} \left| \begin{array}{cc} \overset{>}{\phantom{.}} & \overset{>}{\phantom{.}} \\ \end{array} \right| \textit{etc. simile}$$
$p<ff>pp<ff>pp<ff>$

The end is calculated to leave the listener exhausted, reeling beneath the impact of the relatively huge resources which Berlioz here deploys with such fabulous skill. Were this work to have been written after 1870 it would be justifiable to belittle it on the grounds of its periodical ineptness and occasional miscalculations. History is not to be denied, however, and the inescapable fact remains that in orchestral virtuosity and exploration of tone and rhythm this symphony leapt so far into the future that one can be

indulgent if it loses its footing in places. Its psychological significance is probably equally as great, for with this work, music
plunged headlong into the giddy current of Romanticism; the
intrusion of the composer's Ego in so blatantly autobiographical
a manner was a milestone; it remained for composers of a later
period to unleash the Id.

## CHAPTER VII

# BRAHMS

## Symphony No. 2 in D, Op. 73 (1877)

1. Allegro non troppo. 2. Adagio non troppo. 3. Allegretto grazioso (Quasi Andantino) alternating with Presto ma non assai. 4. Allegro con spirito.

Orchestra: 2 flutes; 2 oboes; 2 clarinets; 2 bassoons; 4 horns; 2 trumpets; 3 trombones; 1 tuba; 1 timpanist; normal complement of strings.

Brahms composed this symphony in the summer of 1877 while staying at Pörtschach, on the Wörthersee. It appears to have caused him little difficulty since it was finished in a matter of months—a striking contrast to the First Symphony, over which he had laboured for fifteen years. The first performance was given on 30 December of the same year in Vienna, with Hans Richter conducting. The work was rapturously received by the Viennese audience, but had a rather chilly reception some ten days later when Brahms himself directed a performance in Leipzig.

IT IS CURIOUS that a composer who is now acknowledged as one of the great masters of form should have been so unsure of himself when it came to writing a symphony. Whether Brahms was really as overawed by the stature of Beethoven as he made out, or whether he felt that the symphony as a form was in a state of decline it is impossible to say. The indisputable fact remains that his first symphony did not appear until he was forty-three years old, and its opus number (68) is clear enough indication of how much music he already had behind him at the time. Once he had tasted success with his initial venture he was quick to follow it up, so much so that his four symphonies were all written within a span of nine years.

In comparison with the sombre, tragic mood of the First Symphony, the Second is an astonishing contrast—lyrical, sunny, and full of a quality of serenity which at times warms to a positive radiance. It is as though Brahms were heaving a gigantic sigh of relief at having overcome the immense obstacle which his First Symphony seems to have represented. To dismiss the D major symphony as a mere divertimento, as some writers have tended to do, is, however, a gross underestimate of its value; the nineteenth-century Leipzig critic who complained about its 'prettiness', claiming that he expected more weighty things from a composer of Brahms's quality, failed to realize that here was a work of truly dazzling craftsmanship, in which Brahms displays a fertility of technical resource which is unfailing in its inventiveness. Of the four, this is the most rewarding symphony to study, not because it says anything more profound than the others, but because in it we can most clearly see the hand of a supreme craftsman at work. We cannot expect to acquire the attributes of genius, however hard we study; what we can do is to see how genius is channelled and directed by technique.

The very first page of the score is as rich a source of material as you will find anywhere. On the face of it, it is simply a disarming melody:

Ex.108

Allegro non troppo

Nothing could be more deceptive; the ear may connect all this up into a continuous strand, but to Brahms it is a series of fragments, each one of which is as potentially fruitful as an acorn.

Thus in the first bar, which also appears in the bass of bars 5 and 9, we find the three-note motive (*a*) from which any number of developments will be seen to grow; in the first seventy bars alone this little pattern appears over thirty times in one form or other. Bars 2 and 3 must be considered as another detachable unit (*b*); bar 4 is yet another (*c*). (The fact that it is also an inversion of bar 1 is, I think, no more than a coincidence.) Lastly, the four-bar woodwind phrase (*d*), though more complete in itself than the mere snippets we have detached so far, is equally liable to be chopped out of its context and developed as a separate entity.

For the moment horns and woodwind continue on an un-troubled course; the violins bide their time in patience. When they do come in, they have a bare suggestion of the bar 1 figure, both elongated and extended.

Ex. 109

This descending chain seems to dissolve as it dies down to a single muttered drum-roll; trombones brood quietly while the woodwind periodically remind us of bar 1 again. Then, in the forty-fourth bar, the sun comes out, and these tentative sugges-tions of melody flower at last into a lyrical outburst from the strings. Even here, though, the three-note pattern from the first bar is of prime importance.

Ex. 110

This new theme overlaps itself very neatly, and Brahms makes a positive daisy-chain out of it, instrument after instrument coming in impetuously, each without allowing its predecessor to finish.

The music grows bolder and more severe; soon we find the three-note pattern striding firmly across the score; matched against it are these choppy quavers:

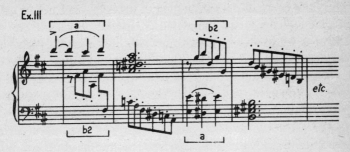

Ex. III

It only takes a little thought to realize that this aggressive new counter-subject, which I have called *b2*, is none other than a contraction of the opening horn theme (*b*) from the second and third bar of the work (see Ex. 108). As the tension increases, the three-note pattern (*a*) gets squashed up, until its condensed version suddenly breaks right across the pseudo-heroic mood of the music and beguiles us with the most enchanting musical chuckles.

Ex. 112

The music seems about to disintegrate as Brahms reduces it to a scatter of brief chords and snatches of the *b2* phrase; then he seems to take a grip on himself in a patch of glorious sustained harmony, and at last the true second subject appears.

Ex. 113

Here the 'cellos steal the violas' glory by taking the upper line; above, the two violin parts interchange decorative fragments which are all based on *b2*. In such a way does Brahms relate these new events with the very beginning of the work. For some thirty bars, he now allows this new theme to have its head; as it grows in assurance it gradually dispenses with its links with the past. The references to the *b2* motive vanish, and wind and strings take turns in extending this gracious second subject. Suddenly a violent new rhythm breaks the spell. Jagged, leaping octaves, harsh syncopations, rough dissonances explode into a tempestuous new version of bar 1.

The rhythm is made even more agitated by tying over the last of each group to the first of the next,

etc. For several pages of the score this savage pattern persists; around it surge uneasy memories of the first three notes of section *d* (Ex. 108)—reappearing for the first time. After a tremendous climax the second subject comes in again, somewhat shaken; an almost feverish counterpoint on a flute harps incessantly on the two adjacent notes of *a* until, exhausted, the music sinks back to an uneasy rest. At this point Brahms demands the classic repeat of the exposition, but in this symphony conductors usually disregard his instructions.

Until now, the composer has mainly occupied himself with the first three bars of the symphony. This may seem a somewhat startling assertion, but apart from the second subject, which

as I have shown is cleverly integrated with the horn-call (*b*) from
bars 2 and 3, practically everything that we have heard so far has
been closely related to those first 'germs' *a* and *b* of Ex. 108. It is
interesting now to see how Brahms transfers his interests to *c* and
*d* when he comes to the development.

The first inkling that we are moving in a new direction comes
with a sudden switch to F major—a fairly positive denial of the
'home' key of D, since it cancels out both F♯ and C♯, the two
salient accidentals of D major. The horn reminds us of the
opening phrases.

As you can see, the oboe at once seizes on the fragment labelled
*c* and extends it into a sequence. This is the cue for a general
increase in severity; the meltingly lyrical quality of the music is
replaced by something much more 'academic', as though Brahms
were addressing himself to some imagined critic—after all, this *is*
a symphony. The other wind instruments take up the oboe's
extension of *c* more strongly; the 'cellos and basses match them
stride for stride. Before we realize it we are pitched headlong on
to a fugal sea; at last bars 6–9 of the first page come into their own
(see Ex. 108), and the neglected phrase (*d*) reigns triumphant.

Even here one marvels at the way Brahms keeps an ever-watchful eye on his material. Many patterns of quavers would fit against a main subject of this calibre, but he chooses one which is still related to what has gone before. The descending pattern (*c*) which had been established by the oboe in the passage quoted in Ex. 115 is tightened up into a brittle counter-subject.

becomes

The struggle continues. Any suspicions we may have had that Brahms was just coasting along writing a sort of glorified serenade must be dispelled by the sense of intellectual grappling which we now experience. At its height, the trombones (which are used with the most masterly economy in this score) suddenly cut into the texture with grinding dissonances that put the bar 1 motive on the rack.

Over and over again these jagged outlines spill through the score—shortened, lengthened, tumbling one over the other, rocks spewed out with volcanic force. In time *a* and *b* are actually combined, as the wind and brass hammer out the first two notes of *b* while the strings hack their way through *a*.

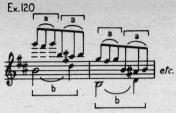

Even the serene melody quoted in Ex. 110 is forced into the minor key by the overall mood of agitation. At last the supreme climax of the movement is reached; the whole orchestra reiterates over and over again the pairs of notes indicated as *b* in the example above. After eight bars of *ff* there is a sudden drop in the tension; horns and trumpets continue quietly with fragments of *b*, but the strings remember once more the slowest version of *a*,

A last convulsive chord leads to a slow descent in the woodwind which brings us back to the recapitulation. The combination of themes here is so masterly that I make no apology for quoting a few bars in short score. There could be no more graphic proof of the concentration that a real master brings to his task. Composition consists far more of rejection than acceptance; anything irrelevant is pushed aside by the composer; everything possible is done to relate theme to theme, pattern to pattern.

The recapitulation follows a roughly similar course to the first few pages of the exposition; in detail, however, it is infinitely richer. What was before a bare sketch is now filled in with intricate counter-melodies, warmer harmony, richer scoring. By chopping out a whole section of some thirty bars, Brahms brings in the second subject much earlier than before, and, since the point has now been made, he no longer bothers to underline its relationship to the first subject. Once again, though, we must realize the danger of sitting back as passive listeners; the recapitulation is not an empty formula, for Brahms has many new pleasures in store for us. In particular we want to look out when the first horn begins to rhapsodize on this version of *c*.

Ex. 123

*dolce*                          *etc.*

From now on, this horn part reaches out further and further until, in a typical Brahmsian sunset, the music dies down to a slower tempo. In a soft haze the violins muse over *b* while the 'cellos and basses extend *a*. With the utmost delicacy the woodwind recall the little chuckling phrase from Ex. 112. All is gentleness and peace, and the movement ends as it had begun, with a tender simplicity that is far from naïve. It seems more as if Brahms had fallen in love with the material of the movement; this affectionate farewell shows his reluctance to part with it.

It is essential to hear a movement like this many times before you can really claim familiarity with it. There is so much detail packed into every page of the score that only close analysis will reveal all its secrets. Such craftsmanship is not merely an incidental facet of the music; it is an integral part of its greatness. If we just sit back and say that this section is pretty, that one is loud, this part is getting slower, or even 'turn the volume down a bit, dear, I'm reading', we are (by our intellectual indifference) reducing the music to the level of any orchestral background noise. Brahms must have exerted every ounce of his mental energy when writing this, and it is our duty to make a corresponding effort to get to the heart of every marvellously constructed phrase. Music is not just an emotional stimulus—a pattern of sedatives and shocks; it is something far more significant. Listen intelligently and with understanding and you cannot fail to feel an intense gratitude that any one man had the vision, the humanity, the intellect, and the craftsmanship that go to make up such a masterpiece.

Of the four movements in this symphony, the second is the most difficult to grasp. One is soon aware of its gravity, of its determination to avoid the type of sentimentality that we find in the long horn solo in Tchaikovsky's Fifth Symphony; but analysis is of little help. What is needed most is simply a willingness to soak oneself in its beauty, to respond to the mood Brahms clearly has in mind. Much of the movement is concerned with shapes rather than melodies—in fact, one of the most important features could be represented diagrammatically by two lines approaching each other.

This contrary motion is of the greatest importance, since it imposes a certain mathematical quality of detachment, of abstraction on otherwise emotional material.

Ex. 124

Brahms seems determined to keep any unduly obvious senti-mentality at bay, and much of this movement is fugal in style. Do not be misled, though, into classifying as new those themes which are actually old ones disguised. For example, half-way through the opening melody, which is coloured in the rich yet sombre hue that only the 'cellos can give, we find this phrase:

Ex. 125

Brahms needs only four notes out of this to build a whole new section, a section which at first glance would appear to be a completely new development. The horn leads off with this curious rocking theme:

Ex. 126

It is taken up in turn by oboes, flutes, and 'cellos and basses—certainly not as a strict fugue, but at least in the spirit of one. Where does it come from? Look at the fifth to the eighth notes of Ex. 125 and you will see at once.

The severity of much of this movement is softened by a delicate contrasting tune in F♯ major. Scored mostly for wood-wind with a *pizzicato* bass giving it a suggestion of a dance-rhythm, it is notable for the gentle syncopations which Brahms may well have learnt from Schumann. The sunnier mood which this tune induces does not last for long, and soon the strings present yet another theme, again of an intensely serious kind. The unity of this movement is remarkable; we have seen how one small segment of the opening melody can be the mainspring of a whole new section. Brahms now accomplishes this same conjuring trick once more. Take the last few notes of Ex. 124:

Although it is quite probable that Brahms had no particular intention of echoing this pattern later in the movement, there is unquestionably a fairly close family resemblance between it and the new serious theme which the strings first present in bar 45. I will transpose it down so that the similarity of contour can be appreciated more easily.

Compare this in turn with the horn theme in Ex. 126, and the feeling of what one might call a musical blood-tie becomes even more striking.

This new theme goes through a somewhat stormy episode in which Brahms makes much use of the three rising quavers with which it begins. There is also a fascinating ghost, an ominous three-note phrase, B♭ A B♭ or E F♮ E, which could conceivably be a memory of bar 1 of the first movement. If the music were by César Franck I would unhesitatingly assert that this was a deliberate back-reference; since it is by Brahms, I tend to feel that it is probably a subconscious echo and no more.[1] It is important in so far as it leads us back to the initial theme whose ultimate unwinding is marked by various decorations and perturbations before it finally sinks to an uneasy rest.

The third movement was an instant success, having to be repeated at many of the earlier performances of the symphony. The mature Brahms seems to have wanted to slow down the hectic scherzo which Beethoven had perfected. Many of his chamber works show a preference for an easygoing amble rather

[1] For a further discussion of this type of 'quotation', see p. 116.

than a breathless gallop, and this movement remains in the memory as a gentle Allegretto even although 142 of its 240 bars are marked 'presto ma non assai'. In form, it is a combination of three things: a rondo, a set of variations, and an inversion of the classical Scherzo and Trio. At first glance it seems to be ABACA, which would make it a rondo. We then realize that B is a variation of A, and that C is another variation; this puts it into the second category. Lastly we remember that it is the third movement of a symphony and consequently that it stems from the scherzo and trio of classical usage; but whereas the trio was traditionally taken at an easier tempo than the scherzo, here Brahms introduces what I have termed an inversion of the form by substituting slow-quick-slow-quick-slow for the more conventional quick-slow-quick-slow-quick.[1] All of which is merely intended to show that there is more originality to this than its attractive presence would suggest.

It begins with an enchanting theme on the oboe.

Ex.129

Meanwhile, the 'cellos are busy pretending to be guitars, their softly plucked accompaniment only emphasizing the serenade-like character of the tune. The upper strings stay aloof from the proceedings for thirty-two bars. When they do come in the mood is broken, and with a lightness that almost suggests Mendelssohn they lift the oboe-tune into more airy spheres.

Ex.130

[1] For a similar example in his chamber music, cf. the second movement of the Violin Sonata in A major, Op. 100.

The 'Midsummer Night's Dream' atmosphere is heightened by a sudden burst of rowdiness, as though Bottom and his troupe had blundered into some fairy glade.

Even this will be seen to be an inversion of the opening theme, albeit a fairly free one. The bustle continues until a few more measured beats from the 'cellos lead us back to the original tempo. This is a moment of pure magic, for Brahms now harmonizes the oboe tune in a subtly different way, changing one's whole conception of its emotional intensity. Its initial purity is replaced by a haunting pathos; daylight gives way to dusk. Compare these two phrases and you will see what I mean.

The tune takes a somewhat different direction now, seeming to become a little more serious with implications of E minor creeping in. In particular, Brahms keeps stressing the little triplet figure from the fourth bar, whose importance we only realize fully when the next Presto section begins. It proves to be the very mainspring of the new tempo as the strings lead the way into a second dance. Equally Mendelssohnian in character, it employs the simplified version, as in Ex. 131a. In time, this is stripped down to a bare skeleton before the gracious opening tune makes its final appearance. As a coda, we find a last romantic paroxysm from the strings—a phrase which seems so akin to the slow movement of Mozart's Piano Concerto in A major (K.488) that one can only assume a subconscious memory on Brahms's part.

Ex. 133

Mozart's rhythm

Such unconscious imitations are not important—Brahms himself said that plagiarism was one of the silliest topics of stupid people —but they are interesting in that they emphasize the almost universally felt emotional patterns that seem to go with certain intervals and harmonies. It is as though composers of different ages and different nationalities were able to draw upon some common store of experience, a store from which a group of notes is indelibly stamped with melancholy, brilliance, tenderness, or pathos, according to its contour.[1]

The finale is a magnificent and complex movement in sonata form. In common with the other movements, it shows Brahms to be much occupied with dissection. We have seen how in the opening Allegro he abstracted small fragments of the first melody and developed them as separate units. Here we find the same technique being employed. He begins with a quiet and mysterious theme, of which the second bar is particularly important in that it frequently becomes a reiterated bass, or *ostinato*, to use the proper term.

Ex. 134

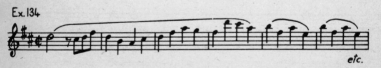

etc.

We must be prepared for bar 1 to be compressed into four equal quavers:

Ex. 135

[1] See Deryck Cooke's most interesting study *The Language of Music* (Oxford University Press, 1959).

Bar 2 we already know is destined to become a bass-line—in fact, the 'cellos and basses are immediately hypnotized by it and go on playing it a further four times while the violins climb up to the high D. Bars 5 and 6 show falling fourths coupled in pairs; these too bear a suggestion of things to come, for from them springs this important if subsidiary theme:

All this is presented with bated breath and an air of mystery that is intriguing to say the least; suddenly this mood is swept aside, and a riotous full orchestra takes up the theme as if to say, 'Why, there you were all the time!' A down-to-earth *tutti*[1] blows all thoughts of fantasy from our heads. The falling fourths are broken up into abrupt little phrases— and much is made of the compressed version of bar 1. There seems no reason to stop the general rejoicing until, with a dramatic gesture that reduces the rest of the orchestra to a sudden hushed *piano*, a single high clarinet introduces a new sustained theme that changes the whole atmosphere. Only a subdued murmur of Ex. 135 in the strings keeps this new idea 'in the family'. A few wide-spaced harmonies on the woodwind lead us to the second subject.

Just as the second subject of the first movement was subtly related to the opening bars (see Ex. 113), so here Brahms unifies the finale by presenting constant reminders of Ex. 135 against this lyrical new theme. At first we assume that this is no more than a characteristic display of craftsmanship, but with the imaginative skill that distinguishes all truly great composers, Brahms seizes on

[1] *tutti* = a passage for full orchestra; a term especially used in concerto-form.

this decorative fragment and develops it in the grand manner. The range of the phrase is widened until it gains a positively heroic stature.

Ex.138

On the face of it this seems a far cry from Ex. 134, but it is a legitimate extension of the first bar of the finale, and must be appreciated as such. The running scales at the end of Ex. 138 are passed around the woodwind section with some enthusiasm before a curious rhythm with a Scotch snap to it rounds off the exposition.

The development is a good deal more involved than is usual in a symphonic finale. After a brief reminder of the first four bars of Ex. 134, the music seems to disintegrate into brief phrases which appear to be leading nowhere. In fact, they are leading to the obscure world of F♯ minor, a wonderland which causes the opening theme to stand on its head.

Ex.139

As will be seen from a closer look at this, the phrases in quavers with a bracket below them are a quickened inversion of the crochet phrases with a bracket above. Brahms plays turn and turn-about with these two fragments until a sudden rather cross entry of Ex. 136 (now in the minor) chases them away. With increasing intensity, and propelled by strong syncopations, the music builds to a passionate climax. Most unexpectedly this leads not to a triumphant restatement of the opening material but to one of the most intimate and magical moments of the entire symphony. In the warm radiance of F♯ major we suddenly find a gently rocking motive that opens a whole new world of emotion.

Ex. 140

What a wonderfully subtle variation of Ex. 134 this is, as the rhythmic pattern below reveals. Intermingled with this touching development we find sundry echoes of Ex. 136, but for the most part they are now in the minor. With an effect of distant majesty, like a great mountain seen far off, the trombones enunciate the first bell-like notes of Ex. 136 in minims; a slow *tremolando* in the violins enhances the impression of distance. It is the dawn of a new day, for in a moment Brahms leads us back to the recapitulation.

This behaves in an orthodox manner, taking a shortened route to the second subject which duly appears in the tonic key of D major. The various developments that we have experienced are passed in review, until in a last blaze of triumph the trumpets and horns lift the second subject from its normal contemplative self to a mood of heroic rejoicing. Whenever Brahms felt particularly pleased with a work he would joke about it in terms that were the exact opposite to the truth. For instance, of the great Scherzo of the Bb Piano Concerto he said that it was 'a tiny wisp of a scherzo'. Of this symphony he wrote that it was so mournful that the score would have to be printed on black-edged paper. To those who knew him, such a remark indicated the special delight that comes with the knowledge of a job well done.

## CHAPTER VIII

# SIBELIUS

## Symphony No. 2 in D, Op. 43 (1901)

1. Allegretto—poco allegro. 2. Tempo andante, ma rubato—
allegro—andante sostenuto. 3. Vivacissimo—lento e soave—
tempo primo. 4. Allegro moderato.

Orchestra: 2 flutes; 2 oboes; 2 clarinets; 2 bassoons; 4 horns;
3 trumpets; 3 trombones; 1 tuba; 1 timpanist; normal complement of strings.

This symphony was written in 1901, two years after the First
Symphony, at a time when the composer was thirty-six years old.
First performance on 8 March 1902 at a concert devoted entirely
to his works. For several years around this period Sibelius was
greatly worried by ear-trouble, and no doubt fears of deafness
afflicted him and caused him a severe emotional crisis. Despite
this, the general impression we gain from this symphony is one
of optimism, an optimism which perhaps reflects the Italian
spring, since it was mainly written in the hilly country behind
Rapallo, where Sibelius had rented a small work-room.

IT IS IRONIC that whereas the inclusion of a Sibelius symphony
in such a book as this would have been regarded as inevitable
in the nineteen-thirties, today one must almost adopt a defensive
attitude to justify his inclusion. For some reason or another
Sibelius has become a rather 'unfashionable' composer, even
though many sincere and knowledgeable musicians believe him to
be truly great. I think the principal reason for this is simply that
the best way to be looked on as unfashionable is to scorn fashion,
and if ever a composer did that it was Sibelius. At a time when
experiments in every aspect of music were rife he stuck firmly to
his own somewhat traditional style. While the First Symphony

shows evidence of many influences—Tchaikovsky, Rimsky-Korsakov, and Grieg are perhaps the most noticeable—once he entered his own particular world, a world which he first saw clearly in this Second Symphony, he continued on his own way. The post-Wagnerian melting-pot, in which every imaginable form of musical experiment was tried, applauded, rejected, and resurrected, affected him not at all. In enviable isolation he went on writing what he wanted to, untouched by the emotional or intellectual excesses that were changing the face of European music. His compositions range from the supremely concentrated distillation of the Fourth Symphony to the unabashed popularity of the *Valse Triste*.[1] On occasion he will despise melody, concentrating all his resources on tiny fragments of a mere three or four notes; in more expansive mood, he can write a long, sustained tune that for sheer melodic beauty knows few parallels. There cannot be many themes as beautiful and yet as intensely personal as that in the slow movement of the violin concerto, in which the rich tones of the solo violin are enshrouded in the romantic gloom of horns and bassoons while the ghostly footsteps of the plucked strings pad furtively through the dusk. Yet although the atmosphere of this movement positively reeks of nineteenth-century Romanticism, Sibelius manages to present its Byronic fantasies in a completely new light. Where a Liszt or a Wagner would have become obsessed with a literary image, and where they would have allowed the musical form to be overshadowed by a picture, a story, or some figment of a non-musical imagination, he keeps the movement under iron control. The sensuous passion may be there, but it is kept in heroic restraint. He is a true classicist; his works are the product of a marvellously ordered mind, and while such control in lesser hands might lead to mere worthiness, in his case it leads to true worth.

The strong classical bent we find in him inevitably drew him towards the symphony as a form, even although it had lost its

---

[1] Those who accuse Sibelius of commercialism in writing the *Valse Triste* should remember that he sold it outright to his publisher for £5, thereby forfeiting any further royalty.

appeal for most other composers. The reason for this mass deser-
tion of a form ennobled by Mozart and Haydn, Beethoven and
Brahms is fairly clear. As I have constantly stressed, tonality or a
sense of key is the basis on which the symphony had been built.
Once the tonal freedom of Wagner had loosened the ties of key
the whole foundation of the symphony was weakened; modulation
ceases to register in music which is in a constant state of tonal flux,
and without significant modulation the architectural implications
of a large-scale movement are changed almost beyond recognition. In the first years of the twentieth century, other composers
were striking out in all kinds of new directions—the impression-
ism of the French, the Russian folk-art of Stravinsky, the neurotic
(and erotic) symbolism of the atonal composers such as Schönberg
and Berg. On all this experimentalism Sibelius turned his back,
choosing to tunnel deeper into the heart of the greatest classical
form.

Like all the major classical composers, he prefers to work with
fragments rather than melodies. It is a basic property of music that
all sounds breed a certain emotion; this group of notes[1] bespeaks
loneliness, another conveys brilliance, another gaiety, and so on.
The problem for the composer, then, is that he is wrestling intellectually with material which is in its very nature emotional.
There is little enough emotional significance in a phrase like

Ex. 141

which is what makes it good symphonic material; there may be
intensity in the *playing*, in the sheer sound of the orchestra, but
the phrase itself is pretty well negative. If a composer writes a tune,
as he does in a slow movement, the tune becomes the master. It
dictates the emotion, and even its creator must follow it, supporting it with suitable harmonies and embroidering it with decorations of one kind or the other. In his First Symphony, Sibelius fell

[1] Even a single chord—a 'bare' fifth, a 'rich' major triad, an 'anguished' ninth.

into this trap, choosing themes that were too positive in their emotional content, and which consequently proved intractable in development. In all the later symphonies he uses much more neutral material—fragments which he presents to us as disconnected, apparently irreconcilable units, and which he then forges before our very eyes into a marvellous cohesion.

Although I have emphasized the conservative nature of Sibelius's genius, it is a fallacy to imagine that his symphonies in any way resemble those of Beethoven or Brahms. His ideas of form are entirely different from those of his predecessors. It is difficult to find an exact simile to elucidate the differences, but even a comparison with something mechanical will help. Suppose that we compare the first movement of a symphony to a watch. In the classical symphony the composer showed you the watch complete in the first section or exposition. 'Look at this watch,' he would say. 'This is one side of it, the first side, and here is the other side, the second; and they are joined together by the bit in the middle.'[1] In the development section he would take the watch to pieces, concentrate on one (or several) of its component parts, or build new patterns from its works. In the third part, the recapitulation, he reassembles the watch in the light of experience gained and gives you the satisfaction of a second look at the completed article —at which point you can lean back feeling that you now know a lot more about watches.

Sibelius has a technique which is almost exactly opposite to this. He starts his symphony by showing you a lot of oddly shaped little bits lying about all over the score; in the development section he puts them together, allowing them to grow and co-ordinate so that you see a watch being built; finally, as likely as not, he takes them all apart again, leaving you with the scattered pieces and a sense of 'Would you believe it? Those different little bits were related to each other all the time.' Naturally, this is something of a simplification, but it should be enough to make Sibelius's individuality as a musical craftsman evident. While it could be argued that Brahms also offers us a number of fragments at the

[1] First subject—bridge passage—second subject.

start of his Second Symphony (see Ex. 108), they at least *sound* like one melody; the essential difference between his technique and that of Sibelius is that the later composer presents his ideas as disconnected gobbets, often divided one from the other by silences. In fact, there is one great historical precedent for the Sibelian concept of form, and that is the B minor Sonata of Liszt. This astonishing work anticipates almost exactly the structural innovations with which Sibelius is normally credited.

The Second Symphony begins with a figure which sounds like an accompaniment but which is actually vitally important.

On top of this unassuming opening gambit a perky little wood-wind theme appears, like a distant fanfare.

The last few notes of this are underlined by the horns, who softly repeat them at a somewhat slower tempo. As if to empha-size the importance of this material still more, Sibelius repeats it a couple more times, albeit with slight modifications of pitch. On each occasion the change of rhythm in the horns gives a curious feeling of uncertainty, as though the composer were still not convinced of the worth of this material. Finally, the music dissolves into a longish silence. Two flutes make a tentative sugges-tion which seems ineffective; bassoons echo it half-heartedly and then launch themselves into a fanfare-like motive which one feels has been stolen from the rightful preserve of the trumpets.

Ex.144

The hollow laughter of the flutes' trill mocks the bassoons into silence, and then, totally unsupported by harmony, the violins suddenly project a long melodic line. Even Berlioz never presented a theme as baldly as this.

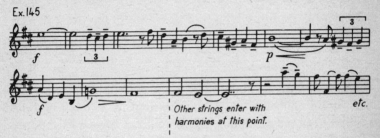

Ex.145

Other strings enter with harmonies at this point.

Classical training might lead us to think (quite wrongly) that this is a second subject, but all in all the whole symphony up to this point would seem to be an extraordinary hotchpotch of disconnected ideas. Any attempt to relate them one to another is sheer folly, for Sibelius intends them to be disconnected. Here, laid out for us to see, are the wheels, the springs, the hands of his watch—little snatches of tunes, harmonies, rhythms from which he will ultimately build a whole movement. To add further to the confusion there are curious vacillations of mood from tenderness to savagery.

The first truly forward impulse of the movement is heralded by a fascinating passage for *pizzicato* strings. A quickening of the tempo leads to the most significant and characteristic theme of all.

Ex.146

Note the reappearance of Ex.142 beneath.

Sibelius seems greatly drawn towards themes which begin with an immensely long note whose tension is dispelled by a sudden convulsion of quicker notes. This particular example generates tremendous energy; the strings begin to whirr with the precision of machinery, while abrupt little phrases on the woodwind cut sharply through the texture. Gradually the calming influence of Ex. 142 makes itself felt. A single oboe reminds us of Ex. 146, only to be answered by a bassoon which drags up a somewhat murky phrase of considerable importance.

Ex. 147

The quiet dynamo hum of the strings continues while over and over again different woodwind instruments reiterate a brief angular phrase in descending fifths.

Ex. 148

(sometimes only five notes)

Above all one gains an impression of tremendous drive and pace, a feeling that is only slightly eased when the music settles down on a constantly repeated G sharp on a solo kettle-drum. From this point an extensive development of Ex. 143 begins. Its treatment involves translation into a minor key, inversion, and an ingenious condensation:

Ex. 149

(bar 1. inverted)

The next stage is more impassioned as the strings vary this pattern still further, goaded by waspish trills from the woodwind. In a continuous ascent to higher levels they at last arrive on a high

B flat, whereupon Ex. 146 appears once more in triumph, while double basses and drums pound out the rhythm with which the symphony had so unemotionally begun. The most dramatic climax of the movement is heralded by a fanfare in which the trumpets and horns at last take over the theme the bassoons had presented so unconvincingly in the early stages (Ex. 144). As is often the case in Sibelius's music, one has the impression of immense natural forces at work as crashing brass chords cleave their way through a haze of trills on the strings.

Suddenly we find ourselves back with the familiar material of Ex. 143, although this time it is deprived of its original support (Ex. 142). Instead, the violins reveal that the last two bars of Ex. 145 can be integrated with Ex. 143. The material is presented once more in what passes for a brief recapitulation, but everything now seems infinitely *closer* than it was before. The quiet ending deliberately leaves us in the air.

The slow movement is perhaps the toughest part of the whole symphony, tough in its intent and the most taxing for the listener. There is very little truly lyrical writing in it, and it is periodically convulsed with violent primeval struggles, as though some mighty glacier were breaking up. It begins with a long drawn-out and seemingly tireless *pizzicato* for the 'cellos and double basses. The Finns are great long-distance runners, and this opening always makes me think of the numb automaton-like feeling of the weary legs of a runner plodding on and on, till at last from his tired mind there emerges a sad dark song.

Ex. 150
Lugubre
*mf*       *dim.*   *pp*

The short square-cut phrases of this folk-like melody are entirely characteristic of Sibelius, as is the gradual increase of tempo that now ensues. The upper strings begin to take an interest in the proceedings until they become positively obsessed with this concentrated and savage little figure.

Ex. 151

It is with some surprise that we realize that so ferocious a pattern can be softened to this:

Ex. 152

This brief interlude of tenderness comes after a terrifying outburst on the full brass—one of the most electrifying moments in the whole symphony. A few bars of almost pastoral music with rippling thirds on flutes and bassoons are still not potent enough to dispel the prevailing thunderclouds. Within a relatively short time the threatening mood returns and the lower strings savagely worry at the bracketed portion of Ex. 152.

This movement is extremely long and dramatic; even in the light of the composer's subsequent achievements it must remain a landmark, for never before had the slow movement of a symphony expressed so graphically the forbidding grandeur of Nature at its most awe-inspiring. Despite its great economy of material, it gives an impression of free composition—an improvisation on the orchestra. Inevitably it will conjure up pictures in the listener's mind, of mountain crags, of dark forests, even of demons. It is, however, not a tone-poem but a symphonic movement, showing a masterly discipline in its handling of immensely striking thematic material.

I have already mentioned in the prefatory note to this analysis that the general impression we gain from this symphony is one of optimism. Although this opinion is fairly universal it is hard to substantiate in detail. It reflects three memorable impressions—the simple gaiety of the opening, the luscious oboe tune in the Scherzo, and the heroically striding theme that begins the finale. Far the greater part of the symphony is occupied with moods of agitation, severity, terror, uneasiness, and melancholy, and yet still the impression of a 'happy' score remains. Such is the potency of a key like D major. I mention this since the Scherzo is a stormy windblown movement of extraordinary concentration. A superficial glance at the score might lead one to imagine that the influence of his Italian surroundings had caused Sibelius to write a Tarantella.

Such a conclusion is quickly proved wrong by the ruthless savagery with which this theme is handled. Even although much of the music is *pp* it has a demoniac quality about it that suggests the winds of Hell. Driven before its perpetual gale, like a hard-pressed ship seen occasionally above the giant wave-crests, is one forlorn phrase that appears again and again in the woodwind.

For ten pages of score little else can be heard but the ceaseless drive of Ex. 153 with occasional glimpses of Ex. 154 scudding above. Suddenly there is a mysterious silence, broken only by five wide-spaced drum-beats which recede to the virtual inaudibility of *pppp*. With a magical release of tension, the famous oboe solo appears.

The nine-times repeated note with which this melody begins is of course a variation on the type of theme I have already described as a Sibelius trademark (see Ex. 146). Instead of a long held note he now gives us a pulsing repetition, but it amounts to nearly the same thing. There is something else more interesting in this tune, for once again we have an intriguing example of the way a composer's mind works. To most listeners, this melody seems unrelated to what has gone before, yet closer examination reveals this to be a false assumption. If we look at the string figuration immediately before the drum-taps, we find an exciting sequence built on this pattern:

Ex. 156

Now look at the second bar of Ex. 155. What is it but an extension of this same pattern, decorated by a simple ornament? If I write it this way you will see the resemblance at once:

Ex. 157 Lento

The Scherzo is structurally simple, consisting as it does of an orthodox ABABA pattern, with A being the *vivacissimo* section and B the lovely oboe tune. However, the final A section is not a conclusion; in fact, it would be fairer to call it C, since it consists of new material whose function it is to carry us willy-nilly into the finale. Insistent segments of rising scales push their way through the score until at last with immense pomp and majesty the great theme of the last movement unfolds. Different though it may be in character, this too is derived from the oboe melody since its first three notes are clearly the same in pattern as the first three notes of bar 2, Ex. 155.

Ex. 158

This invigorating tune is helped on its way by grinding C sharps in the bass, coupled with repeated chords in the trombones which together give an impression of some great engine throbbing. The orchestration increases in intensity until at last a typical disintegration sets in; for the first time we hear a continuously revolving phrase in quavers which Sibelius is going to use to enormous effect. It is no more than a glorified five-finger exercise but in his hands it assumes the majesty of an ocean swell. Above it, the woodwind gradually formulate a clear picture of a most important theme. To start with, we hear no more than tentative suggestions from oboe or clarinet, but at last it becomes apparent that this is more than a random counterpoint and the phrases build and combine into a great span of melody.

Ex. 159

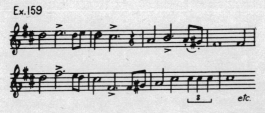

A brief sample such as this gives no idea of the extraordinary way in which Sibelius extends this pattern, spinning it out with an almost relentless quality which is enhanced still further by the constantly reiterated phrase beneath. On paper it seems a boring device; in performance it has a hypnotic power.

Such is the simplicity of the material in this movement that a detailed analysis is not at all necessary. Mention must be made of one further idea, a brief and martial phrase which recurs frequently, usually on the heavier brass.

Ex. 160

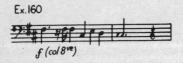

Admittedly the contour of this carries more than a suggestion of Scheherazade, but I have already mentioned the clear influence Rimsky-Korsakov seems to have had on Sibelius. The development section, if one can use such a term for a fairly loosely constructed movement, concerns itself mainly with fragments of Ex. 158 alternating with Ex. 160. It is worth remarking on the beautiful new light which is shed on Ex. 158 by playing it quietly, and with a less austere harmonization. The most memorable feature of the movement, however, is the immense accumulation of sound in the last sixteen pages of the score. Starting from a low *p*, the continuously revolving quaver pattern unfolds itself in seemingly endless repetition. For seventy bars the 'five-finger exercise' continues virtually unchanged until, with stunning effect, a cunningly placed F$\sharp$ switches the music into the major. Meantime, the sheer weight of sound has been growing until we seem engulfed in great waves of orchestral colour. It is an extension of the technique that Smetana uses in *Vltava*, but without the prettiness that tends to make the earlier work pall. There is a ruthless quality about the Sibelius that is extraordinarily impressive. Once the major has been reached, the feeling of extreme severity can be relaxed a little and a deeply satisfying re-statement of Ex. 158 brings the symphony to a triumphant conclusion. Never has emotion governed to the extent of tipping the music over into sentimentality, and the composer's iron restraint gives the whole work immense strength. Certainly in 1901 nothing was being written with greater originality than this, nor was anything more free from the all-pervading shadow of Wagner. This is great music, and it should be unaffected by the vagaries of fashion; to deny ourselves the pleasure it can bring is surely the height of folly.

## CHAPTER IX

# STRAVINSKY

## Symphony in three movements (1945)

1. ♩= 160. 2. Andante, ♩= 76. Interlude leading to — 3. Con moto (♩= 108)

Orchestra: 1 piccolo; 2 flutes; 2 oboes; 3 clarinets, 1 doubling bass clarinet; 2 bassoons; 1 double bassoon; 4 horns; 3 trumpets; 3 trombones; 1 tuba; timpani; percussion; piano; harp; strings.

Notice the characteristic gesture by which Stravinsky dispenses with any tempo indication for the first movement; he regards the metronome mark as self-sufficient. The symphony is dedicated to the New York Philharmonic Symphony Society and was first performed in New York on 24 January 1946. The normal classical orchestra has here been expanded by the use of various instruments, most of which are employed to amplify the range available—e.g. double bassoon, bass clarinet, etc. The piano is used almost entirely as a percussion instrument. The orchestra is substantially reduced in size during the slow movement.

THE CHOICE of a truly representative twentieth-century symphony poses quite a problem; I have already shown[1] that with the collapse of tonality the foundations of the symphony as a form were immeasurably weakened. Two courses of action are now available to a composer wishing to perpetuate this great style of musical architecture: either he can agree to abide by the traditional rules of tonality, which might well cause him to be dubbed old-fashioned, or he must devise some new control which will act as a substitute for the long-established key relationships which have prevailed for a couple of centuries. One such substitute is the entire new grammar and syntax of music which comes under the

[1] See p. 122.

heading of 'twelve-note composition'. Such a fundamental rejection of the known language of music did not appeal to Stravinsky, and only in his seventies has he shown any personal leaning towards systematic atonality—and then possibly out of a desire not to be thought unfashionable.

The fascination about Stravinsky is that all through his life he has delighted in giving audiences something completely different from what they had grown to expect. Just when they had come to understand and appreciate the rich colouring of *Firebird* and *Petrushka* as an extension of nineteenth-century orchestral virtuosity, he shook the world with the primitive barbarity of *The Rite of Spring*. Reconciled at last to that, audiences had next to grow used to the infinitely scaled-down resources of *Les Noces*—four pianos and percussion instead of a ninety-piece orchestra. After all this rhythmic pounding, the dazed public was called upon to accept a reconstitution of eighteenth-century elegance in the enchanted pages of *Pulcinella*. Back went Stravinsky's clock still further, and several neo-Bach works appeared in which austere counterpoint reigned supreme. At least the critics were now confident that Stravinsky had finally turned his back on the highly coloured music of his romantic Russian forebears; judge of their confusion when he next produced *Le Baiser de la Fée*, a ballet based on Tchaikovsky and full of rich orchestration and nineteenth-century sparkle. There seemed no limit to the caprice of this wayward genius; and yet now, with the perspective that time inevitably brings, we can see a fairly consistent line of development, despite occasional excursions off the track.

The basic clue to Stravinsky's approach can be summed up in the word 'simplification'. His palate was quickly sated by the exuberant riot of colour we find in the early ballet-scores. From then on, he imposed ever more severe disciplines upon himself, stripping away everything irrelevant to his purpose. The first magnet to draw him (in *Pulcinella*) was the eighteenth century, the Age of Reason. Then his glance went back across the centuries to the spirit of Ancient Greece. *Oedipus Rex*, *Apollon Musagètes*, *Persephone*, and even the *Symphony of Psalms* all share the quality which I can best describe as being 'written in marble'. There is a feeling of classic detachment in them; the beauty of empty temples beneath hot, open skies; the sharp contrasts of dark green, white, and harsh blues; the measured movement of priests and priestesses in ancient ritual; the eternal stillness of some Homeric figure, whose sightless eyes gaze forbiddingly from the imprisoning stone.

It is paradoxical that the man who in 1913[1] must have seemed like a musical Attila, putting the traditional elements of music to the fire and the sword, should by the nineteen-twenties have become the most classically minded of all contemporary composers. Yet such is the case, and no composer since Bach more aptly illustrates one of the great truths about music—that an emotional response is more frequently an incidental (if unavoidable) by-product of it rather than a primary aim. In other words, a fugue has two sorts of beauty: the mastery with which its musical fabric is assembled, and the beauty of the actual sounds of which that fabric is composed. Of the two, the intellectual mastery is the more important. This is the very rock and foundation upon which Stravinsky's aesthetic is built. He eschews any deliberate effort to evoke emotion in an easy romantic way; for him music is a science, but also he feels it to be endowed with the dispassionate purity of a ritual. Despite the superficial appearance of complexity in his music, the most remarkable attribute of his scores is their simplicity. It is a great part of Stravinsky's genius that he is able to present the most commonplace elements of classical music in a completely new light.[2] Both the *Symphony in C* (1940) and the *Symphony in Three Movements* now to be discussed are notable for the economy with which the composer achieves effects of remarkable originality. Where other composers use materials that are intrinsically complex in themselves, Stravinsky gives us a straight common chord that is completely familiar. It is the angle of approach that is different; just as a camera can reveal new and unsuspected facets of an everyday object, so can Stravinsky uncover aspects of the chord of C major that we have never dreamed of.

---

[1] The year of *The Rite of Spring*.      [2] See Exx. 28 and 29, pp. 31–2.

The first movement of this symphony is strident and savage; it could be said to reflect the machine-like pulse of an industrial age. It is devoid of heart and makes only the smallest concession to emotional appeal. It is useless to seek in its brittle pages either the tenderness of Mozart, the drama of Beethoven, or the passion of Tchaikovsky. What you will find is an immensely exhilarating if somewhat ruthless drive, and a rhythmic vitality that belongs exclusively to our age. Rhythm and sonority have become the prime concern of the composer, and unless we accept this change of bias, unless we go out and meet him on his ground, we are sure to misunderstand his message.

If you were to come across this passage in a romantic piano piece it would seem perfectly orthodox.

Stravinsky would regard this as the tawdry trappings of Romanticism; you can't wear armour in a taxi; you'd trip over your sword getting into a bus. His technique then is to preserve the strength of such an idea but to make its presentation much starker. Instead of a sweeping tune you will find abrupt and incisive chords, cutting like machine tools into any suggestion of a soft core that the melody might have. The 'heroic' quality of Ex. 161 is stripped away and only the bare bones grimace at us.

The upward scale in the first bar, reinforced by a *glissando* on the piano, sounds like the ripping of a giant piece of calico. In itself this scale is important, and it is particularly worth noticing how Stravinsky uses it to break up any undue suggestion of symmetry. After an immensely striking first paragraph, the texture is suddenly reduced to a quiet chopping rhythm on clarinets over which we hear the most important theme of the movement. It is no more than a bare outline of G minor.

Individual brass instruments stand out in turn like heralds proclaiming this vital idea.

Now one of the most noticeable hall-marks of Stravinsky's style is what is called an *ostinato*—a continuous pattern of repetition in one part which goes on regardless of what may be happening elsewhere. Stravinsky will use such a pattern in two ways: either in direct repetition, or by ringing the changes on the *rhythm* while preserving the notes intact. Thus for twenty-three bars the 'cellos and basses pluck their way remorselessly through the three notes A C A.

Above this systematic and regular pattern we find violent cross-rhythms, syncopated splashes of piano chords, and a driving rhythmic urge which is a perfect reflection of modern industrial life. It is to such passages that the ballet sequences in a work like Leonard Bernstein's *West Side Story* owe their inception. As with

Picasso in the world of art, Stravinsky's influence on music extends into the most unlikely fields.

His second treatment of the *ostinato* pattern is shown in this example:

Ex. 165

The intrusion of the occasional B natural does not destroy the essential relationship that exists between this phrase and the preceding one. The basic A C A pattern continues like a carpet underfoot, its very consistency serving to heighten the extreme irregularity of the rhythms above. These are grouped in all sorts of variables of 3, 5, 11, 7, 4, and so on, so that the listener can never anticipate the duration of the next group. At last the *ostinato* releases its grip on the music, only to give way to a bass consisting entirely of segments of the scale of C major. It is interesting to see how Stravinsky's mind works when it comes to 'rethinking' the concept of a simple scale. The familiar outline of our schooldays is made considerably more exciting by this sort of treatment:

Ex. 166

Throughout this first movement an examination of the score shows how extraordinarily simple are the actual materials that Stravinsky uses. For bars on end the strings will have a brittle repetition of an ordinary G major arpeggio of three notes, while above, horns or trumpets will have sharp little outbursts built on conventional triads.[1] Yet despite this reliance on material from a

[1] A triad is the basic three-note chord of music, i.e., any note together with the third and the fifth above it. *Doh-mi-soh* is the simplest example.

first-year harmony book, Stravinsky's score sounds as searingly contemporary as any atonal work.

For development he draws mainly on the three-note pattern of Exx. 165 and 166. It appears both as a brief respite on quiet violas, and as a dry comment on the piano. The whole middle section of the movement is scored for altogether slenderer resources, and Stravinsky suggests something akin to a *concerto grosso* in the clearly defined contrasts of wind against strings, with the piano acting as a go-between. The writing is mostly contrapuntal in a free and fairly dissonant style, but the material is so clean-cut that the ear has no difficulty in disentangling one element from another. One important newcomer should be mentioned since much of the development section is based on it:

Ex.167

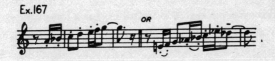

There are so many variants of this ascending scale that it is clearly Stravinsky's intention to develop the *idea* of a rising scale-pattern rather than any specific pattern itself. In fact, we can probably infer a relationship at least between these figures and Ex. 166.

Now it would be foolish to deny that at times Stravinsky's counterpoint is as thorny as a cactus; to ears brought up exclusively on a diet of what I once saw enchantingly described as 'Gilbert N. Sullivan', this score is virtually incomprehensible. However, once you are prepared to go out and meet Stravinsky and to see what his intentions are, you will inevitably find that this music is worth while. Not a note is wasted, and the elaborately spun texture of rhythms grows on one to such a point that in time the lush richness of a Brahms score will seem positively immoral in its hot-house sensuousness. A more detailed analysis of the first movement than I have attempted here would be uninformative and depressing—how else can I convey the arid boredom that comes from pointing out the obvious? Obvious would seem a strange word to use about a work such as this, but its structure is quite clearly defined, and the material easily recognizable. The main problem for the listener is to surrender his prejudices and to absorb the idiom. Unquestionably it is the sort of music where to follow a score is an enormous help; as with most of Stravinsky's works, a miniature score is available,[1] and any serious music-student should study it closely. Suffice it to say for the moment that the opening material returns in a conventional if somewhat abbreviated recapitulation, and that the movement ends with a quiet chorale-like coda that puts us in a suitable frame of mind for the Andante which follows.

This is in Stravinsky's favourite 'antique-restoring' idiom. The fascination with eighteenth-century music that seems to have been induced by *Pulcinella* stayed with him for a long time, and many of his works show him wrestling with the problem of endeavouring to re-create the delicacy and grace of Baroque[2] music in twentieth-century terms. The easy and non-productive way of doing this is to write attractive pieces called 'Dolly's Minuet' or 'The Dresden Shepherdess' and have them played in programmes for housewives; they will not be unduly concerned that you have produced something which is synthetic, plagiaristic, and Bad Art. To recapture the keenness of mind and the elegance of spirit of the Baroque composer is a different question; it means depriving oneself of all that the Romantic movement stands for, and making a conscious return to the stylistic purity of the truly classical composer. Stravinsky accomplishes this partly by using rhythms which we tend to associate with eighteenth-century music in particular (e.g. ♩♫♩♫♩♫♪ ), and partly by a determination to eliminate what I might call the 'personal' element in composition. Classical music is objective, Romantic music is subjective; a return to Classicism involves the re-establishment of the barrier that Beethoven demolished, the barrier that made it seem improper

[1] Published by Schott, Ed. 4075.

[2] A somewhat loose term embracing a period of musical history of approximately 150 years from 1600 to 1750.

for the composer to express *his* suffering, *his* love, *his* joy as opposed to the *concept* of suffering, love, or joy. A cynic might call this barrier Good Taste. The passion in the music of both Mozart and Wagner is patently there, but they inhabit different worlds; I have no doubt that Mozart would have regarded Wagner's music as obscene, not because he was a puritan[1] but because he would never have permitted music to express the carnal passions so openly.

Stravinsky's conscious rejection of the romantic elements in music has often led to the accusation that his compositions are 'cold'. This is not a true criticism, but merely the expression of a preference for music that is 'warm'. Since he is seeking detachment, since he is deliberately avoiding any identification of Self with his music, it will inevitably seem cold after the hot-blooded creations of the late nineteenth-century composers. If, on the other hand, he were not to avail himself of the harmonic liberation of our times he would merely produce a pastiche. Only by combining the weight and texture of eighteenth-century music with the harmony of today can he solve his self-posed problem of re-creating the Baroque aesthetic in modern terms.

This Andante begins with the type of 'neutral' accompanying figure that we might find in many an earlier score:

Ex. 168

*mp*

There is nothing alarming about this; only the bass is unnerving, since its isolated quavers tend to appear after the beat and, on occasion, seem drawn towards F naturals which contradict the D major feeling implicit in the quotation above. The clash of F♮ against F♯ is one long hallowed by Tudor and Jacobean composers; consequently I feel it is a little unreasonable to protest

---

[1] His letters show that he was anything but . . .

when we find it in a work written in 1945. Above this gentle and non-committal accompaniment we find a gracious descent on the flute.

Ex. 169

The answering trills on clarinet and strings sound like little gurgles of delight. This phrase is like the first tentative line an artist might draw on a blank sheet of paper, the starting-point from which all manner of decorative proliferations are to grow. Stravinsky's thinking is almost entirely linear in this movement, and only rarely does he allow himself the luxury of harmonies of any density. A few such bars on six-part solo strings emphasize the crystal clarity of the rest; the same passage reappears later scored for woodwind. A brief 'middle section' is initiated by a low flute hovering precariously around its bottom D. In the entire movement there is no dynamic higher than *mf*.

A seven-bar Interlude bridges the gap between the Andante and the last movement. It consists of a few speculative chords which might be described as an 'awakening', but which are probably nearer to the preliminary waggles with which a golfer addresses the ball.

The finale employs techniques which are familiar to us from the first movement. At a casual glance, the movements would seem to be too alike, and the sense of resolution that we can feel in such a symphony as Beethoven's Fifth is not at all apparent. In performance, the movements do not seem to resemble each other to any special degree, and the extreme contrast of texture they both afford in comparison to the delicate traceries of the slow movement is enough to give them separate identities. Once more we find Stravinsky welcoming the common chord.

Ex. 170

Con moto

This barrack-room ballad has some pretty disturbing things going on underneath, and it would be misleading to suggest that we get an impression of C major unadulterated.

A brief quieter spell shows the bass clarinet trying on a seventh for size beneath a discreet murmur from the strings, and then we are off again on another display of explosive energy.

The indication 'piu presto' ushers in a somewhat disputatious dialogue between two bassoons which, despite its tensions, is conducted in decently muted tones. Other voices join in, and the listener is momentarily baffled by what seems like a confusion on Stravinsky's part as he introduces one fragment after another without seeming to show a particular affection for any one. In fact, he is again using the technique already mentioned on p. 139 by which he deals not with a theme but the *shape* of a theme. Everything here is concerned with three adjacent notes, and the next example shows several themes having this factor in common.

Ex. 171

a) Oboe

b) Horn

c) Flute

d) Vln. Solo

*etc.*

In such a way Stravinsky imposes a feeling of unity over fragments which at a first hearing seem to be unrelated. Gradually the music grows more positive until the horns give voice to a theme which recalls the folk-music of some of his early ballet scores.

Ex.172

The strings join in, in a similar vein, albeit with different material, until the whole orchestra starts to fidget with Ex. 171c. This section ends with some exciting screams from the horns. Propriety is restored by the bassoons who now present Ex. 170 in straight military costume in the typical march style that Stravinsky had so enjoyed in *L'Histoire du Soldat*. Everything seems to be going swimmingly when the triumphant course of the music is interrupted by some doleful sighs from the bassoons. These may be prompted by the sight of the academic task ahead, as though a Boy Scouts' hike had ended up with prep. in the classroom. Over the page there lurks a fugue.

The oboe had already made an unsuccessful attempt to think of the subject in Ex. 171a. Now it is presented in the unlikely colouring of trombone and piano, and although the various entries are by no means exact the theme is always identifiable, since it starts with an indeterminate rocking to and fro on two notes.

Ex.173

A curiously restless *agitato* section abbreviates this already concise subject still further:

Ex.174

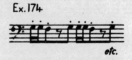

Suddenly Stravinsky seems to lose patience with it all, and some strident chords in wind and piano blow it away. The movement ends in a dissonant blare of sound, its last chord a shattering denial of the C major from which the symphony had sprung. It is strong meat this, and demands a spirit of adventure from its audience; if you like the negative listening of the arm–chair addict it is not for you. Stravinsky takes you by a very firm grip and shouts his message in your ear; those who have taken the trouble to listen with understanding have found that he really has something to say.

PART 2

# TALKING ABOUT CONCERTOS

## CHAPTER X

# ONE AGAINST ALL

ALL MEN are not born equal; even in the somewhat limited field of musical executants, some are endowed with infinitely greater natural ability than others. The concerto as a musical form is a logical reflection of the fact that in any group of musicians gathered under one roof, one or two will outshine the others in technical and musical ability. In the very early days, concertos tended to be for several players rather than one. There is a charming proof of why this was so in one of the Handel concerti grossi for strings; in the slow movement of the piece in question, there is a particularly elaborate ornament given to the solo quartet which at no time appears in the ordinary orchestral parts, for the simple reason that the rank-and-file players would have been unable to play it with the requisite neatness and agility. In other words, Handel had not conceived the form itself as something special; it was simply a composition for orchestra which reflected the superiority of the front-desk performers. Put yourself in the place of a composer like Haydn with a resident orchestra at his disposal in the Eszterházy household, or Bach, working with the local players at Cöthen or Leipzig. It would only have been common sense to acknowledge the fact that Herr X or Dr Y was the outstanding performer on the oboe or the violin; what more natural, then, than to write a work which showed off this greater ability?

Thus the early concertos came about, and herein lies the explanation of the seemingly haphazard choice of instruments which composers so often appear to have made at the time.

The emergence of the soloist into the splendid isolation he came to occupy in the nineteenth century was a slow process. In the Bach concertos for violin or keyboard, the soloist usually plays with the orchestra at all times, establishing the tempo and generally acting as an orchestral 'leader'. Even in such a case as the slow movement of Bach's D minor keyboard concerto, where there is no indicated part for the right hand until the thirteenth bar, it seems certain that the harpsichordist would have played with the accompanying strings, perhaps directing them with an elegant wave of the right hand at times in order to show his complete command of the situation. Gradually the competence of orchestral players increased to such an extent that they could manage without the assistance of the soloist; remember though that the conductor as we know him today was still unknown in 1700. Reports tell us of such barbarous customs as the audible beating of time with a stick upon the floor, or with a roll of parchment on the lid of the harpsichord. Where direction was necessary it would almost invariably come from the keyboard player, but there seems to have been a remarkable absence of formality about musical proceedings, even in the complex world of opera. Johann Mattheson, who was not only a composer, harpsichordist, organist and singer, but a linguist, a dancer and skilled fencer as well, when singing a role in an opera, would periodically leave the stage and direct the music from the harpsichord in the pit. It was on 5 December 1704 that he found an obstinate young man called Handel at the keyboard who refused to give way, thereby provoking the challenge to a duel which is a well-authenticated incident in Handel's life. Honour was satisfied when Mattheson's foil, having easily penetrated Handel's guard, impaled itself on one of his waistcoat buttons. This story is not entirely irrelevant, since Handel was accustomed to delight audiences at the opera-house by performing his keyboard concertos as interval music.

It was Mozart who established what we now think of as the

classical concerto form. In essence what he did was to devise a grand sonata for soloist and orchestra, though there are certain differences between strict sonata form[1] and the normal pattern of a Mozart concerto. What is the normal pattern? It is hard to say, since nearly every work of this kind has points of originality which make it an exception to any presupposed set of rules. For what it is worth, though, here is a rough ground-plan.

An orchestral exposition[2] presents us with most of the salient themes; but whereas in a sonata exposition the second subject will be in the so-called dominant key (a fifth higher than the tonic or 'home' key), in a concerto it is very much more likely to be kept in the original tonality. To make things more confusing, the composer will sometimes refuse to reveal the true second subject at all at this stage, preferring to save it up as a special treat for the soloist. (Beethoven and Mozart both have a lovable habit of fobbing us off with a 'dummy' second subject which, having been hailed with shrill cries of delight by the musical analyst, then fails to reappear until the recapitulation, much to our discomfiture.) On the whole, modulation to remote keys is avoided in the early stages, as this too is that much more effective if kept in reserve for a later moment. What distinguishes good concerto material from purely symphonic music is a very subtle suggestion that something is missing; that the music so far, although beautiful and satisfying enough in itself, has implications of potential decoration in the future. As the simplest possible instance of this I will quote two bars from the exposition of Mozart's piano concerto in G, K.453. They first appear in this very stark guise, and I would like to under-line the fact that their extreme simplicity should plant a seed of suspicion in our minds.

Ex. I

---

[1] See Part I.

[2] Known as the *tutti*, from the Italian word for *everybody* – meaning that all instruments are playing.

When the equivalent moment is reached after the soloist's entry, we find this rudimentary phrase undergoing a delightful transformation. In the first place it is decorated with elegant syncopations:

Ex.2

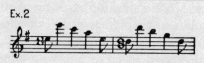

and in the second with something even more elaborate:

Ex.3

Experience teaches us to recognize such moments and to await expectantly the pleasures that lie ahead. In other words, we should not regard the orchestral exposition as something cut off from the main part of the movement, but rather as the framework of a plot into whose events the hero (or soloist) will duly move as chief protagonist. All the same, this orchestral introduction, or *tutti* as it is usually called, will often finish with a formal conclusion, terminating in a polite silence before the soloist plays a note. As composers became more adept at handling the form, the solo instrument's entry was managed with increasing subtlety, as we shall discover in due course.

Now it might be thought inevitable that the soloist should begin with the first subject as presented to us by the orchestra, and indeed there are plenty of Mozart concertos where that is what happens. But in four[1] out of the twenty-three works he wrote for piano and orchestra the soloist begins with completely new material, while in at least five others Mozart has devised some novel entry in which the orthodox presentation of the first subject is effectively disguised. In time, though, the soloist is bound to admit the existence

[1] K. 415, 466, 482, 491.

of the main theme; even so, it is by no means unusual to have it re-stated on the orchestra with the soloist merely adding decorative figures above. Perhaps the most original of all Mozart's variants on this very flexible plan occurs in the A major violin concerto, K.219. The soloist enters not only with a completely new theme, but at a totally different tempo as well. Then, the violin having discoursed most eloquently for a minute or so above a discreetly murmuring and pastoral accompaniment from the orchestra, the opening tempo is restored. Only at this point do we realize that the orchestral exposition, which had offered us what had seemed frankly to be one of Mozart's less inspired themes, was in fact merely an accompaniment, such as might be found at the beginning of an especially elaborate aria. It is the soloist who presents us with the true first subject, which is superimposed above the very same bars with which the orchestra had begun the work. Unorthodoxy can go no further.

Our search for a normal concerto form continues, however, and with the entry of the soloist we have reached what might be termed a secondary exposition. Exceptions there may be, but as a general principle composers at this point will re-state the opening material, this time including the soloist together with any additional comments he may care to make. In character this new statement is often much more akin to a development than an exposition, in that there is nothing to stop the composer journeying off into new episodes that have little or no relevance to what has gone before. One of the great excitements of concerto form is the element of fantasy it so often implies.

The line of demarcation between this secondary exposition and the development proper is a fine one, not always easy to perceive; all the same, there is a difference, and the introduction of new themes, excursions into more remote keys, even changes of tempo, are all more likely to occur in the true development section. Do not expect, however, such a concentration on the matter in hand as we find in the Mozart G minor symphony or Beethoven's fifth. In many concertos the development is an excuse for rhapsodic interludes; showers of notes may fly from the pianist's fingers,

weaving delightful patterns that are in fact no more than decorative
formulae of little thematic interest. If the themes are referred to,
they are more likely to be found in the orchestral part, rather as
though the orchestra was a crowd of anxious nannies trying to
dissuade a capricious child from going too far on its own. Nevertheless, Mozart's greatest inspirations often occur in the development, and it is usually at the moment immediately *before* the
recapitulation that we find those passages whose harmonic tension
(and consequently emotional intensity) are the greatest.

The recapitulation, once reached, will certainly begin with a
re-statement of the first subject, usually with a more co-operative
attitude from the soloist than heretofore. But for the audience it is
no time to sit back; the chance of new happenings at this point is
far greater in a concerto than in a sonata or symphony. Not only
is variety easier to achieve because of the contrast in colours
between soloist and orchestra, but also there is always this element,
already alluded to, of improvisation, of fantasy, which is an intrinsic
part of the form. One thing we can be pretty sure of, though, is that
at some point the soloist will drop out and allow the orchestra its
head for a while. This convention is based on a purely practical
reason in that it is designed to give the soloist a rest before he
embarks on the most strenuous part of the movement, the cadenza.

The cadenza, rather despised by the purists, is for me one of the
most fascinating attributes of the concerto. In the days of Bach,
Mozart or Handel, and indeed right up to the time of Chopin or
Liszt, the ability to improvise or make up music on the spur of the
moment was expected from every musician. Matches were even
held in which two performers would be sat down in turn at the
keyboard and called upon to extemporize on a given theme. The
cadenza gave an opportunity for the performer to display this skill,
and while technical virtuosity was certainly called for, further
development of the thematic material was as important. It is
unlikely that truly improvised cadenzas were ever heard at
public performances, since any sensible performer would presumably have prepared something in the process of learning the work.
But the stimulus of an audience may well have provoked new

flights of fancy, and most particularly the presence of other musicians in the surrounding orchestra would be likely to encourage the performer to new invention. What is undeniable is that the style of composition shown in those cadenzas by Mozart or Beethoven which have been written down is different from their usual manner. This is even true of the three-part keyboard fugue with which Bach's *Musical Offering* begins. It seems almost certain that this is a more or less exact transcription from memory of a piece that Bach had improvised on the spot to King Frederick. In it we find passages of free figuration that are quite un-fugal in character, as though Bach was doodling happily with his fingers while his brain was working out further possibilities of manipulating the fugue subject. Cadenzas, then, are the nearest thing we have to a recording of the great composers, for even if we make allowance for 'improvements' that may have crept in once the notes were put down on paper, it still seems likely that a cadenza by Mozart or Beethoven represents a reasonably honest transcription of what they would actually have improvised.

If the cadenza was a truly spontaneous invention, there had to be some indication to the orchestra that it was time they took up their instruments once again, and so it became established that a trill, or series of trills, was a signal to stand by. In due course the orchestra would enter with a triumphant affirmation of the first subject, whereupon (in nearly all of the Mozart concertos) the soloist would remain quiet till the end of the movement. It wasn't long before composers realized that the omission of the solo instrument from the final bars of a movement was a miscalculation, and Mozart himself, who thought of nearly everything—including serial music according to some wishful thinkers—experimented with the possibility of using the soloist right up to the end of a movement.[1]

The second movement of the classical concerto is designed to show the poetic and lyrical qualities of the instrument. It is often the movement which displays the deepest feeling, but it is misleading

[1] e.g. in K.491, the C minor concerto.

to expect this in all concertos, as sometimes the composer may prefer to write what is virtually a song without words, a movement whose function is decorative rather than contemplative. The early Mozart slow movements conform very much to the fashion of the times; they are elegant, elaborate in decoration, but relatively unadventurous in harmony. Even the melodies lack that truly personal distinction that he found in the last ten years of his life. Once the intensely romantic strain in his nature enabled him to overcome the artificialities and inhibitions of the musical language of his era, he was to write in his concertos some of the most profoundly expressive slow movements that have ever been conceived. As to the form of these movements, it is impossible to lay down any clear ruling. Some are variations, some are rondos, some are sonata movements. A typical example might begin with the solo piano playing the main theme; at its first appearance it will be relatively free from decoration and will as it were simply be offered to the orchestra, who will in their turn play it without comment from the soloist. A so-called 'episode' might follow in which soloist and orchestra will become more closely linked. Further discussion of the first theme could then lead to another more dramatic episode in which the soloist might well indulge in those wide melodic leaps which are so much a hallmark of Mozart's mature style. According to the length and complexity of the movement we could then either return to the opening material for the last time, or be led into new developments. Form in slow movements is of less importance than it is in an opening allegro; there must be a shape that is satisfying to the listener, but the form is not essential to the actual drama as it so often is in a sonata movement. It is usually sufficient for us to sit back and wonder at the beauty of the ideas that are presented to us; we do not need to be so aware of structures and relationships.

The third and last movement (four-movement concertos are a rarity) is most usually a rondo, a form in which one tune appears a number of times with varying 'fillings' between the repetitions— a multi-decker sandwich in which the rondo-theme is the bread, and the layers of cheese, salami and lettuce are the intervening episodes. Mozart also uses variation-form on occasions, and even a sonata movement is not unknown. Professor Girdlestone[1] has classified the one hundred and eleven finales of Mozart's maturity into seventy-six rondos, eighteen sonata-form movements and seventeen which are variations or minuets. Whatever the form, the function of the last movement is clearly to entertain; as in the symphony or the sonata, each movement serves a different purpose, the first to stimulate thought by elegant conversation about serious matters, the second to relax or edify, the third to delight and amuse. But there are exceptions to practically every statement that can be made about concertos, as of all large-scale musical forms it is the most flexible.

We come now to one of the most fascinating aspects of the growth of the piano concerto. If you want to buy a string instrument, and money is no object, you get one that is more than two hundred years old; there have been minor technical modifications to the violin, but basically it has remained unaltered. To buy a two-hundred-year-old piano with the intention of performing on it publicly would be the act of an unpractical eccentric; the instrument has changed out of all recognition and early examples are only really of interest to the antiquarian or the musicologist. The tone was dry and 'woody', it had little sustaining power, its compass was substantially less than that of the modern piano, its volume limited. The piano on which Mozart would have performed bore as little relationship to a modern concert grand as a 1900 Mercedes did to the sports racing car with which Stirling Moss won the Mille Miglia in 1955. This is a fact, but it is a fact from which we must draw the right conclusions. Mozart's scoring is wonderfully calculated in its balance between soloist and orchestra; whenever an important theme is given to the keyboard, the orchestra will either be silent or make sympathetic accompanying noises. On the other hand, many passages where the

---

[1] C. M. Girdlestone: *Mozart's Piano Concertos* (Cassell).

melodic interest lies in the woodwind or strings may be embellished by decorative cascades or notes from the piano, since there was no likelihood of their being obscured. It is these passages that are most liable to be distorted in modern performances; the dazzling technique and prodigious tone of the concert pianist of today causes figures which Mozart clearly intended to be no more than a silver lining to swamp the orchestra. This is especially true in all too many gramophone recordings, where the already disturbed balance is made still more remote from Mozart's conception by artificial means. There is no need to deny ourselves the virtues of the modern piano when it comes to subtlety of touch, beauty of tone and sustaining power. But we must scale down its resources in sheer volume and brilliance, or we will get a totally false impression of the actual musical content of a Mozart concerto.

In his first three piano concertos it is fairly clear that Beethoven had exactly the same problem to deal with as had Mozart. He rigs the balance in just the same way, never allowing the piano to compete openly with the orchestra. In the fourth concerto, which is the last truly classical concerto[1], the implied contest between soloist and orchestra is won by gentleness; this is most notably true of the slow movement in which the aggression of the orchestra is marvellously tamed by a constant turning of the other cheek, a refusal to fight which ultimately reduces the opponent to silence. Between the composition of his fourth and fifth piano concertos Beethoven apparently came into possession of a new piano. Despite his deafness he at once realized the potentialities of the instrument, and in the so-called 'Emperor' we see the result of his re-assessment of the relationship between piano and orchestra. Here for the first time in musical history the piano stands up to the orchestra as an equal, even indulging in open defiance at times. (For a detailed discussion of this work see Chapter XV.)

The last half of the nineteenth century saw a continuous increase in the demands that composers and pianists made upon the instrument, and in all fairness one must acknowledge the efforts of piano manufacturers to meet those demands. Improvements of

---

[1] until Stravinsky!

one kind or another were constantly being made and even in recent years new refinements have been invented. A small price has been paid for the enormously improved quality of sound, for the modern keyboard does have a deeper touch than Mozart would ever have known, which means that more energy is needed in the quicker-moving passages. The aesthetic problems raised by the changes in the instrument remain some of the most eternally fascinating in music, and every performer must come to terms with his own conscience in deciding how to play the classical repertoire.

The popular appeal of the concerto, and the piano concerto in particular, is enormous. The reason for this is fairly obvious. To be a hero one must vanquish an outnumbering opposition. In the public eye, the soloist is a sort of hero, dominating the orchestra, and triumphing despite tremendous odds. An element of self-projection enters in, and the listener gets a vicarious thrill by imagining himself to be in the soloist's place. (Did he realize one tenth of the work entailed in achieving the standard of performance which any concerto demands, he might think twice about it.) To the soloist, the concerto remains the ultimate challenge. There is little logic in this, since to play a solo sonata of the dimensions of the Hammerklavier or the Liszt B minor would seem to be even more demanding. In the long run, it must be this very situation of 'one against all' that makes the concerto what it is, for every story needs a hero with whom the reader can identify himself. The hero in a concerto is just that much more obvious. . . .

## CHAPTER XI

# MOZART

## Piano Concerto in D minor, K.466 (1785)

1. Allegro. 2. Romance. 3. Rondo: prestissimo.

Orchestra: 1 flute; 2 oboes; 2 bassoons; 2 horns; 2 trumpets; 2 timpani; strings.

BEFORE we begin to explore this work in any detail it might be helpful to think about the language of music and the way in which a composer of Mozart's stature uses its vocabulary. For the moment let us confine ourselves to the familiar but sometimes arduous process of learning a language that is foreign to us. The grown-up normally goes through a fairly agonizing period of '*Avez-vous un' chambre avec deux lits pour ce nuit*—or should it be *cette nuit?*—Oh dear, it is so difficult.' The receptionist then says in perfect English, 'Sorry sir, the hotel is full', and you try again elsewhere. The child, on the other hand, absorbs a language without much difficulty, but seldom has an adult perception of its ultimate possibilities. He may have Corneille and Racine crammed into his head at school and be profoundly bored by them, whereas later in life he may regret not having learnt enough French to be able to appreciate them properly. Now it is my belief that a true appreciation of music can only come with a deep understanding of its language, and there is no better illustration of the need to develop a really discriminating ear than the opening of this concerto. All musicians accept that it is one of the great works; they also realize that its greatness lies partly in its unusually romantic and turbulent quality. Yet if we reduce its opening phrases to their bare bones it would seem to be pretty trivial stuff, for this is the framework on which it is built:

Ex. 4

Now it is undeniable that that is pretty poverty-stricken as music, and it is equally undeniable that a great composer can use such a framework and construct a masterpiece upon it. How? Let us return once again to the analogy of language.

Pick a few simple words and throw them into a hat. As nouns we will select 'sun, winter, home, wages, task, heat'; as verbs let us have 'fear, do, go, take, have'. All simple words. Throw in a few make-weights like 'no, the, more' and so on and we still have nothing that is not in common use. Even if we add 'worldly' or 'furious' we are scarcely plunging into the extremes of rhetoric. Let us now make a sentence from these simple components.

'Furious at the winter, I've gone from home to get some sun and heat. I'll take my wages—no more worldly tasks for me.'

As prose, this is grisly, but I have simply tried to assemble the given words into some sort of order, just as the anguished tourist does with his 'Avez-vous un' chambre avec deux lits pour ce nuit'. But what can those same words do in the hands of a master?

> Fear no more the heat o' the sun
> Nor the furious winter's rages;
> Thou thy worldly task hast done,
> Home art gone and ta'en thy wages.

What wonderful stuff it is; and yet the words in themselves are so very ordinary. Now can we improve on Shakespeare? Suppose that instead of 'Fear no more the heat o' the sun' we say, 'The intensity of temperature from the solar system will no longer harm you.' The thought may be the same but the poetry has vanished. It is not the thought, then, that makes the line poetic but the way in which the thought is expressed. With this in mind let us return to Ex. 4. In itself this sequence of chords has little value, but it can be dressed up in a number of different ways. You could decorate it with a long sustained melody:

Or you could turn it into a stately sarabande:

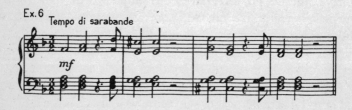

Equally well it can be made heroic, though I will admit that this version smacks a little of amateur theatricals:

This is no more remarkable than it would be to suggest a simple idea such as sunset to three different poets. One might express himself in these words:

> The sun descending in the west,
> The evening star does shine;
> The birds are silent in their nest,
> And I must seek for mine.

Another would choose a different way of expressing the same thought:

> The day's grown old, the fainting sun
> Has but a little way to run;
> And yet his steeds, with all his skill
> Scarce lug the chariot down the hill.

And a third, in a more sombre mood, might say:

> The curfew tolls the knell of parting day,
> The lowing herd wind slowly o'er the lea,
> The plowman homeward plods his weary way,
> And leaves the world to darkness and to me.

The basic idea is the same in all three verses, but the words in each case are different. There is, however, a greater difference, one that can only be appreciated after we become interested in words for their own sake rather than in the thoughts which they are used to express.

Now if, as I have suggested, the effect of a poem depends not just on its meaning as a statement of fact or a description of events, nor even on any intrinsic quality in the words chosen, such as 'fear, heat, sun, west, star, etc.', the clue to its quality must lie more in the order of words and their relationship to each other. The word 'chimney-sweeper' has no great merit; but a genius like Shakespeare will put it in the very next line to a lyrical phrase such as 'Golden lads and girls'—

> Golden lads and girls all must,
> As chimney-sweepers, come to dust.

The bright sunlight in the word 'golden' is, so to speak, cancelled out, blackened by the associations of soot and chimney and the dark enclosing tunnel above the dead ash of the fire. If we appreciate these things we are appreciating the subtlety of the poet's use of language, not just accepting the statement at its face-value. The same thing applies to music; listening to the opening *tutti* of a concerto such as this, we need to take into consideration far more than just the fact that to start with it consists of simple alternations between the chords of D minor and the dominant seventh in A.[1] Here now is Mozart's version of Ex. 4:

Ex. 8　Allegro

In order to appreciate this fully we need to be well enough read in music to be able to compare it with a host of other works. First we need to relate it to Mozart's twenty-two other concertos for piano and orchestra—not necessarily knowing them all in detail, but being aware of their individual qualities, whether lyrical, dramatic, spring-like, immature or tragic. Not one of them begins with this sort of muttering uneasiness, nor with these restless syncopations. This alone, then, should be enough to make us listen with special attention. Next we need to know enough about Mozart's style to realize the significance of this type of figure in the bass.

Ex. 9

[1] The proper term for the chord in bar 4 of Ex. 4.

In his terms, such a figure is not just an empty gesture; rather will it imply a certain dramatic force, and when it is in a minor key, as it is here, there will inevitably be a suggestion of considerable agitation.

If we cast the net a little wider and take in the whole of the opening orchestral chapter, another unusual aspect of the music should strike us. I doubt if there is a single introductory *tutti* in all the Mozart concertos that stays so single-mindedly in the same mood for such a long time as this. It has a length of aim, a fixity of purpose that is remarkable. This is partly because of his refusal to pamper us with a really substantial melody. He constantly leads us to believe that one is going to appear, but all the time the music is driven forward with these uneasy syncopations; never does he allow it to settle. Lastly we should bear in mind the matter of key and all that goes with the implications of D minor in Mozart's world.

This is what I mean by an appreciation of music. Now one has to admit, however reluctantly, that many people in their endeavour to grapple with the language of music never get beyond the 'Avez-vous un' chambre' stage. To them the language will always remain unfamiliar, and the sheer lack of vocabulary will limit their horizon enormously. There are others who press on to the stage of being able to translate reasonably fluently; they can even at times 'think' in the language. But the ultimate appreciation of a concerto such as this demands a complete receptivity to Mozart's thought, so that the placing of every note in its context becomes significant. The proverbial man-in-the-street *can* enjoy this as a fairly typical classical concerto with rattling runs on the piano and a nice tune popping up now and then. This is because the superficial aspects of Mozart's language are now very familiar to us; all the more reason, then, that it should take a particularly perceptive ear to re-assess the striking originality of Mozart's ideas. Enough of preliminary thoughts: let us turn to the work itself.

As we have already discovered, there is an unusual consistency of mood in the opening *tutti*. So often Mozart alternates between a positive heroic statement and a gentle reply; here the music stays turbulent for the first thirty-two bars. There is a moment's silence and then we are introduced to the second subject:

Cast as it is in the form of question and answer, this is ideal concerto material, and it is no surprise that when it reappears it is divided between orchestra and piano. For the moment it is enough that it eases the tension so far generated by the music; what we do not realize at this time is that there is another whole paragraph to this tune that Mozart still keeps hidden from us. It seems too early for this second subject really to establish itself and it is soon swept aside by a new and stormy phrase. With a dramatic intensity that we tend to associate more with Beethoven than Mozart the music drives remorselessly on. Only in the few bars immediately before the soloist's entry do we find any further traces of tenderness, and even here the theme is of such a pathetic character that it does little to soften the impression of a soul in torment that has been so clearly conveyed. And now, at the critical point of the solo entry, what does Mozart have in store for us? Not as might be expected a reflection of the dark uneasiness of the preceding pages, nor even a conventionally heroic gesture such as a scale or arpeggio. In a meltingly beautiful phrase he offers us at least some feeling of comfort, though there is obviously still an element of sadness involved.

This theme is to be the exclusive property of the soloist; at no point of the movement does any member of the orchestra even touch on it. It isn't long, though, before the soloist finds himself very much involved with the orchestra. The strings begin the disturbed rhythms of Ex. 8 once again (the secondary exposition), this time with reinforcement from the piano. The harmonies are strikingly dissonant in Mozart's subtle way, much use being made of sevenths and seconds.

Important though the piano part is, it is the orchestral music that contains the heart of the matter here; the piano figuration merely adds an extra bite to the harmony.

In due course Ex. 10 reappears, this time divided attractively between orchestra and soloist, until we shortly meet the second part of the second subject, an elegant and graceful tune that was well worth waiting for.

This is seized on with delight by the orchestra while the soloist decorates it further with descending scales that are not a bit less delightful for being a convention of the period. For a short time it even seems as though the thundery mood of the opening has been entirely forgotten. But it is not to be; gradually the piano writing becomes more jagged in outline, leading us back inevitably to another section for orchestra alone in which the music of the first pages appears once more. Some of the brooding intensity is dispelled however by the fact that it is now in F major instead of D minor.

We have now met all the main themes of the movement and from here on the interest lies in their changing relationships. One cannot say what the music *means* precisely. We are aware of many fluctuations of mood, of moments of extreme tension, of other periods of relative calm; but it is part of the mystery of music that it can play on our emotions without there being any rational justification for change. It is enough that our response should mirror in detail every subtle nuance of feeling that the music contains, remembering at all times that this is not cold, detached or conventional in its classical perfection, but Mozart at his most romantic and impassioned. The mood remains disturbed right up to the end of the movement, the orchestra having an unusually lengthy concluding chapter (or coda) which in no way lessens the perturbation of spirit that the music has so signally conveyed.

From this dark unease there now emerges a phrase that combines both innocence and beauty. Mozart calls this second movement a Romance, a term to which too much significance should not be attached, as it was in quite common usage at the time. But partly because of its context it seems to have a special quality of sweetness even by Mozart's standards. The melody has two stanzas, each of which is played first by the soloist and then repeated by the orchestra. It is hard to imagine anything more eloquently civilized than this.

Ex. 14

Incidentally it is worth remarking that most performers today are so hypnotized by the word Romance that they probably take this movement far slower than Mozart intended. The time-signature is ₵, which means *alla breve* or two-in-a-bar; we usually hear it as a rather slow four.

Now it makes little difference to Mozart whether he is writing a concerto for piano, violin, clarinet or what; his inspiration always conjures up what is essentially a vocal line translated into instrumental terms. The third piano entry in this movement introduces what is virtually an aria for piano which at a slightly lower pitch could easily be mistaken for one of those marvellous soprano parts that so delight us in operas like *Cosi Fan Tutte* or *Il Seraglio*. The left-hand part is perfunctory in the extreme; all the performer's attention must be concentrated on the difficult task of making the keyboard sing. Meanwhile the orchestra has a supporting accompaniment of apparent simplicity which all the same is full of subtlety. A limpid and effortless return to Ex. 14 concludes this lyrical chapter.

There follows the big surprise of the movement, a stormy middle section which now appears most unexpectedly, disrupting the calm beauty of what has gone before. It is as though the anxiety of the first movement has not after all been forgotten; here it casts its dramatic shadow over the second movement. Mozart gives no indication of a change of tempo, so here is confirmation that a fairly quick pace is justified in the first part. To play a passage of this type slowly is to deny its very nature; one would as soon cry 'Once more unto the breach, dear friends' in tones of milk and honey, for here is Mozart the virtuoso pianist as well as Mozart the composer.

The return to the former calm is wonderfully accomplished, with the soloist gradually easing the pace by a smooth transition through groups of six notes, then four, then three and lastly two to each crotchet beat. The opening tune is re-stated in full, this time with the pianist playing the whole span of the melody without the participation of the orchestra. Together they combine in a long coda in which new and tender themes ease away the last traces of tension.

The finale scarcely represents the joy unconfined we might reasonably expect. Mozart begins with the piano, and at once we are impressed with the urgency of the mood. Quick the tempo may be, but it is anything but cheerful.

\* Mozart also puts a C♮ here with great effect.

The orchestra is quite willing to follow this lead; in a matter of seconds the strings embark on a passage that is every bit as disturbed as anything from the first movement. The syncopations now are even more restless and the tension is if anything increased as one dissonance follows another. Comes the soloist's entry and once again Mozart catches us off our guard. Just as he did in the first movement he introduces a totally new theme. From a structural point of view this is no great surprise; it is the emotional character of the music that is unexpected.

\* The discrepancy of notation between right and left hands seems to be one of Mozart's rare errors—a slip of the pen, no doubt.

It is only a moment, however, before this new theme is rejected and swept aside by a fresh outburst of Ex. 16. An episode in F minor does nothing to reduce the tension, but then at last the sun seems to come out and in the twinkling of an eye Mozart transports us to a different world, a world where care is forgotten and gaiety can at last reign supreme. Surprisingly it is the orchestra that first leads us to this enchanted land.

Ex. 18

The soloist endorses this change of heart, but even a tune as beguiling as this is destined to be soured by the prevailing mood. When this same happy theme reappears once more, it is in the minor, and much of its original character has been lost. Not until after a cadenza (which should obviously sustain the generally turbulent mood) is the deadlock ultimately broken. The key-signature of D major heralds a release from tension and Ex. 18 reappears in its happiest guise. In the last few pages a genuine gaiety is at last established convincingly, and the work ends in an atmosphere of radiant optimism.

What an extraordinary piece it is though for 1785. None of the Beethoven concertos betrays so disturbed a frame of mind, not even the third; as for the works of a still later period, they reflect a different concept of concerto-writing in which the piano part tends to ride roughshod over the orchestra, dominating by brute force where necessary and hogging the limelight most of the time. How can they be expected to rival the profound subtlety of this music, which expresses a state of emotional turmoil that makes it singularly apposite to our times? If only we can penetrate beyond the superficial familiarity of Mozart's idiom we will soon realize how intense and personal the message of this work is. When we do understand the language well enough to perceive its meaning, we shall be moved almost beyond bearing.

## CHAPTER XII

# MOZART

## Piano Concerto in A major, K.488 (1786)

1. Allegro. 2. Adagio. 3. Allegro assai.

Orchestra: 1 flute; 2 clarinets; 2 horns; 2 bassoons; strings.

IF THE CONCERTO in D minor discussed in the previous chapter can be said to show Mozart at his most romantic and impassioned, then this concerto is certainly the most lyrical. It is one of the supremely lovable works and is such an undiluted pleasure to listen to that there is even a danger that we may take it for granted. Has it not always been there, we feel, like summer skies, flowers, fountains and waterfalls? In many ways it is far less adventurous than the other concertos that are its immediate neighbours; it could well be described as the textbook example of the classical concerto except perhaps for its avoidance of virtuosity. Much of it lies within the technical grasp of a musically gifted child of twelve or thirteen, yet despite these handicaps, if handicaps they be, it remains for many people the loveliest of all his piano concertos. Partly this is because the tunes in which it abounds are themselves so beguiling.

These are presented in considerable detail in the long orchestral introduction with which the concerto begins. Nor, as is so often the case in Mozart's mature works for a solo instrument and orchestra, are these proffered riches to be ignored by the soloist; in due course he will welcome them all. Only three themes of real significance are kept in reserve for later in the movement, and each one of these when it does reappear is stated first by the orchestra. Mozart seems deliberately to have abstained from his favourite trick of holding back some especially delicious morsel for the soloist, as though to show a new originality by being entirely orthodox.

The mood of the work, which perfectly evokes that peculiarly Mozartian feeling that I have described elsewhere as 'tears behind the smile', is established by one crucial harmony in the very first bar. Imagine for the moment that Mozart had written this:

Ex. 19

It's all quite smooth and effortless; the tune is undeniably pretty but it hasn't a great deal of character. Let us turn now to Mozart's own version and see what differences there may be.

Ex. 20

The subtle poignancy of the G natural in bar 1 is a masterstroke, as is the clash between G sharp and A in the 4th beat of bar 2, and the less obvious dissonance between the chord of A major and the D in the bass in bar 4. It is these moments of harmonic tension that prevent the music from being merely bland; behind the sunny façade there are shadowy places.

For the first eighteen bars there is nothing of great importance apart from this vital tune; anything else is merely an offshoot from the main stem—what a gardener once described to me as 'unnatural growth', whatever that may mean. In the 18th bar we find an important episode, a passage which the orchestra is going to have several times even although the soloist only decorates it—and then by implication rather than direct statement. This passage too is deeply affected by the G natural we first experienced in bar 1.

Ex. 21

This may appear to be drawn towards D major fairly positively, but it is in fact merely a flirtation, and G sharps in the very next bar restore the momentarily forsaken tonality of A.[1] It is this very ambiguity that makes the music so curiously emotional; the G natural preserves its character of a flattened seventh (which jazz musicians would call a 'blue' note) rather than seeming merely to be the fourth note in the scale of D.

As the music enters its 31st bar, the graceful second subject makes its appearance. Its general air of elegance is again prevented from sounding superficial by the occasional chromatic note and the subtle placing of a dissonance of sorts on the first beat of every bar.

Ex. 22

Two more themes are worth quoting, both of which have suggestions of question and answer in them that lead us to suppose (rightly) that they will later be treated as a dialogue between piano and orchestra.

[1] For an extensive discussion of the importance of tonality in classical music see Chapter I of *Talking about Symphonies*.

All of these ideas are important, all are due to appear in decorated versions once the soloist has entered the scene. The 66-bar introduction ends with a firm no-nonsense cadence in A major and the piano part begins. Not here the çapricious opening of concertos such as the ones in C minor, D minor or E♭ major, in which the soloist denies all knowledge of what has gone before, preferring to state his own material in his own terms. This is a work in which the sense of partnership between solo piano and orchestra is complete[1]; consequently it is with a feeling of welcoming back a dearly loved companion that we renew our acquaintance with Ex. 20, now presented to us in terms of such utter simplicity as to cause composers of later and more complex periods to despair. A few decorative runs of no great difficulty lead us onward to Ex. 21, which is first stated by the orchestra and then delightfully embellished by the soloist. Since the relationship may seem obscure to the uninitiated ear I will clarify it by this little three-part exercise in which the outer parts represent the solo pianist's

[1] In this respect it is interesting to note that in this concerto Mozart retained the old tradition of indicating that the soloist should play *with* the orchestra throughout the *tutti* as a means of holding the work together—a custom discontinued nowadays, of course.

contribution, and the middle line shows the implied reference to Ex. 21.

Ex. 25

This passage is rounded off a little more dramatically, but it is worth remarking the skill with which Mozart allows the frail tones of his fortepiano to penetrate the orchestral texture. For the most part, rests divide each chord on the wind from its next-door neighbour, and in these fractional silences the silvery clatter of leather hammer against string could have been clearly heard.

Ex. 22 now reappears, this time on solo piano and in the expected 'dominant' key of E major. For a few bars the orchestra sit back and listen before taking over the melody in their turn, at which point the piano obligingly decorates bars 2 and 4 of the melody with a shimmering outline of broken octaves. Nothing could more tellingly illustrate the balance between piano and orchestra that Mozart had in mind than this passage, for each party in the conversation must listen to the other. Mutual support or embellishment is perfectly acceptable, a stand-up argument is not.

Episodes based upon Exx. 23 and 24 now add a slightly disturbed air to the music; the mood of sweetness engendered by the second subject is momentarily threatened. Some more robust scale passages bring about a change of heart, though, and a firm cadence in the key of E leads us to a strong orchestral statement of Ex. 21. This dissolves not into the decorative frills of Ex. 25 but into a moment's silence from which emerges an entirely new theme, the first of the three which have already been mentioned as not appearing in the initial *tutti*.

Ex.26

At once the soloist seizes on this, decking it out in the prettiest imaginable two-part counterpoint. Now so far the mood of the movement has been almost entirely free from the dark and brooding style that Mozart increasingly adopted at this period of his life. But here shadows begin to fall—not dramatic ones, but vague intimations of disquiet. The music flirts with minor keys; widespaced intervals abound and the musical interest lies increasingly with the orchestra. The frail voice of the fortepiano hadn't sufficient weight to discuss these more serious matters; for the time being it is reduced entirely to decoration. It is at this point that the remaining two themes that have been withheld are introduced.

Ex.27ª                              Ex.27ᵇ

It will be seen that these two ideas are closely related in rhythm although different in contour and scoring. Both add more than a touch of poignancy to the proceedings and it takes a fairly lengthy bit of passage-work from the soloist to drag us out of the shadows and lead us once more to the lyrical first theme.

This, once reached, brings us to a remarkably orthodox recapitulation where Mozart conspicuously avoids the dramatic surprises which abound in the more stormy concertos in the minor keys. The cadenza most frequently played is by Mozart himself, but I suspect that it was dashed off in a hurry for a pupil, since it is by no means his best. Compared to his magnificent cadenza for the concerto in G major, K.453, it is a shallow thing, having little in the way of new thematic development. A formal close by the orchestra duly rounds off the movement and we who know the concerto sit expectantly awaiting the sublime adagio which lies ahead.

This, one of the most perfect movements that even Mozart ever wrote, begins with the solo piano playing a melody whose opening phrase, once heard, can never be forgotten.[1]

Ex.28  Adagio

Deceptively simple to look at, it demands such subtlety of touch and phrasing that pianists can go on practising it all their lives. One of the hardest things is to connect up the low E sharp in bar 2. It is really part of the melodic line; great swoops of this type are very characteristic of Mozart's vocal writing, and this particular example shows clearly the way in which he regarded the keyboard as a sort of extension of the voice. Twelve bars of this melody lead us to the first orchestral entry. Orchestra and piano in this movement are like brother and sister, alike and yet different. The orchestra never plays the long melody that the piano has stated with such tenderness and melancholy, preferring its own material which in fact is equally beautiful. The texture is full of gentle dissonances and that imitative elegance that is the hallmark of the born contrapuntist.

[1] It is the only occasion that Mozart ever used the key of F♯ minor.

Ex. 29

Everything follows on with what seems like an inevitable logic even although the next piano entry introduces yet another theme. For five bars the solo piano holds the stage alone; then we arrive at a moment of melting beauty as the music turns positively towards a major key for the first time in the movement. This significant change is marked by a hushed chord in the strings; it is not quite powerful enough to shake off the wistful quality that has so far prevailed, and we find ourselves in a sort of limbo half-way between A minor and A major. It is the orchestra that resolves the dilemma, opting firmly for A major with yet another theme given out by the woodwind.[1]

Ex. 30

At last piano and orchestra agree that here is a tune worthy of their united attention, and for the first time in the movement we find a theme shared. It continues, decorated with languorous scales that are like the sighs and flutterings of the heroine of a Restoration comedy. The first theme returns, bringing the same response as before from the orchestra; but whereas the piano had formerly disregarded Ex. 29, this time it extends its strains still further with touching little embellishments that add to its emotional intensity. The coda was only sketched in by Mozart. Time after time one hears performers solemnly plonking their way through a line of

[1] Also used by Mozart in *Don Giovanni*.

single notes that would have been unthinkable to the composer. Since he was usually writing for himself, Mozart often resorted to a sort of shorthand in which he indicated the extreme outer notes of the phrases and no more.[1] All that is left for us at this point is this threadbare sketch.

Ex. 31

To Mozart, a literal performance of this would have seemed an abomination, for the simple reason that it would have sounded atrocious on the piano of his time. Gradually we are finding the courage to add some small elaboration to passages such as this, but usually we are so terrified of altering the text that we tend to drift into triviality. For what it is worth my instinct tells me that we are far too conservative in these matters. I suspect that a performer of Mozart's day would probably have done something more on these lines.

Ex. 32

If Mozart had wanted *less* than this it would have been no trouble for him to write it out—as he did in the subsequent bars. It is precisely because he was anticipating a fair number of notes to a bar that he resorted to shorthand at this point.

[1] There is a notable instance in the finale of the concerto in E♭, K.482.

The movement ends with as sad and tender a leave-taking as parting lovers ever lingered over, a last memory of Ex. 29 which the piano caresses with delicately repeated C sharps.

The final Rondo is sheer joy. The soloist sets the mood with its opening bars.

The orchestra takes up the idea with enthusiasm and embarks on an unusually long *tutti* in which the music stays resolutely in the key of A major without for a moment producing a sense of monotony. One theme in particular stands out as a sort of Instant Gavotte, galvanized at this tempo into new and unimagined activity.

The general air of high spirits is unmistakable. Delightful though it all is, it fails to capture the interest of the soloist, who has ideas of his own. Theme after theme flies from the keyboard in a positive burble of notes. The orchestra can hardly get a chord in edgeways, though at one point they do introduce a new theme.

At once the soloist seizes on it, decorating it with chromatic runs and using the C naturals in the sixth bar as a pivot to open the fairly remote door of C major. There is a brief excursion into foreign territory and then a swift and convincing return to E major, the most closely related key to the 'home' key of A. The chatter continues, the piano part seeming like a veritable *moto perpetuo*. One more theme must be mentioned before we finish our exploration of this totally enchanting work. It is like a children's game of going upstairs and down again. No more than a scale really, it wears an air of being something more important, an air that is completely spurious since its importance is that of a child wearing a grown-up hat.

Ex. 36

*etc.*

The flute is very drawn to this tune and proceeds to play with it in his own time, regardless of the fact that the piano has gone on to other things. To list every tune in the movement would make this a very long and unnecessarily arduous chapter. Mozart was never more generous in melody than he was in this concerto and it is hard to believe that he only had five years to live when he wrote it. It was a time when his inspiration was in full flood. Work after work poured from his pen, and nearly every one a masterpiece. Their craftsmanship and facility have never been surpassed, but as I warned earlier, let us not take such things for granted. Music like this is not common or everyday; if angels dance, this would serve them well.

## CHAPTER XIII

# BEETHOVEN

## Piano Concerto No. 2 in B♭ major, Op. 19 (1795)

1. Allegro con brio. 2. Adagio. 3. Rondo: molto allegro.

Orchestra:   1 flute; 2 oboes; 2 bassoons; 2 horns; strings.

THE FIRST VENTURE into a major musical form is something of an occasion for a composer, particularly if he is young and inexperienced. It may even inspire a certain reluctance—Brahms's refusal to commit himself to a symphony till after he was forty is a well-known example of this. In 1795 a young man called Beethoven, then aged twenty-four, was asked to play at a concert for the benefit of the widows and orphans of the Society of Musicians in Vienna. This was a big opportunity, and he was fired to compose a piano concerto for the occasion. As is so often the case, insufficient time had been allowed for him to write a major work, and with only two days to go the finale still hadn't been written. At this point, the poor young man had a nasty attack of colic. However, 'the show must go on' seems to have been an understood principle even in 1795, and poor Beethoven pressed on with the last move-ment with a doctor by his side, and four copyists in the next room; as each sheet of manuscript paper was completed by the suffering composer it was passed through the door and the desperate process of making a set of orchestral parts was continued.

When it came to the rehearsal another problem presented itself— the piano was half a tone flat. Despite the exhaustion that Beethoven must have felt after two frenzied days of composition, not to mention the aftermath of the colic, he rose manfully to the occasion and rehearsed the entire work, transposing it up a semi-tone into B major. As a feat of musicianship this seems all the more remarkable when we remember that he could have had no time to practise the notes properly and get them under his fingers. He must have been virtually sight-reading as well as transposing. Under the circumstances it is small wonder that the concerto got pushed aside and forgotten; Beethoven probably felt that it had somewhat sour memories for him. Three years later he revised it and issued it as his second, another one having been written in the interim. Ever since, there has been confusion in people's minds, since the concerto we know as No. 1 was actually written second and vice versa. Unfortunately I am not in a position to be able to compare the two versions—in fact I don't know if anyone can, as the original part was probably destroyed. But if the last movement stands more or less as it was when he wrote it, it must be the most entertaining work ever written by a man suffering from colic.

Now this concerto demonstrates admirably the need for the listener to have the widest possible receptivity to music. Composers obviously don't want us to listen to everything in the same mood; and since emotions can change far more rapidly in music then they ever would in a play, we must react more quickly than would the audience in a theatre. There is more to this than merely responding to the prevailing mood; if we look on the different movements as the acts of a play it requires no great critical faculty to be able to say that this act is dramatic, this sentimental and the other comical. We need to go a long way beyond that; for just as when we listen to Shakespeare we appreciate the beauty of language, the subtle inter-relationship of word and phrase, even while we laugh at the antics of Sir Toby and Sir Andrew, so in music we must learn to see in what *terms* a particular passage is dramatic, intense, tender, humorous, ironic, pathetic, or whatever.

In the first movement of this concerto we find an astonishingly rapid alternation of different emotions. The first bar is heroic:

Ex. 37

the next three, tender:

Ex. 38

Bar 5 takes us back to the heroic theme again, followed once more by a tender reply to balance the first. A pattern has been suggested—heroic-tender-heroic-tender, and so you, nice, responsive and intelligent listener that you are, expect a renewal of the heroic mood to conform to the pattern. Instead of complying with the suggested laws of symmetry, Beethoven introduces a melting new theme, all the more touching in that you should be expecting a reversion to the heroic mood at this point.

Ex. 39

A brief extension of this phrase leads us back to Ex. 37; but now what was openly heroic has become taut and nervous. The same pattern has been so translated by a change of orchestration as to produce an entirely different emotional reaction. One could perhaps make a reasonably convincing comparison between music and the theatre by saying that if this theme is our hero, the various versions of it that Beethoven produces show him in different situations which call for different behaviour on his part. Here, he would appear to be in some danger:

Where such comparisons come unstuck is that music is not governed by the logic of action, nor by a plot. What we have to do is to learn to respond in just as receptive a way as we do to a dramatic stimulus in the theatre, but without trying to translate music into the terms of a materialistic world. I regard it as entirely legitimate to say that a passage in music *resembles* a small boy cocking a snook at his elders; but I would regard it as a monstrous misinterpretation to suggest that the composer was actually describing such regrettable behaviour, unless he had given us his specific authority so to do.

That music is a language of a sort cannot seriously be doubted, for it communicates emotion and thought from one human being to another, which is about as good a definition of the function of language as you would arrive at after consultation with a hundred philosophers. Moreover, it is a language which deals largely in emotions, owing to the simple and inescapable fact that sound evokes an emotional response. A quiet sound is a sedative, a loud one is a stimulus; the same obviously applies to slow-moving or quick-moving music. Without becoming too obscure, one could say that the language of music deals with generalizations in a detailed and particular way. Ex. 37 shows us a generalized conception of the heroic, clad in classical dress. Beethoven, having once stated it, will discuss it in great detail, constantly changing our ideas as to its content and purpose. In addition to this he will concern himself with purely musical considerations such as modulation, rhythmic extension, decoration and so on. These in their turn may be said to have certain spiritual implications—the sense of remoteness conveyed by a modulation to a distant key for instance. In the long run then it is impossible to isolate one side of music from the other; its intellectual qualities may very well be the deepest source of its emotional impact. Lovers of Bach will know precisely what I mean. But let us return to the orchestral exposition of Beethoven's Op. 19.

After some fairly stormy excursions into other keys and some eloquent consideration of the possibilities of Ex. 37, Beethoven brings the music to an abrupt halt. Three hammer-blows by the whole orchestra arrest our attention.

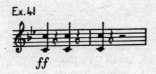

Ex. 41

ff

Tentatively, the pattern is repeated a semitone higher. The intellectual in Beethoven has dictated a strange and disturbing shift of tonality; the emotional effect is to translate us into a new world, as magical as any that Peer Gynt may have entered on his journeys. As graceful as an enchantress the second subject appears —or what we are justified in believing to be the second subject.

Ex. 42

pp    p    etc.

This theme is in D♭ major, and its key-note of D♭ soon becomes the crucial minor third of B♭ minor—an easy step towards the original key of B♭ major in which Ex. 37 again appears in the somewhat perilous version already shown as Ex. 40. Further exploration of its possibilities brings us to a display of bombast by the full orchestra which is calmed by a last allusion to Ex. 39, now happily wedded to Ex. 42.

Ex.43

Two resounding chords of B♭ major awake the soloist from his reverie.

The entry of the piano is an entirely logical development of the traditions established by Mozart; a new theme, never even remotely suggested by the orchestra, and in no way attempting to impress us by weight or volume since these were the least striking qualities of the early pianos. What is perhaps un-Mozartian is Beethoven's use of the highest register available to him. The F an octave higher than the top line of the treble stave was a risky note that Mozart hardly ever used—indeed most of the keyboards of the time stopped at the E a semitone below. Its quality must have been thin and it is unlikely that it ever kept in tune for any length of time. The mere fact that Beethoven begins the piano part on this note is evidence of a sort that the instrument had already begun to improve. An elegant little solo leads us by easy stages down to a good fat chord of B♭ major, all in the bass stave. The ensuing phrase in the orchestra, though an unimportant link to Beethoven, interests us greatly nowadays as an early harbinger of his fourth piano concerto. It has the same insistence on repeated notes and a remarkably similar outline.[1]

Ex.44

The piano brushes this aside and embarks on a busy extension of Ex. 37, indulging in Scarlatti-like leaps and most of the conventional flourishes of early classical pianism.

[1] Beethoven may have 'borrowed' it subconsciously from Mozart's piano concerto in C, K.503, which he almost certainly would have known.

Composers are notorious for their refusal to comply with the examination requirements of academic boards. Hitherto we had been reasonably confident that Ex. 42 was the second subject, but in comparing it to an enchantress I was speaking more truly than I knew. Like most enchantresses she has vanished, leaving only a fragrant memory. 'Here', says Beethoven as the orchestra introduce a new refrain, 'is the true second subject.'

Ex. 45

The pianist tries this out and finds it to his liking, but again the decoration of it is very Mozartian. An abrupt and stunningly beautiful twist into D♭ major restores the true image of Beethoven though, and it isn't long before the pianist finds himself faced with some very awkward passages, with waspish runs and sharp-edged rhythms in each hand in turn.

Apart from giving a bar-by-bar commentary (which would be boring and unnecessary) there is little more that I need to say about this movement. There is an interesting reappearance of the pianist's opening phrases, now in the dominant key of F major. Another point worthy of mention is that Ex. 42, the 'enchantress' theme, does turn up again, although the pianist treats her in a more matter-of-fact way than did the orchestra. Choppy chords in orchestra and piano alike suggest resemblances to the finale of the 'Moon-light' sonata, but the importance of such oblique relationships is an illusion. What is perhaps a comfort to the analytically minded is Beethoven's ultimate affirmation that Ex. 45 is in fact the genuine, true, and guaranteed unmistakably authentic second subject. It happens like this.

At one moment we reach what is clearly the recapitulation. The orchestra pick up the identical phrases which had begun the work; Ex. 39 is assigned to the piano, but apart from a few decorative arpeggios things remain much as they were. But at approximately

the place where we might have expected some reference to the
hammer-blows of Ex. 41, Beethoven leads directly to Ex. 45
and the enchantress, for all her beguiling appearance, is never
heard of again.

The second movement begins rather as though Beethoven had
just returned from a performance of *The Magic Flute*, and was
recalling the solemn music of Sarastro. It is in no way a quotation,
but the almost religious mood is suggested in terms that are remarkably near to the language of Mozart. The piano writing is
much more complex in decoration than any movement in a
Mozart piano concerto however, and bars which have no less than
36 demisemiquaver triplets in them look bewildering to the eye
to say the least. The movement is an extension of Mozart's language
rather than a denial of it, and passages like this clearly reveal their
ancestry.

But whereas some of his contemporaries were producing empty
imitations of Mozart's style, Beethoven had the individuality to
bend it to his own will, and there are many passages that are
stamped unmistakably with the hallmark of his genius. Of these
the most conspicuous is a sort of anti-cadenza near the end of the
movement. The indication *con grand' espressione* shows us Beethoven's intentions, and while the orchestra recall the very first
phrases of this adagio, the piano interleaves with them profoundly
expressive figures of this pattern, in the unadorned simplicity of
single notes.

Ex. 47

The finale of the concerto begins with the piano in a very skittish mood, presenting a tune which the orchestra takes to most enthusiastically:

Ex. 48

Having even outdone the soloist in a display of exuberant enjoyment, the orchestra seems to pause and take thought; with an almost ecclesiastical gesture they pronounce this solemn phrase:

Ex. 49

The piano part, unimpressed by the change of mood, has a brief clatter of broken octaves that sound to my ear more like an irrepressible fit of the giggles. The orchestra, not amused by this rebuff, re-affirm Ex. 49, whereupon the piano goes dancing off on its own until almost shamefacedly the strings consent to join in with a sort of 'pom-ching' accompaniment.

Beethoven now introduces a new tune:

Like a mocking child giving an exaggerated imitation of a friend's walk, the orchestra give out a derisive version of this phrase. It is Beethoven's way of making the 'wrong note' joke that is the stock-in-trade of so much musical satire. The spirit of mockery is the same whether we find it here in this movement or in Poulenc's *Mouvements Perpétuels*. What we need to do is to clean our harmonic palate enough to be able to appreciate the spiciness of Beethoven's harmony; to regard it as ordinary in comparison to the more exotic fare of more recent years is less than just. Anyway, this slightly grotesque dialogue continues until the pianist in a burst of high spirits starts to play a game that involves hopping a step further each beat.

The split note at the top is part of the fun, giving an impression of fumble-fingered inaccuracy that is denied by the agility of the subsequent passages. These show some inspired extra frills that ultimately reduce the orchestra to an awestruck silence. Not until the pianist has condescended to repeat Ex. 48 can they be persuaded to join in again. At this point things take a more serious turn, and for a moment or two the orchestra builds a climax on some well-used clichés of classical rhetoric. This is too much for the piano altogether; in protest against this unwanted eruption of academic jargon it resorts to a sort of eighteenth-century boogie:

Ex.52

Once again we have a contrast between the irreverence of the piano part and the rather sober comments of the woodwind, who seem not to approve of these new-fangled high jinks at all. Between each new outburst from the piano we find a self-righteously proper phrase from oboes and bassoons; I need hardly say that it has no effect on the irrepressible high spirits of the piano. Impudence beats dignity every time.

As the movement progresses much the same material appears again, although there are some enchanting new twists in places. One particularly delightful moment comes when the orchestra have been silent for a few bars. The pianist seems suddenly to notice their absence and in a couple of rising phrases seems to say 'Don't you want to play?' The impassive silence that greets each query is a perfect example of the subtlety of musical humour. Finding no response, the pianist proceeds to upset the balance of the tune by transferring the accent into a different place, changing 'Humpty Dumpty sat on a wall' to 'Hump-tee Dump-tee sat on a wall'. The orchestra express some interest in this, whereupon the pianist prevails upon them to join in once again.

Most beguiling of all is the last page, where the piano seems to cheep like a sparrow in a perky comment on the orchestral tune. The music fades away into virtual silence, broken only by tiptoe chords from the keyboard. Two quiet chords from the orchestra show them entering into the spirit of this game of grandmother's footsteps. Then with a sudden shout of triumph, 'CAUGHT you!', they explode into an *ff* cadence that only serves to underline the humorous content of the whole movement. No music can do so much to destroy the popular misconception that a composer uses music as a means of reflecting his mood of the moment; it is only in Hollywood that a composer needs to feel sad to write sad music and exalted to write exalted music. Here is the music of a sick

man, written under great stress; yet its character is one of capti-
vating gaiety, infecting us all as we listen with its exuberance and
vitality.

## CHAPTER XIV

# BEETHOVEN

## Violin Concerto[1] in D major, Op. 61 (1806)

1. Allegro ma non troppo. 2. Larghetto. 3. Rondo: Allegro.

Orchestra: 1 flute; 2 oboes; 2 clarinets; 2 bassoons; 2 horns; 2 trumpets; 2 timpani; strings.

THIS WORK, surely one of the two greatest violin concertos ever written, took even longer than usual to be accepted by the musical public. Its first performance was singularly unfortunate; the orchestra was sight-reading without a rehearsal—even the soloist didn't really know it, and it was regarded as so long and diffuse that the audience would get bored hearing it all at once. Consequently the first movement was played in part one of the programme, and the Larghetto and the Finale in part two. In the middle of the concert the audience was regaled with a sonata for violin, to be played on one string only with the instrument held upside down. This circus trick was probably regarded as much more remarkable than the concerto—certainly the violinist had practised it more assiduously since it was his own composition. The next day, the critic of the Vienna paper wrote:

> Among other excellent pieces the remarkable violinist Clement also played a violin concerto by Beethoven which, owing to its originalities and wealth of beautiful passages, was received with exceptionally great applause . . . The opinion of connoisseurs . . . admits that it contains beautiful passages but confesses that the context often seems broken and that the endless repetition of unimportant passages produces a tiring effect.

[1] Beethoven also made an adaptation of this work for piano and orchestra in a bid to increase its popularity.

I like that bit about '*also* played', as though the concerto was a rather light encore. However, despite the 'exceptionally great applause' Beethoven had the greatest difficulty in even getting the work published: several printing houses turned it down, and no full score was actually engraved until 1894, 88 years after it had been written. As for performances, various violinists attempted to popularize it, but all were met with indifference until Joachim, as a twelve-year-old prodigy, performed it with Mendelssohn conducting.

I suppose one of the reasons it was slow to catch on is that it is difficult without being showy, and that much of it takes place in a world of serenity and peace that is at odds with the rather brash exhibitionism associated with the nineteenth-century concerto. It is to violin concertos what Beethoven's fourth—the G major one—is to piano concertos; and just as that began unexpectedly with the piano playing quietly and alone, so this begins with four undemonstrative taps on a drum:

The subsequent phrase on the woodwind is the most important theme in the movement, firmly establishing the tonality of D major and conveying a feeling of tranquillity that is the most noteworthy feature of the work. A balancing phrase leads to the first string entry, a four times repeated D sharp on the violins about which any amount has been written already—and deservedly so since it is a remarkable example of Beethoven's individuality. To understand its full significance one must realize how important a sense of key was in Beethoven's time. This concerto is in D major, and to move out of that key into another one is a form of musical drama every bit as important as any *fortissimo* climax. The note

D sharp is a rank intruder in the scale or key of D major, and Beethoven as it were flirts with danger when he now gently insinuates it into the musical texture. The rhythm he uses refers back to the opening drum-beats, but the note itself is an outrage to the whole concept of D major. The other strings react in a fascinating way—it's as though they were trying to cover up for the indiscretion committed by the first violins. 'It's D major we're supposed to be in,' they seem to say, and they reassert the key by playing the dominant seventh quite strongly. Beethoven again persists in his gentle tugging at the sleeve of D sharp, and again the music brusquely regains its balance in a satisfying cadence back into D.

Ex.54

The woodwind now restore order by playing some straight-forward scales of D which first climb up and then dip, only to climb again. All seems peaceful enough when a sudden _ff_ from the full orchestra catches us by surprise. Beethoven cuts right across the pleasant and pastoral country of D major, and with a violent change of mood bursts into the fairly remote key of B flat. As a result of this excursion the surface of the music remains somewhat ruffled and it's a moment or two before the violins again calm things down and lead us into the second subject proper. This too is wedded to the drum-tap motif, which is destined to be of enormous importance throughout the movement.

Ex.55

Beethoven develops this lovely tune at some length, putting it into the minor and giving it an increasingly complex accompaniment. It is towards the end of this section that one mystery is solved. The baffling D sharp of Ex. 54, which had caused such bewilderment so early in the concerto, is now integrated perfectly into the texture.

**Ex.56**

As if in triumphant vindication of himself—'You see, I knew it would fit'—Beethoven has a splendid full close in the key of D major, and then several times repeats a new theme of considerable importance.

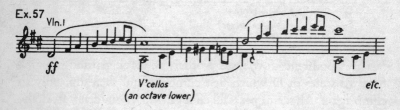

**Ex.57**

The music dies down and the solo violin is heard for the first time. After so lengthy a preamble it is only right that the soloist should have a share of the limelight straight away, and Beethoven allows the violin to soar high into its most ethereal register before settling down to the matters of the moment with a gently decorated version of the original first subject (Ex. 53). The four drum-beats are usually to be found in the background somewhere, while the orchestra recall the first sixteen bars of the movement in virtually an exact repetition, though now the music is enhanced by decorations from the soloist.

Really to understand how a work of this scale is constructed, one needs to make a bar-by-bar comparison between the orchestral exposition and this secondary exposition involving the soloist.

The first significant change comes with the rising scale-passage that originally appeared on clarinets and bassoons (soon after Ex. 54). Initially this stayed firmly in D major. Once it is given to the soloist we find it being twisted away into new directions, and there is quite a display of agility before things calm down and the second subject (Ex. 55) is allowed to reappear. Again it is scored for woodwind, and it is notable that in a violin concerto, orchestral themes are frequently given to flute, oboe or clarinet in preference to the strings, simply because they offer a better contrast to the tone of the soloist. On this occasion the violin obligingly takes over the melody in its highest register, finishes it off, and then embarks on a long and serious passage in triplets, made up for the most part from broken octaves and somewhat angular arpeggios. Meanwhile violins and violas in unison have a quiet think about the possibilities of putting Ex. 55 into the minor. This leads us towards the fairly remote key of C major—remote in that it cancels out C sharp, one of the most powerful influences on the key of D which is the tonal centre of the concerto. Now all of this had appeared in a comparable form in the orchestral exposition. There too the violins had a minor version of Ex. 55 that was markedly similar to this, in outline at least.[1] But the triplet accompaniment, from which later the embellishments of the soloist are due to spring, was very much smoother and more orthodox as a counterpoint. Horns, trumpets and timpani constantly reiterated the drum-tap rhythm of the first bar, and despite the quiet playing that Beethoven demands, we received an impression of firmness and authority. Now all seems changed; in some extraordinary way the music gives an impression of far greater mystery, and the omission of the drum-tap rhythm (which Beethoven doubtless feels we should now be capable of imagining for ourselves) makes the whole phrase seem much less substantial.

A meltingly beautiful reference to Ex. 56 leads us to something of a climax, but surprisingly it peters out into a quiet recollection

---

[1] The difference being, of course, that one is in the 'tonic' minor of D, the other in the 'dominant' of A.

of Ex. 57 which, since its original function had been to conclude the exposition, must now be made to serve a different purpose. Sure enough, Beethoven uses it to start out on a new journey, the 'cellos being mainly responsible for moving us on into new fields. The writing for the soloist is fairly active though relatively unimportant; the firm line of Beethoven's thought is to be found in the orchestra, and the use of themes that by now should be thoroughly familiar makes the whole passage perfectly clear. But soon we are going to be initiated into a secret and mysterious world, and here once again I must stress the significance of modulation in classical music. While I freely admit that it isn't necessary to know the technical terms for these procedures, we must experience their effect. For instance, we have now reached a point where, by all the laws of musical convention, Beethoven would seem to be heading for a nice safe cadence in A. To simplify reading, I will bring the violin part down an octave and close up some of the gaps.

Ex. 58 Vln. solo

This sit-down on A, while certainly gratifying expectation, is entirely predictable. It is at just such moments that a composer of Beethoven's calibre will prefer to avoid the obvious path home. To move into the unknown, he likes to use something that is familiar; the four repeated notes that began the whole work are the key that opens the door into a new world. Beneath the trill in bar 3 of Ex. 58, the violins play an E four times. They are answered by a low and ghostly F natural from the 'cellos and basses. Hypnotized by this spellbinding note, the violins move upward to F themselves, where in hushed tones they are joined by the other strings. It is like a patch of cloud, ominous and grey until the sunlight of A major is reached again. All through these mysterious happenings, the violin has been trilling like a lark far above the disturbing harmonic

changes in the orchestral part. A few gentle scales against a background of sustained chords from the woodwind lead us to another
violent interruption. In a way it is a pity that we should know a
work like this too well, as inevitably some of the surprise we should
feel at such moments is lost. When Beethoven rocks the whole
fabric of the music with a convulsion of this nature we need at least
to be aware of the shock it must once have caused, even if its impact
on our own ears is somewhat dulled by familiarity.

Mind you, it is an interruption that Beethoven himself has
prepared us for; it has already appeared in the exposition, and
to a superficial glance the ensuing pages would seem to be little
more than a re-hash of part of the opening chapter. There are
variants in the orchestration, and passages that had once been soft
are now loud. However, we need to beware of assuming that the
tunes themselves are the only things that matter in music of this
period. Again it is a question of key; Beethoven ultimately intends
to return to the soaring opening phrase with which the violin
had made its first entry. While on the face of it the orchestra seems
to be going over well-tried ground, there is one profound difference. The music is turned away from the expected home
territory of D major and ends up in C instead. We know therefore
that all is not what it seems and that this, far from being a true
recapitulation, is rather going to lead us still further afield. So it
turns out. A brief cadenza, closely resembling the one which the
violin had originally begun with, leads us to a long development
of bars 2–5 of Ex. 53. The thematic interest lies for the most part
in the bassoons. The strings constantly remind us of the four
drum-taps, while the soloist indulges in very much the same sort
of decorative figures that one might find in a Mozart keyboard
concerto. The music seems to grow in intensity, and then, at the
very moment when we feel that it is going to emerge from the
shadows, it grows quieter still, settling down into G minor. The
horns play four repeated D's beneath a trill from the solo violin and
there begins one of the most beautiful pages that Beethoven ever
wrote. This extraordinarily romantic section is as expansive as a
Chopin nocturne and yet as simple as something by Mozart. All

the time, like a restraining hand that keeps this idyll relevant to the movement as a whole, the horns quietly reiterate the four repeated notes with which the work began. Not only is this the emotional core of the movement; it also fulfils a valuable architectural function, for in its course Beethoven finds his way back to the tonal centre of the piece. Slowly the soloist climbs back towards daylight and the final confirmation of the long awaited D major. This is a moment of triumph, and Beethoven hammers home its importance by asking the whole orchestra to play those first repeated drum-notes. The serene mood of the opening is quite forgotten in this impassioned reprise.

In many points of detail the ensuing pages are different from the original statement of the material; but the big surprises are over. Still to come, though, is one of the most original moments of all, the re-entry of the orchestra after the cadenza is finished. Beethoven never bothered to write out a cadenza, as Mendelssohn and Tschaikovsky did in their violin concertos. There are at least thirty in existence now from which violinists can choose one that suits them best; the most played is one by Joachim, but the cadenza by Leopold Auer runs it close in musical ingenuity. The one significant lead that Beethoven gave was that the cadenza should end quietly, for after the concluding trill he gives the violinist another chance to browse over the lyrical second subject (Ex. 55). The accompaniment is a mere sketch of plucked chords into which the woodwind instruments gradually interpolate a more sustained line. A solo bassoon reminds us of Ex. 57 once more, and then with a brief flourish the movement is over.

The slow movement is a remarkably strictly organized piece of music that still manages to sound like an improvisation. Beethoven accomplishes this paradox by choosing a theme that moves by such gradual steps that we are scarcely aware of any real forward impulse at all. Above it he places a number of profoundly expressive decorations which sound as though they were spontaneous inventions on the part of the soloist. Tovey describes it as one of

Beethoven's cases of 'sublime inaction'. The theme is sixteen bars in length, and full of those pregnant silences which always show Beethoven in his most soul-searching mood.[1]

Ex. 59

As one might have expected, these silences are destined to be filled by comments from the soloist. Meantime the theme is repeated with virtually no alteration other than its scoring. The plan of the movement is this:

   I. Theme on strings only.

   II. Theme on horns, clarinet and strings while the soloist adds decorative figures high above (Var. I).

   III. Theme on bassoon, violas and 'cellos with still more complex decorations from the soloist (Var. II).

   IV. Theme on orchestra, quite strongly, but without soloist (Var. III).

So far the form has been so circumscribed as to seem positively restricting, were it not for the beauty of the theme and the marvellous freedom of the solo part that lies above it. Beethoven now has an inspired moment of unorthodoxy. He has given us enough to make us assume that we are listening to a strict set of variations, but now a simple cadenza leads us to a completely new theme. To call this Variation IV would be too far-fetched altogether, although one can force it into the framework of the first four notes by Procrustean methods.

[1] Cf. the slow movement of the piano sonata in E♭, Op. 7.

Ex. 60

This type of analysis can prove practically anything. However, attractive though it is to those of us who are anxious to twist the evidence to suit our purpose, I refuse to believe that Beethoven intended any such relationship. This theme is an interlude whose function is to create a mood of even greater stillness than before, as well as to focus our attention on the soloist for the first time in the movement. Up to this point the music he has had to play has been purely decorative; now he has a theme, and to catch our interest it is a new theme. Once the point has been made we return to the original idea, and Variation IV appears. Plucked strings remind us of the outline of the tune while the solo violin plays a lagging version above, so drugged with beauty that it can scarcely bring itself to move to the next note. Another short interlude follows, at the end of which the soloist recalls Ex. 60, caressing it with loving embellishments before returning once again to the preceding interlude. We must therefore add these further sections to the plan above:

   V. Brief accompanied cadenza, leading to—
   VI. New tune on solo violin.
  VII. Var. IV on plucked strings with soloist following like a shadow.
 VIII. Interlude.
   IX. Elaboration of VI.
   X. Return to VIII.

This last section seems about to dissolve into nothingness when muted horns followed by violins remind us once more of the first two phrases of the movement. We are on the edge of Paradise when with a cruel blow Beethoven snatches us back. *Fortissimo* chords shatter the mood irrevocably, and the violin is goaded into a brief cadenza that confirms that it too must come down to earth. That Beethoven should leave this vital link to the inspiration of the performer seems rash to the point of lunacy, but I suppose he realized what he was doing. At any rate the die is cast, and the violin leads the way into the finale.

Only the 'cellos seem prepared to follow his lead, and the rudimentary accompaniment they provide to the theme is reminiscent of the spontaneous music-making of country-folk in a pub. Delicate and remote though the sounds still are, they contain subtle suggestions of rhythms slapped out by bare hands against thighs clad in well-worn *Lederhosen*. There's a pint of good German beer on the table, and I can't help feeling that Beethoven whistled this tune in such surroundings when it first came to him, rather than imagining the golden tones of a Stradivarius violin in a concert-hall.

Ex. 61

Tentatively the orchestral violins decide that perhaps they would like to play as well, whereupon the whole orchestra comes thumping in with the theme, extending it with rustic divisions that would have delighted Bottom and his artisan friends. In due course the music quietens down and a sense of expectancy is created by a repeated pattern of tonic and dominant:

Ex. 62

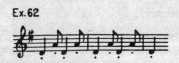

The violinist takes this phrase and throws it high into the air, while underneath a fanfare on the horns suggests a passing group of the gentry bound for an afternoon's sport. As always, I would underline the danger of reading pictures of this type into the music, but Beethoven was not entirely hostile to the idea of pictorial suggestion in his compositions, as the Pastoral symphony and the 'Les Adieux' sonata show. It would be as foolish to deny the obviously outdoor implications of this movement as it would be to try and devise a scenario that would explain them in terms of a plot. The sound of horns may project an image of horse, rider and hound into our minds, but flashing semiquavers from the violin soon bring us back to the world of music, and to a realization that this is no more than an episode in a rondo. For some time the violinist is kept busy with a passage of considerable difficulty, until first the violas and then the violins and 'cellos in turn remind him with increasing firmness that the real matter under discussion is Ex. 61. Sure enough, the soloist takes up the theme once more and for a little while things are just as they were at the beginning.

An ingenious series of modulations brings us to the next episode, a slightly forlorn tune in G minor which one feels should really be attached to a limerick of sorts—

> A certain young lady of Bonn
> Went to bed with her riding-boots on . . .

Ex. 63

*etc.*

Such frivolity may seem appallingly irreverent to the ardent Beethoven-lover, but the fact remains that too often we enclose a work of this quality in a sacred casket, making it seem less human than it is. It is Beethoven who decides the content of a movement, not us, and I am convinced that if he had intended a genuine pathos at this point he would not have elected to accompany Ex. 63 with the type of vamped waltz figure that any pub pianist could improvise on the spur of the moment. The minute that he wishes to turn the music in a more serious direction by making it genuinely lyrical, we find sustained chords in the accompaniment and sophisticated ornamentation in the solo part.

Ex. 64

After the first bassoon and the solo violin have danced their way through this section, the strings remind the soloist somewhat peremptorily of the rhythm of Ex. 61. In an amusing weight-lifting contest, soloist and orchestra drag the theme upwards until it regains its proper pitch; once again, Beethoven starts the rondo in its original guise. All goes as one might expect with a substantial recapitulation of most of the earlier material including the hunting horns episode, which is taken over by the entire orchestra to build up a sufficiently impressive entry to the cadenza. This ends with the usual trill, and we are entirely justified in expecting a conventional rounding-off of the movement soon afterwards. (It is worth joining bar 280 to bar 314 to see the sort of thing I mean.) Instead, Beethoven gives us another surprise; 'cellos and basses come in confidently enough with a reference to Ex. 61. Receiving no recognition from the soloist they gradually lose all confidence, getting on to a very false track.

Ex. 65

*f*                                    *diminuendo . . . . . . p*

The violins properly express a certain incredulity about this, but the soloist obligingly meets them half-way by changing the trill from E natural to E flat. All is explained, and the music proceeds quite happily in A flat major, the most remote key from D that it is possible to find. Psychologically this is a master-stroke, for it means that the final return to D will be that much more effective, since the journey back must now be made from the furthest possible point.[1]

An enchanting duet between oboe and violin re-establishes the tonality of D. The mood grows more boisterous and all seems set for a rowdy ending. But Beethoven has one more surprise for us. A sudden diminuendo takes away any suggestion of the uncouth or vulgar. In a moment of supremely imaginative composition we see a glimpse of something of exquisite delicacy, not unlike that fairy world that Mendelssohn was to make so much his own. A last tiptoe version of the theme is given to the soloist, completely without accompaniment, and then two whacking great chords effectively decapitate the movement. It is as though Beethoven had simply said, 'That's enough'; in all his compositions there is no more beautifully calculated an ending than this, the last perfect touch in a work which is as near to perfection as can be.

---

[1] See *Talking about Symphonies*, p. 13.

## CHAPTER XV

# BEETHOVEN

## Piano Concerto No. 5 in E♭ major, Op. 73
## (1809–10) (The 'Emperor')

1. Allegro. 2. Adagio un poco mosso. 3. Rondo: Allegro.

Orchestra: 2 flutes; 2 oboes; 2 clarinets; 2 bassoons; 2 horns; 2 trumpets; timpani; strings.

THE VERY different relationship that exists between piano and orchestra in this concerto as opposed to its four predecessors has already been discussed in Chapter X. Right from the start Beethoven establishes the fact that the piano is now on a new footing; it is as though the instrument had finally come of age. Nowhere in the third or fourth concertos do we find passages of a comparable virtuosity—there may be sections that are as difficult to play, but that is not the point; their function is different. What had previously been purely decorative has now assumed the mantle of authority. As for the orchestra, their first few chords reduce them to the level of lackeys opening doors, harmonic doors through which the pianist lets loose a flood of sound. Cascades of notes gush forth from three massive orchestral chords in turn. For a listener of Beethoven's time, brought up on a more orthodox diet, the shock must have been considerable. Revolutionary though this was, Beethoven was not prepared to sacrifice the orchestral exposition as some of the later composers of concertos did. At the end of the third flourish from the pianist, the orchestra take over and there begins an unusually rich and comprehensive *tutti* in which the main themes are all paraded for our inspection. First and most memorable is the characteristic tune which at once establishes a feeling of nobility and heroism.

Ex. 66

Beethoven underlines the importance of this theme by the emphatic accents in the last two bars, and at once repeats it with different orchestration employing brass, woodwind and timpani to make the point doubly clear. The sequel to this phrase will prove to be significant, although at first glance it would seem to be little more than a classical convention of broken chords.

Ex. 67

The lack of padding in this exposition is remarkable considering its length, and each idea must be stored away for future reference as it appears, even passages such as this next one which seems to be a bridge to something else rather than a phrase of any intrinsic importance.

Ex. 68

The second subject, towards which Ex. 68 is a bridge, proves to be a strange little affair, a ghostly march which circles round and round the same group of notes.

Ex. 69

The horns smooth this out into a sustained melody with a gently rippling accompaniment from the strings, when suddenly the music becomes strangely sinister. Nervous fragments of Ex. 66 appear in violins and 'cellos in turn; but with the re-establishment of E flat major all becomes clear again, and Beethoven gives us a substantial development of the first bar of Ex. 66 in particular.

Two more themes are important, one descending and the other rising. Both are based on scale patterns, and once again it is unlikely that if we were hearing the work for the first time we would attach any great significance to either.

We can sense that the exposition is nearing the end as it climbs down towards a final cadence in E flat major; but Beethoven averts the solo entry a little longer yet. One more theme has still to be heard, even though the 'cellos are so impatient to get on that they keep reminding us of the opening figure from Ex. 66. It is a smooth and lyrical phrase in Beethoven's blandest style.

The abrupt final rhythm cuts the melody short and is in turn taken up by woodwind and horns as the soloist enters unassumingly with a long quiet chromatic scale. A sustained trill on a high E flat leads to a singularly calm statement of Ex. 66, now stripped of heroic pretensions and imbued with the classic serenity a composer of Beethoven's maturity knows so well how to impart. Not for long, however; the mood changes, and a series of energetic thrusts explodes into a spattering of chords and octaves that tumble down the keyboard. The music dissolves into a mist of scales backed by quiet harmonies from the strings, until a sharp call to action brings in the full orchestra with Ex. 67.

We shall now see how skilfully Beethoven has planted the basic material of this movement in the opening pages of the exposition. It is always interesting in a concerto to compare the orchestral *tutti* with what I have called the secondary exposition, and never more so than in this magnificently planned work. The two columns in the following table make a comparison between primary and secondary expositions a simple matter, and it will be seen that the 'order of events' is identical in both. Any sense of dull repetition is avoided by the insertion of cushions of new material from the soloist between each of the numbered themes; these introduce that element of fantasy (already mentioned on page 154 of Chapter X) which is so essential a part of concerto writing.

| ORCHESTRAL EXPOSITION (or 'tutti') | SECONDARY EXPOSITION (with soloist) |
|---|---|
| Ex. 66. 'First subject'. Loud and energetic; played twice. | Ex. 66. Calm and serene; played once and followed by new material from soloist. |
| Ex. 67. Full orchestra, but with the interest in 1st violins and brass. | Ex. 67. Full orchestra, but then extended by soloist modulating through various keys and changing mood. |
| Ex. 68. 'Bridge passage'. | Ex. 68. Now in G♭ major and accompanied by decorative figures from soloist. The original ending (not shown in the example) is converted into a short fierce cadenza taking us to B minor. |
| Ex. 69. 'Second subject'. First version mainly in strings followed by smooth version in horns. | Ex. 69. In piano part followed by a variation in B (actually C♭)[1] major, leading to a very violent version for full orchestra. |

[1] See p. 218 Ex. 74.

Bars 57–60 Not shown as a = Bars 174–183 Extended into a
music example, but re-
ferred to as 'sinister' on
p. 63, para. 1.

series of quiet arpeggio
figures over sustained
chords; sudden change of
mood leads to

Bars 62–74 Not shown, but men- = Bars 184–195, a striking passage
tioned as development of
1st bar of Ex. 66.

for piano and orchestra
which is also a develop-
ment of Ex. 66, though far
more heroic in character.

Bars 74–78 Not shown, but a = Bars 195–205 Elaborate exten-
passage for full orchestra
featuring (usually inaudible) syncopations in woodwind.

sion, with the syncopated
figure in right-hand part,
followed by a complex
series of broken chords
which finally melt into

Ex. 70$^a$

Ex. 70$^a$ in the piano part; this,
extended and then played
by the woodwind, brings
us to a lengthened version
of

Ex. 70$^b$

Ex. 70$^b$ Quiet descending scales
(bars 217–220) lead us to a

[Ex. 71 is NOT used here, except
for its final rhythm.]

passage in which the closing rhythm of Ex. 71 is
given at half speed—
♪ ♩ ♪♩ instead of ♪♪♩
coming to a powerful and
dramatic close in the
dominant key of B♭.

It is not until this point that any fundamental change of plan is
to be found, and some idea of the relative proportions of the two
expositions can be gained by simple statistics. The orchestral *tutti*
up to the end of the section of which Ex. 70 is the starting point is
79 bars long, the secondary exposition over the comparable
distance consists of 116 bars. The changes have been of two
principal kinds, changes of direction involving modulation to

more remote keys, and changes of content brought about by introducing the element of fantasy that the soloist brings.

Beethoven now decides to put the clock back, making what may seem a somewhat strange decision about the structure of the movement. For the moment, the soloist is allowed to rest; the orchestra have what is virtually a re-statement of a large section of their original exposition, although naturally it is now in a different key. The passage concerned is similar to the one shown in the preceding table as beginning at bar 62, and it runs on for a further 37 bars until the next solo entry which exactly matches the one with which the first *tutti* had ended. We are on the threshold of the development.

At this point it is worth while to pause for a moment and survey the shape of the movement so far. Basically it is a normal sonata-form movement, although one of great complexity. The exposition alone is over 250 bars in length if we include the primary and secondary versions. Presented in the form of a diagram we now have something like this:

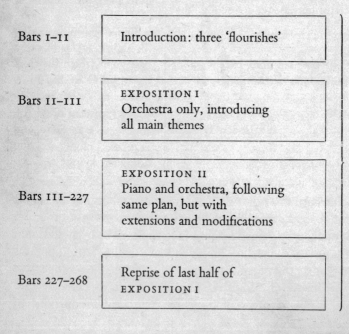

| Bars 1–11 | Introduction: three 'flourishes' |
|---|---|
| Bars 11–111 | EXPOSITION I<br>Orchestra only, introducing all main themes |
| Bars 111–227 | EXPOSITION II<br>Piano and orchestra, following same plan, but with extensions and modifications |
| Bars 227–268 | Reprise of last half of EXPOSITION I |

The whole making one sonata-form exposition.

It is worth noting that Beethoven leads into Exposition II with a long, quiet chromatic scale on the piano which is like the drawing of a curtain. He uses the same device at the start of the development and lastly to introduce the final coda; three of the most significant moments are thus 'unveiled'.

The development begins with quiet and mysterious passages in G major, a less remote key than it would seem since it soon proves to be merely the dominant of C minor—a key which shares the same key-signature of three flats that the 'home' key of E flat major has. Clarinet, flute and oboe in turn now begin a long development of Ex. 66, concentrating on its first two bars and in particular extending the second bar into long and distorted shapes. The atmosphere is almost desolate, the pianist providing a misty background of quiet figuration through which the solo woodwind phrases stalk forlornly. A sudden outburst in F minor brings a tougher mood, more and more instruments joining in as the pianist's arpeggios grow increasingly brilliant. The tension builds to such a degree that it flares into open violence; woodwind and horns, trumpets and timpani fiercely declaim a chord of C♭ (B)

major to the rhythm ♪♫| ♩ ♫♩ ♫| ♩ which will be seen to be

derived from the last notes of Ex. 71. For the first time in the history of the piano concerto, the soloist is able to stand up to this show of force as an equal. Yielding nothing, the piano thunders back, ultimately silencing the opposition as it embarks on a series of dramatic scales in double octaves. While Beethoven appears to have accepted that the new piano for which he was writing could match the weight of orchestral tone in *dialogue*, he still seems to have doubted its capacity to make itself heard *above* any substantial sound. Consequently we find in this next passage a fascinating example of a rigged fight. The piano's octaves are marked *ff*, or very loud.

Ex. 72

The comparable passage on strings with which this constantly overlaps is marked *p* or soft, with only the peak-note of the phrase loud; even that is qualified by the instruction *fp*, which can roughly be translated as 'look as if you are playing loud but don't.'

Ex.73

I am completely convinced that we are justified in changing Beethoven's markings here. It is surely evident from the patterns of the music that this section is conceived as a struggle between equals. I would even go so far as to say that had Beethoven ever been able to hear this passage in his own lifetime he would have allowed the orchestra to play louder; with the resources of a modern concert grand available there can be no doubt that he would have welcomed a stand-up fight between the piano and strings. Only when the pianist's octaves begin a long and beautifully graded diminuendo need the orchestra follow suit. The tumult and the shouting die, and for the first time the soloist is entrusted with Ex. 71. For some twenty bars he muses over it, disregarding the ominous mutterings about the start of Ex. 66 with which the 'cellos and violas occasionally disturb the atmosphere. Nevertheless they are to have their way in the end; in a moment the whole orchestra take up the insistent rhythm and we are snatched from a dream-like trance to the harsh reality of bright daylight. Before we realize what is happening we are thrust willy-nilly into the recapitulation.

Here Beethoven plays a master-stroke. Too often, flourishes such as those with which the movement began seem, on mature consideration of the overall shape of the work, to be an irrelevant appendage. Only by truly integrating them into the whole plan can this potential hazard be overcome, and that is precisely what Beethoven does. In even grander terms than before, the three flourishes reappear, this time thickened by sustained chords on the wind which also serve to bind piano and orchestra more closely together.

It would be laborious to produce another detailed comparison between the secondary exposition and the recapitulation—not only laborious but more difficult, since there are greater differences involved. These differences are not so much in the material as in its relative proportions; for instance, there are now a mere eight bars of orchestral music before the soloist re-enters. When he does so, it is with a totally new and expressive development of Ex. 66. What is interesting is Beethoven's decision to take the responsibility for the cadenza out of the soloist's hands. It was the start of a new order, and from now on composers habitually wrote out their cadenzas as an integral part of the work,[1] or dispensed with them entirely. In this concerto, there is a passage of less than twenty bars before the orchestra rejoin the fray, and of those twenty a mere seven-and-a-half are concerned in any way with the display of virtuosity.

Opinions may differ as to where the coda of this immense first movement begins. To my ear, Beethoven achieves a striking balance by once again repeating the last half of Exposition I as he had in the diagram on p. 214. It is at the end of this that the third chromatic scale already mentioned leads to a quiet and shimmering passage of great beauty, and this, if only for the fact that it is new, I prefer to call the start of the coda proper. The long descent accomplished, the music gathers its strength for the last time before coming to a triumphant conclusion; history had been made, for never again would composers feel the need to 'protect' the soloist in a keyboard concerto.

To write a cold-blooded analysis of the slow movement would seem to be an unforgivable act of vandalism. This sublime music presents no problem, except that of comprehending how the human mind can visualize and then transcribe such beauty. However, since it is the purpose of this book to try to see a little

[1] The sole important exception is in the Brahms violin concerto, where the composer relied on his friend Joachim to fill the gap.

way below the surface, let us at least catalogue the main events together with their implications. The key is B major, a choice that Beethoven doubtless made for very good reasons. The note E flat, which was of course the tonal centre of the first movement, now becomes D sharp, the crucial major third of B major, and in order to make the relationship quite clear, Beethoven begins his slow movement with this very note. He has already flirted with this key a number of times in the first movement, usually preferring to write it in the somewhat confusing notation of Cb. This is not just an intellectual quirk on his part, but a practical way of underlining those elements that are common to both keys. Here are three scales, of which the first and last are identical on a keyboard whatever their theoretical differences may be. It will be seen that there are no points of resemblance at all between the scales of B and Eb, whereas there are several between Eb and Cb.

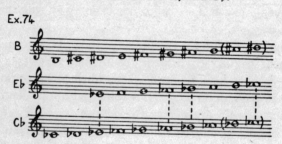

Ex.74

This may seem to the layman to be little more than juggling with notation, but to a composer such distinctions have a practical and sometimes even a spiritual significance.

The first theme, which appears three times in all, is a melody of the most classical perfection.

Ex.75

Beethoven is so reluctant to finish this that he has some difficulty in bringing it to a close; like a fond lover snatching ever one more embrace in parting, he has four cadences in all before allowing the piano to enter. Over a left-hand part of extraordinary restraint, the right hand sings a melody that is half-way between a theme and a decoration.[1] It is a supreme example of the sort of classical doodling that in the wrong hands can be disastrous. Here, by some inexplicable alchemy, it becomes not a slightly disorientated scale over a conventional and pedantic accompaniment, but one of the most exquisitely beautiful passages ever written. In time it flowers into a melody whose rising sequences might run some risk of banality were it not for the beauty of the setting in which they are placed.

Two sighs of contentment from the orchestra translate us into the colder light of D major where the same misty scales cast their spell. The music grows more emphatic, climbing high on spiralling trills until it descends once more to a decorated version of Ex. 75, now appearing for the first time in the piano part. A few bars of seeming improvisation from the soloist lead us to the third full statement of the theme; this time it is accompanied by a gentle bell-like figure from the keyboard which slowly lulls us into a positively hypnotic trance. The music comes to a point of total rest, a long sustained B on two quiet bassoons. Almost imperceptibly the note shifts to B flat, but if we were not wise after the event, we could well believe it to be an A sharp, a note which might indeed take us to a convincing end, albeit an unimaginative and boring one.

Ex. 76

In fact Beethoven exploits precisely the same type of harmonic twist that he had used at the beginning of the movement. By

---

[1] Shown in Ex. 106, p. 241.

changing E♭ to D♯ he had then opened the door to the 'sharp' key of B major; now, by thinking of A♯ as B♭ he reopens the way back to the 'flat' key of E♭, a tonality which he needs to regain for the finale. Very quietly, as though considering for the first time an idea whose implications are by no means fully realized, the pianist puts forward a speculation about the theme of the last movement. Twice the phrase is heard, illuminating the final bars of the slow movement like the first warmth of the sun before its rim appears above the horizon. We are spellbound, as Beethoven must have known we would be; suddenly, and with characteristic humour, he shouts '*Wake* up!' and whirls us into a dance of extraordinary abandon.

Ex.77

One brief portion of this tune (some seven bars later) is worth mentioning in that it is quoted by Schumann in his *Carnaval*. In his March of the Davidites against the Philistines he had no hesitation in enlisting Beethoven's support; he knew it would have been given willingly.

The orchestra is a little laggardly in joining in, but in due course they are galvanized into action, even extending the tune by a substantial margin. The piano re-enters, throwing off a few exuberant scales before introducing a new and particularly delightful theme—one however that is to remain its own preserve entirely.

Ex.78

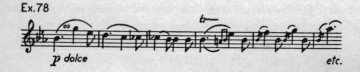

Tempting though it must have been to give this to the orchestra, Beethoven prefers to keep it exclusively for the soloist. The course of the movement remains remarkably simple to follow, even if it is extraordinarily difficult to play; the rondo theme (Ex. 77) is seldom far away, but its various entrances are divided one from the other by passages of considerable virtuosity. It reappears in keys as diverse as C major, A flat and (most mysteriously) E. One rhythm

of the greatest importance needs to be quoted:

This crops up in a multitude of places and in a variety of moods. Towards the middle of the movement there is a long sustained trill on the piano, and with a wonderfully calculated piece of craftsmanship Beethoven reintroduces the vision of the theme that had initially been suggested by the piano in the closing bars of the slow movement. In its way, it is as notable an example of integration as was the incorporation of the preliminary flourishes into the middle of the first movement.

It seems to be a characteristic of Beethoven to have a quiet passage just before the final triumph; in this movement there is a wonderful contemplative passage when the piano has a series of descending chords over the softly reiterated beat of a drum. The impression given is one of utter contentment coupled with a pleasant exhaustion; for the moment the busy fingers of the pianist need some respite, but this does not mean that all joy has gone out of the music. Then suddenly, 'That's enough of that,' Beethoven seems to say; 'Let's finish the thing off.' And without more ado, he does.

## CHAPTER XVI

# SCHUMANN

## Piano Concerto in A minor, Op. 54 (1841-45)

1. Allegro affettuoso. 2. Intermezzo: andantino grazioso. 3. Allegro vivace.

Orchestra: 2 flutes; 2 oboes; 2 clarinets; 2 bassoons; 2 horns; 2 trumpets; timpani; strings.

IT WAS in 1829 that Schumann, then only nineteen years old, first turned his energies towards writing a piano concerto. An abortive attempt in F major was followed by another failure started in the next year. Both works were left unfinished, as was a third concerto which he began in 1833. Thus discouraged, it is scarcely surprising that he should have decided to postpone any further attempt until his technical command had increased, and it wasn't until 1841 that he tried again. This time he simplified his task by writing a one-movement Fantasy for piano and orchestra, something which he may well have felt was less of a challenge to his skill than a full-scale concerto. The truly Romantic composer is seldom at his best in the larger musical forms, and the title of Fantasy gave him a certain freedom which he must have found comforting.

At the time Schumann was writing with extraordinary facility; the desperate battle for Clara had been won and the couple had been married at last after years of opposition and discouragement. He had loved her since she was fifteen; now his dream was realized, and with his twenty-one-year-old bride beside him he was able to fling himself into composition with renewed fervour. In the early months of 1841 he produced his first symphony, an overture, scherzo and finale for orchestra, and then the Fantasy for piano and orchestra which took little more than a week to write. Clara tried it out with the Gewandhaus Orchestra on 13 August of that year but it seems to have made no great impression, and was laid aside.

Three years later Schumann again turned his thoughts towards the combination of piano and orchestra and wrote a Rondo in A major. It was at this point that someone, probably Clara, suggested joining these two movements together by the addition of a third to make a proper concerto. The happy result of this inspired idea was the concerto as we now know it; under the circumstances its unity is remarkable and nobody would ever deduce from hearing the work how curiously it came to be assembled. The first performance of the final version was given on 1 January 1846; strangely enough it still seems not to have inspired any great enthusiasm. Even ten years later, a critic was to write of Clara's performance of the concerto in London:

> The chief novelty of the evening was Madame Schumann's performance of Dr Schumann's Concerto in A minor, which was received with a warmth well merited by the Lady's playing. Because we cannot fancy that the Concerto will be adopted by any performer in London, we will forbear to speak of the composition as a work.[1]

There are none so deaf as those that will not hear!

Since the first movement was designed as a Fantasy there will be little benefit in searching in it for the normal landmarks of concerto form. In fact it is remarkably concise and well-planned, admirably demonstrating that Form is not something superimposed from outside at the behest of musical pedants but a shape which the material itself has much to do with devising. Fantasy or not, Schumann had learned much from Beethoven, as we shall discover presently.

The first note on the orchestra is like a catapult, launching the soloist into a brief flurry of chords which instantly arrests our

[1] H. F. Chorley in *The Athenaeum*, quoted in Nicolas Slonimsky's *Lexicon of Musical Invective* (Coleman-Ross).

attention. In a matter of seconds the orchestra presents us with the most important theme of the movement.

This is at once repeated by the soloist before Schumann plunges us into more disturbed waters. Now one of his most notable characteristics as a composer is his great flexibility of rhythm, a flexibility which at times can be positively misleading. Since we shall find a number of examples of this in the concerto, it will be worth while to consider the very next phrase from this point of view. Here is the melody as Schumann wrote it; below it, the numerals indicate several different ways of 'thinking' the tune with regard to rhythmic stress.

Certainly it seems a more natural solution to place the stress on the minim E both times, treating it as the first beat in each case; but ambiguity could hardly go farther. Gradually a brief but significant phrase emerges from this deliberately vague background:

In time this is taken up very strongly by the full orchestra while the piano writing becomes more virile with two short octave passages. We then find a long and expressive declamation by the pianist in a rhythm which may well remind us of Beethoven's fourth piano concerto—a work with which this has a certain amount in common. Ex. 79 reappears, now in the more confident guise of C major, until a positively Wagnerian sequence of descending phrases brings us to what might be called Chapter II. (The movement actually falls into nine sections, so we may as well think of them as chapters.) This consists of a long and free development of Ex. 79 in which the thematic interest is largely in the clarinet. Only the first part of the theme is used, the tail-end being changed to a rising leap of a tenth.

Ex. 82

The piano part meantime gallops along in a characteristic figuration; gradually out of this accompanying pattern a theme grows: to start with one can hardly put one's finger on it, when all of a sudden one is aware that the piano part has become increasingly lyrical, even although its bustling arpeggios have not ceased. Nowhere will you find this theme written out in the exact terms in which it appears as Ex. 83, but this is the sound that the ear picks out even though the eye may not be able to trace it.

Ex. 83

etc.

This rhapsodic interlude ends with a further statement of Ex. 82 from the clarinet, at the end of which an oboe introduces a variant of Ex. 81ª. An interesting example of the way a composer's subconscious mind works is to be found at this point. The piano is shortly to introduce what I am fairly convinced Schumann believed to be a new theme, but it would seem to be derived from Ex. 81 despite its apparent differences. The link lies in three notes.

Thus do fairly large musical oaks from very small acorns grow. The new theme builds up to an exciting climax on the orchestra in which yet another variation of Ex. 81ᵃ appears in triumph; gradually the music climbs down until a gently rocking figure is all that is left. The mood changes and Schumann embarks on what amounts to an extraordinarily beautiful Nocturne for clarinet, piano and strings. Needless to say this is entirely suitable for a fantasy, if a mite unorthodox in a concerto movement. It is far from irrelevant, however, since it is a skilful development of Ex. 79. This then is Chapter III, in which a new light is shed on a familiar character, and in which, were we to think of it in terms of Dickensian chapter-headings, 'our hero has an amorous encounter in the moonlight'.

Now I said earlier that Schumann had learned from Beethoven in this concerto; we have now reached a moment that demonstrates this. We have seen in the previous chapter how Beethoven integrated his three opening flourishes into the movement by introducing them on an even grander scale midway. Schumann employs the same device. That first brief flurry of chords that had preceded Ex. 79 at the very start of the work now reappears in a sudden and violent entry that shocks us out of the trance that Chapter III has induced. For a few moments there is a hot argument between orchestra and piano, each vying with the other until a cascade of octaves from the soloist quells the orchestral opposition. Chapter IV then is by no means uneventful, even though it is the shortest episode in the movement. The excitement is maintained throughout the next section—Chapter V, to continue the analogy —in which our hero would seem to go for a wild ride in the woods.

One would hesitate to use such words about the music of a truly classical composer, but Schumann was very much the Romantic, his imagination being fired as much by literature and painting as by music. So many of his works bear titles that indicate some extra-musical stimulus that we have less cause in his case to be wary of dragging in non-musical images. If we wish to be coldly analytical we simply acknowledge that here is a new variation on Ex. 79.

Ex. 85

Gradually the excitement dies and we find ourselves back at the beginning once more, although this time there is no preliminary flourish, Ex. 79 simply emerging quite satisfyingly from a long-drawn-out descent. For some time the music now pursues exactly the same course as before so that, apart from transposition, Chapters VI and VII are identical with Chapters I and II. But at the very moment when we feel that perhaps the composer has settled into too easy a rut of repetition, we suddenly find ourselves being swept up into a glorious climax that leads us into something quite new. We have reached Chapter VIII, the cadenza, which is, surprisingly enough from this most romantic of composers, a classic model of perfection.

It starts with a seemingly extempore passage in which Schumann suggests most skilfully that the pianist may well be improvising after all. The phrase that he would seem to have invented spontaneously is not as irrelevant as it would seem, however, as a comparison with Ex. 84 will show.

Ex. 86

* By a curious coincidence this phrase appears note-for-note complete with the same harmonization in Mozart's fugue in C major, K.394.

The soloist seems to meditate on this for some time before a spectacular passage of flying chords brings us to a series of trills, beneath which Ex. 79 reappears as an expressive solo for left hand. Some last impetuous runs lead in to Chapter IX, with which the story ends—or did so until the last two movements were tacked on. The orchestra take up the thread with a quickened version of Ex. 79, of which Schumann once again uses only the first three notes, and the piano part gallops home to a highly effective if relatively unspectacular finish.

The second movement, the last of the three to be composed, is an enchanting intermezzo in which piano and orchestra enjoy a closely-knit dialogue. If the first movement can be said to be mainly concerned with three descending notes, C B A, this is largely built on a pattern of four rising notes, a pattern which the piano states with beguiling simplicity from the very first bar.

Ex. 87

This most elegant conversation is continued for some twenty-eight bars, with the soloist waxing lyrical at times in elaborately curving phrases of great beauty. For much of the movement, however, the piano part is entirely subsidiary to the orchestra. First the 'cellos and then the upper strings sing their way through a most mellifluous melody, whose stanzas are occasionally interspersed with disarming phrases on the piano.

Ex. 88

The serenade continues, with an especially melting effect when the violins take the melody from the 'cellos as it rises beyond their convenient compass. The opening dialogue is resumed and finally disintegrates. It is at this moment that Schumann brilliantly solves the problem of joining up the last two movements to the Fantasy written three years before. Once again his model seems to have been Beethoven's fifth concerto—those wonderful closing bars of the slow movement in which the piano seems to see the theme of the finale in a golden glow before it bursts into life.[1] Now this is a *forward* look, and if Schumann had copied it exactly, his slow movement would have ended with an anticipation of the finale, something on these lines perhaps:

I would even hazard a guess that something of the sort may have passed through his mind. His real problem, though, wasn't to link the last two movements but to join them to the first. Suddenly the inspiration must have come to him; instead of Beethoven's forward look, his was to be retrospective. And so we have the lovely moment where the orchestra looks back to the main theme of the first movement (Ex. 79), only to put aside such nostalgic memories and burst through into the exultant finale.

This is a movement of great brilliance and gaiety. For the pianist it is enormously difficult, not so much for its technical demands as for its somewhat repetitious sequences in which it is very easy to take a wrong turning. Orchestra and piano frequently have to play so much 'across' the beat that it destroys all confidence to look at the conductor, whose gestures often seem to be entirely

[1] See p. 219.

disassociated from the sounds that we can hear. The themes are clearly differentiated one from the other and not even the most dyed-in-the-wool Philistine could claim that this movement was difficult to listen to. It begins with a trumpet-like fanfare in which the piano speaks to us with tones of brass.

These athletic leaps across the keyboard are most exhilarating in their effect, and the rhythmic vitality of the music is enormous. Soon the piano embarks on a long *moto perpetuo* whose span grows increasingly wider the further it goes. At last the music spins to a stop, whereupon the orchestra present the second main theme—another splendid example of Schumann's rhythmical ambiguity.

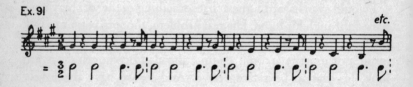

The fact remains that had he used the more logical notation I have indicated beneath, something of the bounce might be lost. As it is, a powerful amount of sniffing on silent first beats goes on in the early stages of rehearsal.

The piano chatters on gaily against fragmentary syncopations from the orchestra until suddenly Ex. 90 bursts back into the fray. Having convinced us of its heroism, it retires into a bookish study and becomes (of all things) the basis of a fugue. This worthy exercise in counterpoint soon loses interest for Schumann, however, and is displaced by a new melody, first heard on the oboe.

Ex.92

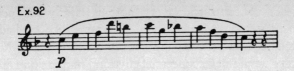

The piano seizes on this happily, sometimes overwhelming it with rushing arpeggios and sometimes babbling away in its upper register.

It is the horns who finally put a stop to this by recalling Ex. 90 once again, the piano part meanwhile grumbling mightily about being taken from the ballroom to the parade-ground. Something like a recapitulation ensues, the music being for the most part transposed up a fourth. It is in the following section that the soloist can most easily go astray, as inevitably his fingers suffer from a feeling of 'I have been here before'. The sequences pound on with the energy of a fast-running tide, the notes rising and falling in wave-like patterns. Finally, by one of those nice, almost mathematical coincidences which music seems to abound in, we find ourselves triumphantly back in A major once more with Ex. 90 reigning supreme. A brief rest for the pianist allows him to gather strength for the coda, which is unashamedly a waltz. In some of the most enchanting music ever dignified by the name of concerto, the notes whirl on, circling and dipping like a ballerina, the orchestra occasionally interjecting fragments of Ex. 90, now wearing its dancing shoes.

Ex.93

Notice that although the piano-leaps are here turned downwards instead of rising, this does nothing to lessen the exuberance of the music. Now and then delicious fragments of waltzes flash past, beguiling the ear, until a last authoritative passage brings the concerto to a stirring close. The whole work has been quite unlike any other concerto and every note is clearly stamped with Schumann's very personal style. If for instance he had never bothered to write the second movement, I am sure no other composer would have conceived anything on the same lines. Yet if we are seeking for comparisons it can truly be said that this concerto is the Romantic equivalent of the last truly Classical concerto, Beethoven's fourth. Needless to say, the whole style of Schumann's composition is far more romantic; the orchestra is less important and the moods are more changeable. It is the absence of force that is common to both. The piano prefers to woo the orchestra, often blending with it in an inconspicuous manner, like a dearly loved queen who mixes with her subjects on the most easy terms. The dominating ferocity that we find in concertos such as those by Liszt or Brahms just doesn't appear in the Schumann. Partly this may be due to the fact that Schumann wrote it for the greatest woman pianist of the age; it must not be forgotten though that it was a tribute not of admiration but of love. That this tribute should come from the most poetic of all composers ensures a work that is unique among concertos—perhaps not an Emperor but a most beloved Princess.

## CHAPTER XVII

# BRAHMS

## Piano Concerto No. 1 in D minor, Op. 15 (1854–58)

1. Maestoso. 2. Adagio. 3. Rondo: Allegro non troppo.

Orchestra: 2 flutes; 2 oboes; 2 clarinets; 2 bassoons; 4 horns; 2 trumpets; timpani; strings.

IT IS hard to believe that a guide-book has been published for intrepid English explorers in which are to be found the names of those restaurants in France considerate enough to serve fish and chips. The sad fact has to be faced that the rich delicacies of continental cuisine are not to everybody's taste; nor is the music of Brahms. To some people his compositions remain turgid, sentimental and overpadded, while the music critic of a leading Sunday newspaper even called the Double Concerto sterile and arid. If this be true, welcome sterility. However, the most imperceptive and biased listener would find it hard to use any of these adjectives about the first piano concerto. It is spare, lean, taut, athletic, certainly not sentimental, and intensely dramatic without ever resorting to the empty gestures of rhetoric. Its initial reception, which was cold and hostile, must have been a bitter blow to Brahms; the general complaint was that the music was dissonant, eccentric and without melody, although in all fairness it must be added that some of the opposition to the work appears to have been dictated by considerations other than musical. Brahms wrote to Clara Schumann describing the first performance at Leipzig:

> My concerto went very well. I had two rehearsals. You have probably already heard that it was a complete fiasco; at the rehearsal it met with total silence, and at the performance (where hardly three people raised their hands to clap) it was actually hissed.[1]

[1] Quoted in *Brahms—his Life and Work* by Karl Geiringer (Allen & Unwin).

Now it is certainly true that the audience would have been expecting something more in line with the fashion of the day, a work in which there would be at least some concessions to surface glitter and virtuosity. There are no such compromises in this concerto, and in effect it is more like a symphony for piano and orchestra than a concerto in the Lisztian manner. Perhaps this was inevitable since the music was originally planned as a symphony. Brahms had a tremendous struggle getting to grips with this piece, and when the first monumental theme came to him he saw it as the start of a purely orchestral work. With much labour he sketched out the three movements, and as composers often do he laid out this first score for two pianos, to save time and effort as much as to be able to try it out. It is what is called a short score, the music being on four staves instead of twenty-four, while instrumentation is suggested by abbreviations such as 'Vn.' for violins or 'W.W.' for woodwind. Conceived as it was at the piano, pianistic figuration kept breaking through; hard as he must have tried, Brahms could not restrict the texture of the music to purely orchestral terms, and what you might call his 'manual imagination'—the sense of what hands can do on a keyboard—kept getting the better of him. The work was re-cast as a piano concerto and ultimately, after much revision, appeared in the form we know today. Its symphonic origin still shows in its almost total denial of the conventionally showy passages in which the later nineteenth-century concertos abound. In concertos such as those by Liszt, Grieg, Mendelssohn or Tschaikovsky, we invariably find the soloist asserting his dominance at an early stage. Not so in the Brahms, where, after an unusually long orchestral introduction, the piano enters with a calm and undemonstrative theme whose spirit is nearer to the spirit of the St Matthew Passion than the glamour of the concert-hall.

We have seen how the Schumann piano concerto was influenced (however indirectly) by Beethoven. The link in this case is much clearer, for the first movement is in the direct line of descent from Beethoven's ninth symphony. Apart from the similarity of key, the emotional resemblances are very strong, and it is an instructive exercise in musical aesthetics to hear the first movement of Beethoven's Op. 125 immediately before listening to the Brahms first movement.

The work begins with an awe-inspiring rumble on drums, horns, 'cellos and basses. The subject is a magnificent one, torn by convulsive trills and shouting defiance at a thundery sky.

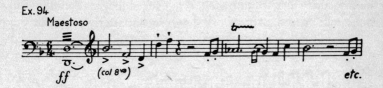

The bass shifts down a semitone to C sharp and the trill theme becomes the subject of a tug of war between various sections of the orchestra. The tension increases until at last the music explodes into two great chords from which there emerges a strange sad theme, apparently unrelated to anything we have heard so far and as bleak as Sibelius in his most forbidding mood. The texture is utterly unlike anything that had ever been written before, so gaunt and austere does it seem. Skilfully Brahms integrates this new idea with the first pages by a subtle relationship with Ex. 94; compare these two figures and you will see what I mean.

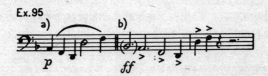

Here is the theme that is laid above this bare accompaniment.

The one pale touch of sunshine in this grey world—the F sharp
in the fifth bar—is quickly extinguished, as can be seen from even
this brief example. The phrase continues to reach upward as though
our gaze were scanning the forbidding rock-face of a mountain, the
eyes rising towards the mist-enshrouded peak. We come now to a
very Brahmsian passage in the dark key of B flat minor. The
orchestral colouring is wonderful here and it is hard to understand
the insecurity that Brahms felt about his ability to handle a full
orchestra when so early a work shows such masterly originality.

For some time Brahms seems to brood on this theme, when
suddenly our thoughts are violently disturbed by a brutal *fortissimo* and three great hammer-blows from the full orchestra, as
though some giant Nordic hero had battered down the door. The
opening theme blazes up again with renewed incandescence; it is
followed by a terse, abrupt theme in quavers, granite chips from
the sculptor's chisel.

Coupled to this is the one truly optimistic tune of the movement,
a call to action that recalls Tennyson's words 'Blow, bugle, blow,
set the wild echoes flying'.

Ex. 99

This, harmonized in D major, is combined with both Exx. 95 and 98 in a masterly fusion of ideas. Gradually the excitement dies and the music grows darker once more; quietly and unobtrusively the soloist enters with an extension of Ex. 98.

Ex. 100

This beautiful and contemplative section continues for some time, but it cannot deny the tremendous forces which it has momentarily tamed; a long-drawn crescendo extending over eight bars leads to a clamorous return of Ex. 94, which storms from piano to orchestra and back again. Here in musical terms is the tempest from King Lear, and its impact is overwhelming. For a few bars the orchestra rages by itself, the next entry of the piano being one of the strangest bits of keyboard writing ever to have come out of the nineteenth century. In the right hand we find Ex. 96, but it is accompanied by a gawky angular figuration in the left hand which is notable for its avoidance of any suggestion of softness in the harmony. It is as bare and uncompromising as even Stravinsky might wish it to be. We are in the throes of the secondary exposition and need feel no surprise at the arrival of Ex. 97, now decorated, as might be expected, with additional notes from the piano. A series of rising trills leads us to a sudden patch of warmth; the comparative oasis of F major has been reached and Brahms is ready to introduce his second subject, a glorious melody which up to now he has kept concealed. It is the soloist's privilege to reveal this treasure:

Ex. 101

Although Brahms clothes this in rich harmony he has not conceived it in entirely vertical terms, and the left hand frequently follows the curve of the melody like a shadow. At one point in this long and expansive line there is a possible reference to Ex. 98, now smoothed out almost beyond recognition, and then the soloist embarks on a version of Ex. 99 which climbs ever higher until, like Icarus, it has to fall once more. A brief interlude in D flat major allows us to draw breath before the orchestra in its turn takes over Ex. 101. It is in a somewhat truncated form which soon breaks out into a series of fanfares based on Ex. 99; meantime the soloist chatters away in swift-running thirds. For several pages Brahms occupies himself almost entirely with Ex. 99, moving through various keys before he settles once again into F major. Its softening influence has brought warmth and tenderness in its wake, so that even Ex. 97 now seems to have thawed, losing its grey and forbidding look in a beautiful orchestral cadence.

The new mood is suddenly shattered by an outburst from the piano in double octaves—the only conventional concession to virtuosity in the movement; it begins with a pattern taken from Ex. 99, so that even this is relevant to the issue. A long development of the opening theme follows in which the angular and choppy writing for the piano, while being ungrateful to play, is strikingly effective. Ex. 96 is also extensively discussed by piano and orchestra together, one passage being possibly the first occasion where a composer has written a simple unison tune of this type in a concerto.

Ex. 102

R.H.

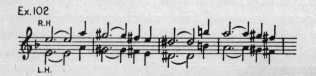

L.H.

This is a device much favoured by more recent composers, and examples by Rachmaninoff or Bartók come to mind readily; unison passages in Beethoven's fourth concerto are not directly comparable as their function is not so purely melodic as it is here.

Another interesting development is Brahms's new treatment of Ex. 97 which, by a process of compression, becomes very much more energetic in character.

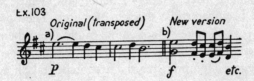

This is so much to the taste of the orchestra that they turn it into a suggestion of a waltz, while the piano part, momentarily released from the brooding and thunderous atmosphere which pervades the rest of the movement, indulges in some delightful and light-fingered passage-work which is a welcome patch of sunshine in an otherwise sombre composition. The passing happiness is not long-lived, however, and a sudden dramatic build-up leads us to some tremendous chords. We have arrived at the greatest moment of the whole movement, the recapitulation. Brahms's avoidance of the obvious here is sheer genius. Everything converges on the home note of D, and not unnaturally we are expecting the theme to reappear as it originally did in Ex. 94, starting on B flat. The complete unexpectedness of the piano entry on E is one of the great shocks of the entire literature of music, to be compared to the effect of entering a room by jumping through a plate-glass window instead of walking in through the door. The music explodes into greater violence than before, such violence that even the gentle phrases of Ex. 100 are transformed by the orchestra into a passage of searing intensity.

A gradual lessening of the tension brings us in due course to a reprise of Ex. 101 and for a moment or two we can relax again and enjoy the sensuous beauty of this most Brahmsian tune. The

composer has by no means finished with us, though, and before
long we are again caught up in the demonic trills and thundering
octaves that we have inevitably come to associate primarily with
this work. The movement ends as it had begun, 'in thunder,
lightning and in rain'.

The slow movement can be reasonably assumed to be in the
nature of an 'In Memoriam' to Schumann, whose attempted
suicide had been a terrible shock to Brahms. The opening bars
have more than a suggestion of choral music about them; indeed,
Brahms even went so far as to write the words 'Benedictus qui
venit in nomine Domini' over the first orchestral phrase.

Ex.104

The mood is markedly similar to parts of the Requiem that he
was to write some seven years later.

When the piano does come in, the style of writing is again
extraordinarily original, the conventional clichés of pianism being
brilliantly avoided. Both hands play virtually identical parts,
separated from each other by a gap of an octave. The texture that
Brahms uses here, and even more so in a few later passages, may in
itself be intended as a tribute to Schumann, since it resembles parts
of his great C major *Phantasie*, Op. 17, a work which Brahms
would certainly have known intimately. Such links in no way
detract from the quality of the piece, being matters of influence
rather than plagiarism. Where they can become interesting is in
detecting not similarities but differences between composers. This
second movement provides a classic example of this in the next
piano entry.

Ex.105

It seems to me perfectly legitimate to compare this to the slow movement of Beethoven's fifth concerto as well as to the finale of the Schumann *Phantasie*, Op. 17. Here first is the Beethoven, whose absolute simplicity breathes a spirit of classical purity.

Ex.106

Certainly this is romantic music in that it is deeply felt and expresses a profound emotion. Despite this the idiom remains entirely classical, conveying by its very restraint a special quality that makes it quite different from later, more overt expressions of the same mood. Turn now to the Schumann:

Ex.107

The much greater span of the accompanying left-hand part, the cross-rhythm of three against two, as well as the G sharp in the melody, make this more flexible and more openly romantic. It is the 'warmest', the most personal of the three examples, having neither the restraint of the Beethoven nor the angular distortion—and consequently greater sense of anguish—of the Brahms. Yet on the face of it there are close resemblances between them; each begins with a spread octave, each traces a long and expressive descent in the right hand and each has a simple accompaniment on roughly similar lines.

If we want to find Brahms writing in a way that has no parallel we do not have to look far, for a strange episode soon begins in which a curiously shaped melody rides uneasily above gaunt syncopated octaves and a rising chromatic bass.

It reads rather like an orchestral transcription for piano solo, but in fact it remains the exclusive property of the soloist.

There are several climaxes in this movement, including one magnificent passage of chords leading to a series of wave-like arpeggios, which suggest the prow of a ship dipping and plunging into an ocean swell. A strange and highly original cadenza consisting of loops and swirls of notes ultimately unfolds into the closing phrases from the orchestra which bring this unique movement to its final resting-place.

The finale has in its opening bars a certain affinity with the third movement of Beethoven's concerto in C minor (No. 3). The piano kicks off with the principal theme, strutting tenths in the left hand giving the music a marvellous bounce at times.

Ex.109

In a Rondo, the theme is seldom developed in the true sense of the word; it is used as a landmark to come back to after each of a series of journeys, as though one were staying in a hotel surrounded by walks. The hotel is the Rondo theme which one returns to after each outing; sometimes it may look a little different because of the light but you know perfectly well it's the same hotel.

In this movement, the first 'walk' is quite a long one. After several repetitions of Ex. 109, it begins with a gentle rise until gradually it emerges on to a lovely plateau where we find the second principal theme, a wonderfully relaxed singing tune.

Ex.110

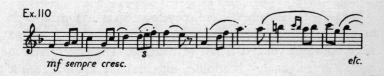

For some time the pianist extends this melody, his left hand assisted by pizzicato 'cellos, but otherwise alone. Only when the excitement has increased substantially do more of the orchestra join in. A quiet interlude follows with the strings rocking gently through a very Schumannesque phrase, when suddenly a suspiciously Wagnerian horn-call[1] summons us, and a precipitate descent back to the hotel begins; after a long unwinding Ex. 109 is safely resumed.

Walk number two takes us through some very beautiful and pastoral country, first revealed to us by the orchestra.

---

[1] Actually derived from the first three notes of Ex. 109.

Ex.111

Brahms shows his usual mastery of counterpoint in his treatment of this essentially lyrical theme, having any number of shadows and reflections of its outline in the supporting parts. After dallying with it for some time in the most affectionate manner, he suddenly decides to make it the basis of a scholastic argument, as though two professors had stopped in an idyllic setting to discuss the nomenclature of a botanical specimen.

Ex.112

In its way this is as unexpected a development as the fugal episode in the finale of the Schumann piano concerto, to which it bears a resemblance of context if not of material. The pianist tries to inject a little light and cheerfulness into the increasingly academic atmosphere by producing a deliciously lyrical version of Ex. 109—not, as one might say, a return to the hotel, but a reminder of its delights. In due course the main theme is regained, but this time Brahms presents it to us in its most stormy guise. Even Ex. 110 is affected by the extreme severity of the music at this point, translating itself into the minor with striking effect. A Bach-like cadenza, having towards its close passages not unlike some of the writing in the slow movement, leads us to a new version of Ex. 112, now seen in a golden sunset such as Brahms was to create in the final pages of a number of his works. For a long time it even seems as though we are coming to a quiet ending. The music grows slower in tempo, while pastoral horns and oboes start a country dance that is full of old-world charm. A long passage of descending trills drifts quietly downwards like the sound of sheep-bells as the flocks come down the mountain-side. Just as the feeling of twilight reaches the point of nostalgia, Brahms decides to whip up the pace and the last revels begin. A final dance of great energy and excitement rounds off this remarkable work. How could the audience at Leipzig have refrained from applause?

## CHAPTER XVIII

# BRAHMS

## Violin Concerto in D major, Op. 77 (1877?–78)

1. Allegro non troppo. 2. Adagio. 3. Allegro giocoso, ma non troppo vivace.

Orchestra: 2 flutes; 2 oboes; 2 clarinets; 2 bassoons; 4 horns; 2 trumpets; timpani; strings.

THE OPUS NUMBER 77 indicates that this is far from the youthful work the D minor piano concerto had been; in fact Brahms was forty-five when he started the first draft. Revisions with the great violinist Joachim's collaboration were to take nearly a year, the composer apparently being quite willing to bow to Joachim's judgement on anything to do with violin technique. A letter accompanying a first copy of the solo part reads: 'Of course you must correct it, not sparing the quality of the composition; if you don't think it's worth orchestrating, say so.'

Another letter of a later date tells us that Brahms revised the work extensively, whether as a result of Joachim's suggestions or not we do not know. 'The middle movements of the work are failures,' Brahms wrote; 'I have written a feeble adagio instead.'

The two rejected movements were later used in the second piano concerto; as for the 'feeble' adagio, one can never be sure how serious Brahms was in the frequently deprecatory remarks he used to make about his music. I tend to think that the more pleased he was with a work the more it amused him to run it down. Although Joachim's first reactions to the manuscript were dubious, he cannot have failed to be impressed with the immense scale of the piece. His first introduction to the concerto was, as I have implied, through the violin part alone; he can have had little idea of the richness and beauty of the orchestral introduction, nor of the profoundly satisfactory solution of the problems of relating violin and orchestra to each other, without too obviously rigging the contest in the soloist's favour. A violin concerto is a notoriously tricky problem for a composer, and it is notable that although each wrote more than one piano concerto, Beethoven, Brahms, Tschaikovsky and Mendelssohn[1] all suffered from once-bitten-twice-shy feelings about violin concertos. The technical reasons for this are fairly obvious; it is a difficult instrument to write really virtuoso music for unless you are a first-class performer yourself,[2] and the problems of balancing one violin against an orchestral background containing thirty or forty more of them are considerable. Brahms's solution to the first problem was to seek the help of Joachim in all matters relating to the technical requirements of the solo part. As to the question of balance, that was a challenge to his skill as a composer, a challenge he met brilliantly—the usual criticisms that it was *against* the violin, that it was impossible and so on notwithstanding.

The work begins with such an air of peaceful serenity that we might be on the threshold of a slow movement rather than one of the grandest movements ever planned for violin and orchestra. Violas, 'cellos and bassoons are soon joined by horns in this essentially pastoral theme, the first of the three which together make up the first subject material.

Ex. 113

[1] I do not include Mendelssohn's concerto in D minor written when 13.

[2] Composers who were violinists themselves, and who consequently had no hesitation in writing more than one violin concerto, include Paganini, Vieuxtemps, Wieniawski, Vivaldi, Mozart and Bach.

The second element, which immediately follows after this, flirts with C major, thinks better of it and then turns the tonality unexpectedly towards D minor.

Ex. 114

The last note of Ex. 114 is also the first note of Ex. 115, for now we meet the third of these three themes. It is of a much tougher fibre with its strong leaping octaves and its typical syncopation.

Ex. 115

Ex. 113 returns in triumph, the impact of the full orchestra seeming to change its character entirely. Brahms chops out four notes from the theme and worries at them like a terrier. Suddenly the music is arrested in full flight by a single note from horn and oboe and we find ourselves translated as if by magic into the world of the second subject; this too consists of three ideas, the first of which contains one ingredient common to all.

Ex. 116

The five notes contained within the square bracket will readily be seen to be the main component of the next example.

Ex. 117

The joining together of these various brief episodes that comprise
the second subject group is marvellously subtle in its craftsmanship. We have seen the link between Exx. 116 and 117. Brahms
now uses the falling fourth in bar 5 of Ex. 117 as a further bridge,
stretching its span by making it into a series of dotted minims (notes
to the value of three beats). From this moment of extreme stillness
there now emerges another important idea, the third of our trio.

Ex. 118

The eye can perhaps spot even more quickly than the ear the
relationship that exists between this theme and its immediate
predecessors. It leads us into a dark and mysterious passage of
haunting beauty; the atmosphere is hushed and still. The spell is
broken abruptly by a fanfare-like theme, imaginatively scored
for strings rather than brass in order not to put the soloist at too
great a disadvantage.

Ex. 119

This breaks off into a tremendously strong figure in semiquavers beneath whose angry tumult there is a somewhat angular
rising phrase, the shape of which has some bearing on the soloist's
now imminent entry.

Ex. 120

The eight examples which it has been necessary to quote in order to be able to explore the orchestral introduction show just how concentrated Brahms's thoughts are. Every one of these is destined to find an important place in the scheme of the movement as a whole, and while the *tutti* has seemed exceptionally rich in material there is not an irrelevant or unnecessary note to be found.

With the most electrifying entry ever devised in a violin concerto, the soloist now flings himself into the fray; the mood is heroic, stormy and yet magisterial. It is not easy to realize that these lightning-flashes stem from the gentle curve of Ex. 113.

Ex. 121

The orchestra fling back their defiance with furious snatches of Ex. 119, the first note of the rhythm being amputated to allow the soloist a clear first beat in each bar (see bar 5 of Ex. 121). Battle is truly joined as it had never been before in a violin concerto. A struggle of such intensity cannot be continued indefinitely, however, and it is not long before an extended passage in rippling arpeggios proclaims an uneasy armistice while solo woodwind play sad distortions of Ex. 113. At last, in a translucent shimmer of sound, this first theme returns, climbing its way down through the orchestral strings; peace is restored, and the way is now clear for the soloist to present us with Ex. 113 once again, clad for the first time in those warm and tender harmonies which have been there by implication since its inception.

A brief and ethereal meditation divides Exx. 113 and 114 from each other in the secondary exposition which now begins. The order of events is, as might be expected, comparable to what happened earlier, but there is not a bar that is the same. The original scoring was so felicitous that it is hard to believe that Brahms could improve on it in any way, yet there is if anything an even greater richness of colouring. Meanwhile the soloist provides not only the most sensuously beautiful decoration at times, but a considerable strength as well. Ex. 115 is flailed by the violin, first with strident chords and then with a hailstorm of semiquavers. Gradually this demonic energy is stilled with a gentler figuration that almost caresses Ex. 116, until the rapt hush of Ex. 117 engenders an absolute calm. A distant mutter of drums, and we are gracefully led towards what might be termed the true second subject. Like Mozart and Beethoven before him, Brahms here delights in reserving the most precious treasure for the soloist. Ushered in by the first curving phrases of Ex. 118 a new melody appears; it is Brahms *par excellence*, most especially in the heart-touching tenths (bars 7 and 8) whose emotional impact on the violin far transcends anything that the piano could do.

Ex.122

This radiant theme appears like a newly opened flower, all the more beautiful in its contrast to the sombre phrases which have previously been associated with the first two bars of Ex. 118. Over an accompaniment of the utmost delicacy, the violin has a long and tender extension of the cross-rhythm that ends Ex. 122. The music turns towards the minor; not to be denied, the sad refrain of Ex. 118 reappears, supported by gaunt double-stopping from the soloist—a marvellously calculated effect.

Our memories of the exposition should now tell us that Ex. 119 is not far away, and sure enough it again cuts violently across the prevailing gloom. Despite its chordal texture it proves to be wholly suitable for the violin[1], as a knowing ear might have guessed even from its orchestral presentation. Ex. 120 is now divided between soloist and orchestra in a passage whose great dramatic force ultimately explodes into an outburst from the full orchestra. First and second violins show those of us who hadn't realized it that Exx. 121 and 113 really were related; trumpets and horns unleash the most savage version of Ex. 119 that we have yet heard; alternations of Exx. 122 and 118 take us through patches of sunshine and cloud. In one of the most intensely romantic phrases in the whole work the violinist takes bar 3 of Ex. 118 and clothes it in black velvet, a dark elegy even by Brahms's standards. Then, with a touch of caprice as the orchestra picks up the thread once again, the violin goes off into a fey little dance, like one of those rather sad fairies in *A Midsummer Night's Dream* who are given the less enjoyable chores at Titania's court. This meltingly beautiful section, which lasts some twenty bars, is suddenly shaken by a series of stabbing trills from the soloist. The effect on the orchestra is immediate; those very pairs of notes which so beguiled us in the preceding section are seized and torn apart. Was there ever a better demonstration of the flexibility of music than this, for the same basic pattern serves equally well to convey an infinite tenderness and a savage pride.

Ex.123

---

[1] It actually appears as Ex. 124.

A massive chord for brass and wind brings us again to Ex. 115 in the orchestra with the solo part striding ruthlessly across the marching octaves in the bass. If ever the violin has been in the position of a dominant conqueror of the orchestra this is the moment; no one who is the least bit sensitive to music could fail to be thrilled by it. Heroism is not a quality one normally associates with the sound of a violin, but the subsequent octaves (based on Ex. 119) have an unquestionably heroic effect. The bow has become a rapier, the orchestra a swarm of adversaries who must be quelled. This section, culminating as it does with a triumphant return of Ex. 113, is the dramatic core of the movement.

The recapitulation is as orthodox as we might expect it to be in the hands of a composer as classically minded as Brahms. We meet a number of old friends again; but there was never a better example of the significance of transposition than this. For many people, transposition is a technical term that describes some rather vague and mystical aspect of music that can surely be no concern of theirs. They know it has something to do with themes appearing in different keys, but little more. Turn back to Ex. 119 though, and having played it in that key, try it in A minor (Ex. 124). Even on the keyboard it sounds strikingly different, and when we hear the two versions on a violin the additional change of colour that comes about by moving to the three lower strings[1] is remarkable.

Ex. 124

* In avoiding unnecessary duplication of examples a misleading impression may have been given. The actual *order* of keys is: (1) D minor in orchestra, (2) A minor on violin, (3) D minor on violin. It is these last two that sound so markedly different.

In due course we arrive at a traditionally placed cadenza. It has already been mentioned (p. 217n.) that this concerto is the last truly

[1] i.e. as in Ex. 119.

great work in which the composer was content to leave the cadenza to the performer; to have done so was the nicest compliment that Brahms could have paid to his friend Joachim. Now it is only too easy for a cadenza to seem, in the classic phrase of the American courts, 'irrelevant, incompetent and immaterial'. In this case it would show an extraordinary insensitivity to the music to produce a cadenza that was nothing but a virtuoso showpiece. Throughout the movement the concentration on the material in hand has been remarkable and there has hardly been a single passage in the solo part that has not been of genuine thematic interest. In the circumstances the masterly cadenza that Joachim provided is less of a feat that it might otherwise have been; all he had to do was to select and rearrange. The one clear lead he had was that it was essential to finish quietly. The re-entry of the orchestra is one of the most sublime moments in the whole work; obviously it must be suitably prepared. It would not surprise me if Brahms had Beethoven's fourth piano concerto in mind here; both works have the same quality of a golden sunset at the aftermath of the cadenza, both allow a last concession to virtuosity in their final bars, blowing up a flurry of notes which dispel the magic of the quiet passage preceding them. In this concerto it is Ex. 113 that has its last tender apotheosis at this point; it climbs higher and higher, attaining a celestial top C sharp before starting a gradual descent. Themes that have almost dissolved in this all-pervading warmth gradually reform into more substantial shapes. The soloist responds to the changing mood, and a brilliant spatter of double-stopped notes brings the movement to an end. Even this is not irrelevant, being a more extrovert form of a phrase that has so far been a gentle counterpoint to Ex. 113.

Brahms originally planned four movements for this concerto, but the two central movements were dropped, the themes thereof being transferred to the B flat piano concerto (see p. 246). He was ever a perfectionist, hating a work to be performed until he was satisfied that everything was just as he wished. In the event, the

slow movement that he finally wrote is as perfect as any in the
repertoire. Only in the thirtieth bar do the orchestral strings make a
discreet entrance; up to then, the music is scored entirely for wind.
It would be absurd to describe this as a welcome relief from string
tone, but the skill with which Brahms varies his tonal palette by
this discipline is worth mentioning. The oboe takes the limelight
in the presentation of this memorable melody. (The two introductory bars have been omitted.)

Ex. 125

Once this tune has run its full course the strings gently remind us
of the two chords with which bassoons and horns had begun the
movement; it is a clue that we should not disregard, for Brahms
now turns back the page, beginning what is in fact an ingenious if
free-sounding variation on the melody just heard. His technique
is a highly sophisticated one, by means of which one bar of the
theme is frequently expanded into two in the variation. It would
be wearisomely pedantic to trace its entire span, but a comparison
of the first few bars should give us sufficient idea of his method.

Ex. 126

Once we have reached the equivalent of the eleventh bar of
Ex. 125, the music starts to change direction, much use being made

of the supporting chromatic figure shown in the example. It settles somewhat uneasily into F sharp minor, at which point the violin introduces a rhapsodic episode whose sole link with past experience lies in its first three notes,  which are presumably related to the second bar of Ex. 125. But while the violin part may seem to trace its elaborately decorative patterns at will, the orchestra become obsessed with a diminutive version of that same chromatic figure that first disturbed the secure world of F major—bar 11, Ex. 125. Over and over again we hear it, now in the strings, now in the wind, conveying to an increasing degree an anguish of spirit to which the soloist responds in ever widening loops and coils of notes. Some tortuous modulations lead us at last back to F major, a return to normality which allows Ex. 125 to reappear in full once again. Over a serenade-like accompaniment from plucked strings, the solo violin produces a glorious extension of the tune.

Ex. 127

poco a poco crescendo      etc.

It is the last flame before the fire dies; the oboe seems to want to begin Ex. 125 once more, but after a mere five notes the music starts a long-drawn-out descent whose nostalgic cadences suggest that sweet sorrow at parting that Shakespeare expressed so touchingly in *Romeo and Juliet*. Bassoons and horns again remind us of the two opening chords; a last word from the soloist, and the movement is ended.

It must be confessed that finales are seldom the best of movements; so often inspiration seems to flag; so often the determination to be gay and brilliant at all costs leads to a loss of quality in the music. In this work Brahms keeps his astonishingly high standard right to the end. The enormous technical difficulties involved frightened most fiddle-players away for many years after the concerto appeared. As always, technique caught up with the demands in the end—so much so that in the late years of his life Brahms had the delight of hearing it played by the twelve-year-old Hubermann.

Having stood in silence for a considerable time at the start of the two previous movements, the violinist is impatient to begin; for once, he has the theme 'from the top' as the orchestral players say. It shows Brahms in that gipsy mood that he so enjoyed.

The orchestra by common consent agree that this is a splendid tune, whereupon the soloist expands it a bit further, indulging in some fearsome exercises in double-stopping as he does so; Brahms's warning against taking the music too fast must have brought solace to many a player here. The theme is taken up again by the full orchestra, who proceed to jazz up the sequence in bars 5-8 in a somewhat disrespectful manner. Sparkling arpeggios from the soloist keep the texture as light as a well-made *soufflé*, until the sudden emergence of a much tougher theme reminds us that this is a concerto and not a rather high-class café piece.

It will be seen that the orchestra enthusiastically turn this phrase upside down as soon as they have cottoned on to it. For some time the music stays in a pretty stormy mood, but it is an exhilarating storm, quite free from the menace that Brahms had conveyed so clearly in the opening pages of the D minor piano concerto.

A return to Ex. 128 leads us, after some discussion, to a fascinating new tune, fascinating in its unexpected time-signature of three-in-a-bar.

Ex. 130

The strings try to cover up this apparent aberration on the soloist's part with urgently whispered reminders of the 'proper' rhythm in $\frac{2}{4}$; but the soloist persists in this wayward disregard of convention. The oboe betrays his colleagues by finding Ex. 130 very much to his liking and it isn't long before there seems to be a general approbation in the orchestra.

A few flashing scales lead us once more to Ex. 129, and the buffetings of the March gale beat about our heads again. A long and triumphant development of Ex. 128 leads us to a brief cadenza which so demoralizes the orchestra that they can only resort to vague mutterings about the start of the original theme. Meantime capricious little arpeggios and trills from the soloist give the music an elusive will-o'-the-wisp character that is curiously unlike our normal conception of Brahms. For quite a while we have the impression that Ex. 128 is on the brink of returning; it is vaguely reminiscent of amateur theatricals at a village hall. We sit awaiting the entrance of a principal character, our expectations clouded by uncertainty as the audible whisperings in the wings fail to produce any visible result.

A change of tempo, a few train-like chuffs from the orchestra and our theme appears at last, clad in hunting-costume astride an uneasily jogging steed.

The joyful ride home begins. Even Ex. 129 becomes positively frivolous under the influence of these infectious rhythms. Only one surprise remains, and that is on the final page. Taking a last leaf from Beethoven's book (see p. 208) Brahms unwinds the music completely just before the last triumphant chords. Fragments of Ex. 131 drift down like autumn leaves, accompanied by a sad chromatic descent in the woodwind. It would be presumptuous to interpret this in other than purely musical terms; it is simply a vision of a very special type of beauty that reminds us that life is more than beer and skittles.

## CHAPTER XIX

# DVOŘÁK

## Violoncello Concerto in B minor, Op. 104 (1894–95)

1. Allegro. 2. Adagio, ma non troppo. 3. Finale: Allegro moderato.

Orchestra: 2 flutes; 2 oboes; 2 clarinets; 2 bassoons; 3 horns; 2 trumpets; 3 trombones; 1 tuba; timpani; strings

IT WAS a strange chain of events that took the son of a village butcher and innkeeper from a remote part of Bohemia to the go-ahead world of New York, but Dvořák was one of the happy band of composers who have achieved success in their own lifetime. Recognition came late, but once it did come he was lionized and fêted in many countries. Perhaps the most striking material proof of this fame was the invitation to become the director of the National Conservatory of Music in New York, a post which Dvořák held for three years from 1892 to 1895. While there he wrote seven works of which this concerto was the last; it was written in almost exactly three months, during which time Dvořák worked on it without pause. On his return to his native Bohemia he made substantial alterations to the finale, as a footnote to the manuscript score tells us: 'I finished the Concerto in New York, but when I returned to Bohemia I changed the end completely as it stands here now. 11th June 1895.' The first performance of the concerto was actually given in London on 19 March 1896, Dvořák having had some disagreement with his fellow-countryman Hanuš Wihan, to whom the work is dedicated. Wihan was a renowned 'cellist and made many suggestions to the composer about technical matters; however, when he proposed the insertion of a large-scale cadenza in the last movement, Dvořák had to insist on having his own way. He stated most emphatically in a letter to the German publisher Simrock that he had not authorized anyone to make any changes.

'I told Wihan straight away when he showed me his cadenza that it was impossible to stick bits on like that,' he wrote (3 October 1895). In spite of the quarrel Wihan's name appears on the title-page as dedicatee, though it was not until some three years later that he actually played it in public.'[1]

The first problem in writing a 'cello concerto is balance, for it is more or less true to say that the lower the pitch of an instrument the less penetrating its tone is likely to be. One piccolo can make its small shrill voice heard above a vast orchestra; but a solo 'cello is hard put to it to stand out from the orchestral mass. The reason for this is due partly to acoustics, and partly to the fact that our ears are not normally attuned to melodic listening in the lower registers. Dvořák solves the problem magnificently in this work; even in a concert-hall, the 'cello is hardly ever over-balanced. If there are weaknesses in the concerto they occur at moments of self-indulgence in which Dvořák perhaps has one 'dying fall' too many; it needs a cold and unsympathetic ear to spot them, however, and in performance one usually surrenders to the warmth and charm which so pervade this delightful score. When Brahms first came across it he said to his friend Hausmann, 'Why on earth didn't I know that one could write a 'cello concerto like this? If only I'd known, I'd have written one years ago.'[2]

The construction of the first movement is on traditional lines to start with, the main themes being clearly stated by the orchestra. The hues at the beginning are sombre, clarinets in their darker register accompanied by soft chords on the lower strings. The theme makes an immediate impression even though it is still only stated quietly.

[1] For some interesting correspondence about this between Dvořák and his publishers see *Music and Letters*, April 1958.

[2] Recounted by Sir Donald Tovey in *Essays on Musical Analysis*, Vol. III (Oxford University Press).

Ex.132

Violins and violas extend this, stretching the third bar in particular and whipping up a fairly dramatic state of tension in a comparatively short space of time. Within twenty-three bars we find the full orchestra taking part with a grandiose version of Ex. 132; Dvořák makes it abundantly clear that this is a theme of some importance. Suddenly the music breaks off into a shimmering descent with typically bird-like trills on the woodwind. As is so often the case, Dvořák suggests a pastoral outdoor world to us; one feels that he must always have composed with the windows open. 'Cellos and basses recall us to a more severely academic mood with a rising scale-passage that sounds far more important than it actually proves to be; a few wisps of Ex. 132 remind us of the first subject. There is a feeling almost of hesitancy as the strings sigh their way through a long sequence of descending fourths, and those of us who have not heard the work before may perhaps look expectantly towards the soloist. Then from the back of the orchestra there emerges a radiantly beautiful tune; this and the slow movement of Tschaikovsky's fifth symphony must be among the most worth-while moments of a horn-player's life, for it is to a solo horn that Dvořák first entrusts this melody:

Ex.133

The utter simplicity of this melodic line shows one of Dvořák's most beguiling assets. As with Schubert, one feels that composition comes so naturally to him that the song in the bath at eight o'clock goes straight on to the manuscript paper at nine; whereas Beethoven or Brahms might mull over the same idea for days before finally committing it to paper. The danger of so uncritical an approach is that it can on occasion lead to moments of banality. There is an example of this very shortly when the whole orchestra rejoins the fray with a rustic and unpolished tune which I suspect may have caused Brahms to raise an eyebrow when he first perused the score. Even Dvořák may have thought better of it, for it never reappears; it is perhaps more of a boisterous welcome for the soloist than anything else, as though the orchestra were to say, 'Here he comes, let's give him a hand.' The noisy greeting dies down, giving way to a hushed chord of B major whose relative brightness is hardly noticed, so darkly is it scored. In a passionate and declamatory style the soloist enters with a dramatic version of Ex. 132. It isn't long before the rhythm of the third bar is condensed,

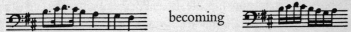

The quickening pulse of the music prompts a brief cadenza from the soloist into which Dvořák interpolates fanfare-like figures that are skilfully scored for woodwind rather than brass so as not to imperil the balance. Some climbing trills, against which flute and clarinet in turn continue to remind us of the important opening theme, lead to a gay and lively idea that might strike the uninitiated ear as something new. In fact it is a variation on Ex. 132, as this comparison plainly reveals; traces of the original pattern are still shown in Ex. 134b.

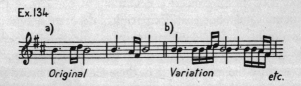

This episode has no counterpart in the orchestral exposition and is a delightful example of that element of fantasy that crops up so often in concertos. For some time the mood of frivolity continues until the 'cellist dramatically recalls the original shape and rhythm of Ex. 132. It is the last gesture of strength before the graceful descent to the second subject (Ex. 133) which the 'cello accepts gratefully, as well it might.

Now an essential aspect of a concerto is the display of virtuosity; there must of course be musical interest as well but a concerto that is just easy isn't really a concerto at all. While it is only too simple to write passages that *are* difficult for the 'cello it is a different matter to write ones that *sound* difficult. To be honest, the instrument lacks the facilities for display that the violin has; the sheer distance that the performer's hand has to cover presents one problem, while a string that is more than twice as long as a violin's cannot be expected to be as responsive in passages that demand rapid articulation. I say this not as a criticism of what is in fact my favourite string instrument, but rather in its defence, lest it should seem to be outshone by its more nimble sister. For instance, at the end of the second subject, Dvořák embarks on a long exploration of a tune whose salient feature is a rocking alternation of two adjacent notes; beneath it, the 'cello supplies a delicate and fluttering accompaniment.

Ex.135

There is a passage that is directly comparable to this in the Tschaikovsky violin concerto, beginning at bar 107 of the first movement. Quiet but sparkling triplets decorate a tune which again is mostly concerned with notes that are next-door neighbours but the difference in sheer brilliance is remarkable and can only be appreciated by the ear rather than the eye. It is in broad singing themes that the 'cello reaps an advantage, for in them its greater size is an asset and not a handicap.

Obviously Dvořák would have been very aware of this sort of problem, and it is interesting to look at the many revisions that he ultimately made to some of the more recalcitrant passages. Here are four different versions of bars 166-167. The first one is unenterprising and conventional and it is no surprise that he wanted to improve on it; the second is more difficult but not all that effective; the third is the suggestion of the 'cellist Wihan. Doubtless it lies well under the fingers, but it is a little turgid in texture. Dvořák's final choice is not only musically more interesting than the other three but is the most lyrical. His decision seems to have been governed then by a consideration of the specific virtues of the 'cello more than by anything else.

Ex. 136

The development proper begins with a longish orchestral section in which Ex. 132 goes through a number of transformations, moving to increasingly remote keys. There are moments of great beauty here, especially when Dvořák first begins to feel his way towards the unexpected tonality of A♭ minor.

Ex. 137

These sighing phrases are interspersed with that same fanfare figure that was mentioned earlier; it is still scored for woodwind, although it is only fair to say that it has also appeared on the horns on a couple of occasions. At last the soloist makes his long-delayed re-entry, this time with a particularly expressive version of Ex. 132, whose note-values are now doubled:

♩. ♫♩                    becomes                    ♩. ♫ | ♩.

This lyrical episode, in which the solo 'cello and the first flute share the melodic interest above a discreetly shimmering accompaniment from the strings, leads to a change of tempo. The music becomes more animated, even though for the most part it remains quiet. For some time the themes lie entirely in the orchestra while the soloist is kept busy with one constantly reiterated figure. Suddenly an increase of tone leads us to a more dramatic passage, and with a great wash of sound the full orchestra overwhelms the soloist with a triumphant version of Ex. 133, now in B major.

It is at this point that Dvořák introduces a remarkable modification of conventional 'sonata' form. What it amounts to is a by-pass in which he finds his way round the normal recapitulation of the first subject group and drives straight on to the second subject. Here is a rudimentary plan of a sonata form movement, with Dvořák's short cut shown in dotted lines.

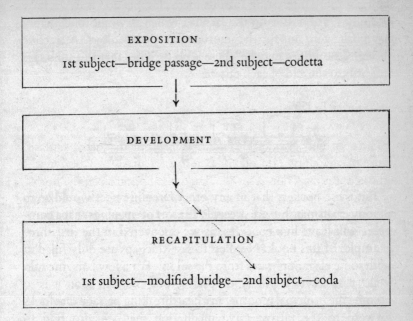

The final peroration is for the most part massively based on Ex. 132, and the movement comes to a magnificent conclusion without recourse to a cadenza.

The slow movement is rich in melodies, having a number of tunes of various shapes and sizes. First to greet our ears is a simple and pastoral affair scored for the woodwind family.

Ex.138

Almost immediately this is echoed quite simply by the soloist. A second phrase now appears and it is a matter of personal taste whether you regard it as a new theme or an extension of the old.

What is more interesting than its mere classification is to see how skilfully Dvořák fills up the lacunae which it would undeniably have if it were not for the intervention of the soloist. Attractive though its outlines may be, there is no denying that this tune sags mightily at the end of each phrase.

Ex.139

But these pockets that in any other circumstances would seem shoddy craftsmanship are precisely the sort of openings that a composer will leave in a concerto, as we discovered in the first three examples of this book. Needless to say, the gaps are duly filled in with some elegant phrases from the soloist. For a few bars, the solo 'cello part serves a purely decorative purpose, but soon it is to become the principal mourner in a heartbreaking passage that looks forward to the introspective meditation that we also find so movingly in the Elgar violoncello concerto. It is a strangely emotional theme to find after so unsophisticated an opening.

Ex.140

The woodwind make a forlorn attempt to remind us of Ex. 138, but Dvořák's imagination has turned to darker things and a dramatic phrase from the full orchestra puts us firmly in G minor. As a foil to this, the soloist offers a sustained melody which is actually an exact quotation from one of Dvořák's four songs, Op. 82. The composer had just heard that his sister-in-law, a charming young actress called Josefina Kounicová, was seriously ill, and with this song he was obviously expressing a nostalgic longing for his homeland. (There is a further quotation from Op. 82 in bars 468–473 of the finale of this concerto.) The movement alternates between the lyrical and the passionate, a series of falling semitones being a particularly beautiful example of musical lamentation. Towards the end there is a fascinating accompanied cadenza in which, within the limitations of his idiom, Dvořák anticipates an idea that we tend nowadays to regard as an invention of Bartók— or perhaps even Messiaen, since it is birds rather than insects that we hear. Above the broad elegiac phrases of the 'cello, a flute warbles like any thrush while bassoons croak like bullfrogs. It is a sudden evocation of the countryside in which we can detect Dvořák's dissatisfaction with the New York setting in which he found himself. As such, it is directly comparable to the second movement of Bartók's third piano concerto which, like this work, was written far from home. The final pages do, however, return to G major and the pastoral mood of the opening.

The finale starts as a march, somewhat *alla* Tschaikovsky. Over the distant tread of 'cellos and basses, the horns present us with a sketch of the main theme, a sketch since it lacks some important details which are kept back for the soloist to reveal. Here is the final version:

Ex. 141

The orchestra confirms this with due ceremony and then we begin a journey that takes us from one melody to another. It would be laborious to list them all here as subsidiary theme A, B, C and so on, since this would merely create complexity where in fact all is crystal clear. The music may not always comply with the proprieties of academic theory, but since it is utterly delightful to listen to why should we worry? Dvořák by now had his honorary

Doctorate (in Philosophy incidentally, but no matter) so he scarcely needed to supply proof of his ability to comply with the conventions. In fact the movement is a perfectly acceptable Rondo; it is merely rather more richly endowed with themes than most. I have counted no less than ten melodies which could be quoted as having some importance, but several of them appear only once and are then discarded.

A change of tempo in the middle of the movement leads to one especially charming episode. As is so often the case in Dvořák's music, the melody seems to be a genuine folk-song.

Ex. 142

But this is soon displaced by a cocky little tune on the flute against which the soloist practises his finger exercises in vain. There are perhaps more passages of sheer virtuosity in this movement than in its two predecessors, but Dvořák's natural fertility of invention ensures that we are never bored. Towards the end the music unwinds into an easy-paced Andante as muted trumpets give out a gentle version of Ex. 141; it evokes a truly romantic atmosphere—the golden glint of an evening sun touching a metal breast plate against a darkly wooded background. Clarinets remind us of the opening theme from the first movement, a recollection which is taken up in turn by a solo horn and then by the first violins. At last, with a great convulsion as though some giant wave were gathering itself to beat against the shore, the music builds to a tremendous climax. We prepare for a noble apotheosis, when 'Let's not take it too seriously', says Dvořák, and mischievously he caps the movement with a delightfully flippant ending.

There had been earlier 'cello concertos than this but nevertheless the Dvořák concerto must be accounted a notable step forward in the genre; it will remain a firm favourite with 'cellists and audiences alike as long as we continue to value emotional intensity, melodic inspiration and rich colouring. These it has in abundance.

## CHAPTER XX

# RACHMANINOFF

## Piano Concerto No. 3 in D minor, Op. 30 (1909)

1. Allegro ma non tanto. 2. Intermezzo: Adagio leading to poco piu mosso. 3. Finale: Alla breve.

Orchestra: 2 flutes; 2 oboes; 2 clarinets; 2 bassoons; 4 horns; 2 trumpets; 3 trombones; 1 tuba; timpani; percussion; strings.

CRITICAL ATTITUDES towards the music of Rachmaninoff are seldom wholly favourable. His music has been variously described as decadent, syrupy, diffuse, or garish; even in the supposedly unprejudiced pages of Grove's Dictionary we find mention of 'artificial and gushing tunes', 'an enormous popular success that is not likely to last', and other equally patronizing remarks. Yet to the despair of the critics, audiences continue to love this music while pianists still enjoy the challenge that it represents. It is so wonderfully written 'on the hands' that it gives an extraordinary physical pleasure to train the fingers to overcome the phenomenal difficulties. The third concerto is often summarily dismissed as a re-hash of the second; there are certainly resemblances of style between the two works, as there are between the first and second concertos of Beethoven for that matter. Both are constructed with an ingenuity that is masterly, and in the development of his material Rachmaninoff shows a far greater technical skill than we would imagine if we were to base our judgement solely on critical opinion. In this chapter I hope to show both the strengths and weaknesses of this work.

Two bars of softly murmuring accompaniment introduce the long first subject, a characteristic melody that is shaped very much as though it were a Russian folk-tune. The accompanying pattern, based as it is on the notes D F E, even suggests the outline of the melody to us before we actually hear it.

Ex.143

It is essential that we should store this in our memory, long though it be, for the first movement is as much a set of variations on this theme as it is an example of normal concerto form. Once the pianist has disclosed the full twenty-four bars of the melody, the orchestra takes it over more or less intact, the soloist meanwhile decorating it with a striking pattern of quick-moving notes that has the purity of a Bach toccata. The writing becomes increasingly complex as, with quickening tempo, notes pour from the keyboard in a seemingly continuous flood. A quiet but important fanfare now catches our attention, first on horn and clarinet, then more clearly on trumpet and oboe.

Ex.144

The orchestra settles into a soft chord of A major, the so-called 'dominant' of D minor, and a brief cadenza at last calls a halt to the rapid flow of notes that has streamed from the piano. In dark tones the 'cellos and basses recall the shape of the first few bars of Ex. 143 before a sudden surge of warm and voluptuous harmony suggests the imminent appearance of the second subject. Rachmaninoff's craftsmanship here is notable. Ex. 144 has planted a rhythmic seed in our minds; the strings now present us with a crisp and precise little march rather than the languorous melody which the preceding bars have prepared us for. Its relationship to Ex. 144 is clear enough.

Within a matter of seconds the dry rhythms of Ex. 145a have been translated into the lyrical expressiveness of Ex. 145b, and what had seemed to be no more than an episode is revealed as the foundation of the true second subject.

If to be original is to forge a style that is instantly recognizable as one's own then Rachmaninoff is an original composer, for no other hand could have penned this next passage. Perhaps it is over-ripe, perhaps to some tastes it may seem altogether too lush, and yet of its romantic type it is a notably successful example. We tend to forget that it was written in 1909 not 1929; World War I had not yet left its mark of toughness and cynicism on the face of European art.

A quickening of pace and a flash of quicksilver from the keyboard bring us to an extension of Ex. 145b that is frequently cut in performance.[1] This dissolves into a few glittering passages that dart around a brief snatch of melody on the clarinet; the music settles down quietly into D minor once again and the development begins. Rachmaninoff first reminds us of Ex. 143; with a touch of real magic he changes one note in the tune—the C sharp in bar 4 becomes a C natural. The resulting modulation into C major is one of those moments that stays in the memory long after a performance, so simple and yet so effective does it prove to be.

[1] I have only once heard a performance of this concerto without any cuts at all (Van Cliburn's).

At first glance most of the material that now appears seems to be new and even irrelevant. In fact it is all closely connected to the first theme. What Rachmaninoff does is to select small fragments, groups of three notes or so, from Ex. 143 and build them into sequences. The following example should make the process easy to follow.

Ex. 146

These two derivations (146 ᵃ and ᵇ) are closely interlocked in a long and fascinating episode before the pianist embarks on a new figure of great complexity. This shows an even more ingenious variant on Ex. 143—which is here transposed into A minor so that the relationship is easier to follow.

Ex. 147

Time after time this pattern unfolds until the music spills over into a great climax of stamping chords which consist of a further extension of Ex. 146ᵇ. A battle royal develops between soloist and orchestra, a battle which resolves itself into a strangely bleak passage in which wisps of counterpoint float above lamenting semitones. Divided strings play some chords that have a curiously gasping effect; the cadenza begins.

This too is a set of skilful variations on Ex. 143. To begin with, the theme is there by implication even although it isn't actually stated; two bars should be enough to show Rachmaninoff's intentions.

This figure persists for some twenty-four bars of brilliantly conceived piano writing; suddenly the pulse of the music changes and a more immediately recognizable variant of Ex. 143 appears, the hands playing alternate pairs of two-note chords that have the curious effect of breaking the tune into fragments. The music builds once more to a climax that gives dramatic evidence of Rachmaninoff's formidable technique, especially in the rapid playing of big chords, until a series of D major arpeggios brings us to one of the most original passages in the whole concerto. The cadenza seemingly continues in silvery ripples of notes that gradually descend into a lower register, but against this harp-like background other instruments gently join in to share the soloist's limelight. Flute, oboe, clarinet and then horn in turn each play a derivative of Ex. 143. In a typically rich cadence the piano part resolves into the key of E flat major and we hear (for the first time in the cadenza) a reference to Ex. 145b.

The cadenza says so much that Rachmaninoff feels no need for any great extension afterwards. The coda is brief and to the point, consisting of a reprise of Ex. 143 followed by no fewer than ten references to Ex. 145a, above which the pianist indulges in some glittering *chinoiserie* that makes an admirable warming-up exercise for aspiring performers. The movement ends as quietly as it had begun.

In the first movement we have encountered some clearly defined musical ideas which have already been developed with great ingenuity. In the remaining two movements we shall meet them again, for the concerto is conceived as one organic whole. Perhaps this is the moment to consider the enigma of Rachmaninoff's music. Why is it that critics tend to adopt so patronizing an attitude towards it? Is it just because by the hazards of their profession they hear too many performances of the piano concertos? In fact there are sound technical reasons for criticizing Rachmaninoff's composition at times; he has a tendency to 'sit down' too often and too obviously in long-drawn-out cadences that are far too self-indulgent. His themes depend overmuch on a step-by-step progress that makes them little more than disguised scales. The texture of the music is often too rich, and any pianist who has worked at this third concerto will say 'Too many notes' with considerable emphasis. One other fault we shall consider in detail in analysing the last movement. Now these criticisms are perfectly valid, but against them we must weigh other equally important considerations. I have already suggested that we tend to be a little confused in our placing of these works historically. Because Rachmaninoff was so dominant and memorable a personality on the concert platform right up to the nineteen-forties we forget that the second concerto was written as long ago as 1901. I suspect that if one took into consideration every composition written between the years 1900 and 1909 it would be impossible to find two major works that have been so frequently performed as the second and third concertos of Rachmaninoff. How then have they survived when a critical ear can so easily discern weaknesses of one kind or another?

There is in most of us a sybaritic streak that revels in soft cushions, luxurious beds, perfume and sweetmeats. The voluptuous, opulent quality of Rachmaninoff's music appeals to this side of our natures. Maybe Czarist Russia was a decadent state, founded on corruption, injustice and cruelty; but for the nobility it was a world in which beauty and sensibility were highly valued, if in a somewhat self-indulgent way. Something of this is reflected in this music, and we may enjoy it in much the same way as we might enjoy a good film about Russia at the turn of the century. The actual construction of the music is often remarkably ingenious, and it is a serious error to dismiss these concertos as mere claptrap. In the long run it comes to a simple matter of taste, by which I mean not that bane of our times, 'Good Taste', but personal preference. The diet may be too rich for some stomachs, but if some of us do not care for peach melba we still have no right to condemn it as a dish. One must accept, however, that Rachmaninoff cannot make a dish that will suit all tables, as Beethoven or Mozart can.

The slow movement begins with a long orchestral introduction that is not by any means the finest page in the concerto—here are those self-same repetitive cadences of which one can legitimately complain. The orchestration is beautiful but the content is too dependent on drooping phrases that get nowhere. But once the piano enters there are some marvellously conceived passages for keyboard; in particular, the conflicting rhythms of three against five, five against eight and so forth, are wonderfully effective in conveying an impression of spontaneity. In due course the pianist reveals the full span of the melody at which the orchestra has been hinting for some time. It begins and ends in D flat major and its adherence to that key is confirmed by no less than six cadences. This again must be counted a weakness in construction, for the ear must tire of being told the same thing over and over again. Yet these cadences are a hallmark of Rachmaninoff's style and we must accept them as such unless we are prepared to lose the good things as well.

The writing for the piano grows increasingly rhapsodic until at one point (again omitted in most performances) the first violins reintroduce Ex. 143 from the first movement. The reason for the cut is tragically obvious when we realize that the root of the harmony here remains firmly on F for eighteen bars; the richness of the decoration that floods from the keyboard cannot disguise the poverty of the bass that underlies it. It was Stanford who used to cover the upper parts of a pupil's composition and expose the bass in all its naked inadequacy, and one cannot help feeling that in this one respect Rachmaninoff might have taken a useful lesson. There follows, as if by some law of natural compensation, one of his finest climaxes; three rising waves of melody in the piano part gather their strength slowly, to break in a great wash of sound in the remote key of D major before a skilful change of harmonic direction brings us back to D flat again and an even more exultant version of the main theme of the movement.

The mood suddenly changes as mercurial triplets dance from the pianist's fingers. A scherzo is ingeniously fitted into the middle of the slow movement. The strings begin a quick waltz accompaniment, while beneath the glittering figuration from the piano, clarinet and bassoon play a delicately syncopated tune.

Ex.149

Closer inspection shows this to be Ex. 143 wearing fancy dress; rhythm and pitch have changed but the contours remain the same.

Ex.150

Play Ex. 150 on the piano and it will sound a somewhat distorted version of the theme from the first movement, for as a further disguise Rachmaninoff has moved the tune up a note in the scale, as though one were to play the National Anthem like this:

Ex.151
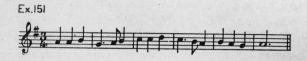

No explanation or analysis can diminish the ingenuity of this passage, which introduces variety by its change of mood and tempo, but which also serves to cement the two movements more firmly together. Rachmaninoff even throws in a few fleeting references to the original form of Ex. 143 in the pianist's left hand just to show willing. They are seldom appreciated by an audience, but they are there for his own satisfaction.

Ex. 152

The fireworks splutter and die, the orchestra resumes the initial mood of the movement. We seem about to embark on a lengthy recapitulation when some abrupt octaves from the piano cut sharply into the prevailing melancholy. With a whoosh and a roar we are launched into the finale.

This begins with a strong rhythmic background in the wood-wind against which the pianist discharges a fanfare-like figure that periodically spills over into handfuls of chromatic notes. After some thirty-eight bars of this, a splendid new theme appears.

Ex. 153

Exciting though this is, it is no more than an interlude; indeed it is difficult to decide precisely what form this movement belongs to, since it is neither a rondo nor a sonata-form movement. A series of themes appears one after the other, each one being destined to return at least once later in the proceedings, sometimes in a rather different guise. Of these two more must be quoted. The first begins with three repeated minim chords before getting under way, but these do not appear in the example.

Ex. 154

The syncopations are heavily underlined by stamping chords in both hands, the left hand giving an athletic character to the phrase by means of some awkward leaps down to the low C which is the harmonic foundation of the whole theme. As a foil to this we find a more lyrical tune which however shares something of the same contour in its rise and fall.

Ex. 155

Climbing ever higher in mounting sequences, this melody has the true Rachmaninoff touch, and despite a plethora of notes in the keyboard part is marvellously scored. A continuation of the urgent syncopations from Ex. 154 lies beneath it, effectively preventing sentiment from getting too much of an upper hand. The opening rhythms return in a brief outburst from the orchestra; the marching phrases grow quieter, and in a rather too obvious cadence the music settles a little ponderously on to the chord of E flat major. We have arrived at an extreme example of Rachmaninoff's ingenuity and ineptitude; seldom can any composer have shown the two characteristics in such equal measure at one time. The ineptitude lies in the orchestral part which stays firmly rooted on an E flat bass for what seems like an eternity—in fact it is virtually thirty-three bars of slow four or six. There are a couple of minor diversions but they quickly return to base. The ingenuity, which I freely confess is much more evident in performance, consists of a fascinating piano part in which Ex. 145$^b$ from the first movement reappears in an enchantingly capricious guise. Ex. 156 shows the two versions side by side, the second one being simplified a little in its notation so that the comparison is clearer.

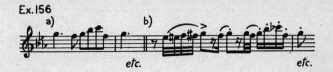

Ex.156

Above the luxurious cushion of harmony provided by the strings, the piano part swoops and darts in little scurries of notes; it is a wonderfully imagined bit of keyboard writing, only spoilt by this regrettable inability to escape from the deadening continuity of E flat that lies beneath. Ex. 156b is developed still further against a background of watery runs of great delicacy before we settle down once more on to a firm cadence of Eb major.

The following section, a more rhapsodic treatment of Ex. 156b, is usually cut since it too finds it difficult to break away from the E flat bass. Suddenly a familiar theme appears as violas and 'cellos reintroduce a brooding version of Ex. 143, the very first theme of the concerto. This kindles nostalgic memories in the pianist, and the expressive second subject (Ex. 145b) duly appears in the welcome tonality of E major, the first significant departure from E flat for a very long time. The music accumulates into an impassioned climax which disintegrates into one last mercurial section of quicksilver writing for the keyboard.

A sort of recapitulation follows in which we meet all the themes of the finale once more. The order of events remains unchanged, though needless to say some details are different. A simpler treatment of Ex. 155 is even more effective; but its lyrical outpouring is suddenly halted by a series of abrupt disjointed phrases that sound remarkably like the noises made by a departing train. These are immensely exciting but seem to be irrelevant. Actually they represent the most cunning join of all from first to third movements, for it is the cadenza which now reappears. A comparison of the following chord sequence with Ex. 148 will prove instructive.

Ex.157

*etc.*

Rachmaninoff gains little credit for so masterly a feat as the average critic is so busy looking down his nose at the tunes that he fails to notice the clever bits. I hope that this essay has given due weight to the composer's virtues while admitting his weaknesses.

The movement ends with an apotheosis of Ex. 154, its syncopations now removed, and the whole arch of melody smoothed out in such a way as to suggest a marriage between it and Ex. 155. A last torrent of octaves and chords causes the audience to give an ovation to the pianist—for this concerto is one of the most formidable challenges in the entire repertoire. Uneven it may be, diffuse and over-full of notes, but its virtues remain evident and its appeal enormous. Not even its most disparaging critic can deny that the imprint of the composer's personality is clear in every bar.

PART 3

# TALKING ABOUT SONATAS

## CHAPTER XXI

# A MATTER OF FORM

THE WORD SONATA embraces so many different types of composition, of such infinitely varied proportions, that it has become virtually meaningless as a definition. There are sonatas for piano, for piano and another instrument (ranging from flute to trombone and including all the members of the string family), sonatas for solo violin, solo cello, for string orchestra, for organ, and even one unique example, by Medtner, for voice and piano. Evolution in music moves at a very much quicker rate than it does in the animal kingdom; the transition from the crab-like trilobite which was the earliest known life-form to the giant dinosaurs took many millions of years. While it might seem discourteous to both composers to pursue the analogy too far, nevertheless, there is nearly as wide a gulf between one of the briefer keyboard sonatas of Scarlatti and the third piano sonata of Brahms; this evolutionary process took a mere century and a quarter. In this short period of time, the sonata emerged as the most important musical form, and rose to a supremacy so total that it became the framework of every large musical structure, whether for orchestra, soloist and orchestra, a small group of players or a single performer. What are symphonies but sonatas for orchestra, what are concertos but sonatas for a soloist and orchestra, what are quartets but sonatas for four instruments? If I equate Brahms' third piano sonata with a dinosaur, it is not entirely irreverent, nor facetious. The dinosaur must have been an awe-inspiring and wonderful creature, and those are both adjectives which I would readily apply to Brahms' magnificent work. But as with the dinosaur, sheer magnitude leads to obsolescence, and while the Brahms piano sonatas are the logical outcome of a line of progression stretching back for over one hundred years, they also mark a point at which composers instinctively realized that a limit had been reached. A few statistics bear me out; if we confine ourselves to keyboard sonatas (which for reasons I shall explain later I have decided to do in this book), Haydn wrote approximately sixty, of which some have been lost, Mozart produced about twenty, Beethoven thirty-two, even if we omit some earlier works, Schubert fifteen, Brahms three, Chopin three (of which one is never played), Schumann three plus several abortive efforts, Liszt two, one of which is really a programme piece based on Dante. In the twentieth century, only Prokofiev has added substantially to the repertoire, the sonatas of Skriabine, Rachmaninoff or Hindemith all having failed to survive the hazards of changing fashions. Where once the young composer, striving to establish his right to be taken seriously, would automatically turn his thoughts to the sonata as a suitable form,[1] nowadays the passport to success lies in thinking up a title with vaguely scientific connotations— Polymers II, Octogram, or Extrapolation would all do nicely.

Unlike Gibbons though, I prefer not to concentrate overmuch on the 'Decline and Fall', but rather to focus my attention on the period when the sonata was the predominant form, whether in the guise of orchestral symphonies, quartets or as a solo work. I lay no great claim to scholarship, nor is this intended to be a scholarly or definitive book; but a brief historical survey would seem to be demanded at this point.

The word Sonata itself simply means a 'sounded piece', as opposed to Cantata, 'a sung piece'. In other words, sonatas began life as instrumental compositions of no determined form. The word first crops up with any regularity in the early seventeenth century, and the one relevant factor that is worth mentioning is that these very early examples did have a tendency to consist of several clearly defined sections of music of varying speeds. As the term became more widely accepted, a division between secular and sacred became apparent; the *sonata da chiesa* or church sonata contained music of a consciously lofty tone; the *sonata da camera* or chamber sonata tended to be more dance-like. It would be dangerous to pursue hereditary principles too far, but in the matter

[1] For example, Brahms, Op. I, Alban Berg, Op. I, Prokofiev, Op. I.

of content and intention, I suppose one could say that Beethoven's Op. 31 No. 3, one of his lightweight sonatas, is descended from the *sonata da camera*, while Op. 110 is certainly a *sonata da chiesa*. But as I have already suggested, the evolutionary process moved at such a pace that it is difficult to trace the sort of consistent thread that would appeal to a logical and scientific mind. If we start with Domenico Scarlatti, which for all practical purposes is a reasonably sensible place to begin, the great majority of the compositions which he called Sonata are single movements, very often limited to one rhythmic or melodic idea, pattern music of enormous vitality and inventiveness, but having no relationship to textbook concepts of sonata form. Indeed, they emphasize how important it is to keep a clear distinction between the Sonata, which is a genre, and Sonata Form, which is a plan. However, there are certain of the Scarlatti sonatas which do contain clearly defined contrasts of theme which it would not be too presumptuous to label first and second subjects. C. P. E. Bach, Haydn and Mozart brought the traditional shape of a sonata form movement into being,[1] while at the same time creating a three-movement pattern, normally conceived as a fairly quick and positive first movement, a lyrical and elaborately decorated slow movement, and a finale which could be a dance movement of some kind such as a jig or minuet, or that multi-decker musical sandwich known as a rondo. The essential difference between this new three-movement plan and the long established Suite lay in the size of the movements and the limitation of their number. A suite might well consist of six or seven different dances, Allemande, Courante, Bourrée, Sarabande, Menuet and Gigue; a sonata tended to be limited to three movements, of which only one might be in a recognizable dance rhythm.

Paradoxically, the next step might be argued to be retrogressive, for it involved adding a fourth movement, which would seem to indicate a hankering after the greater variety offered

---

[1] I am not discounting the previous contributions of Wagenseil, Hasse, Kuhnau, Galuppi and others; the idea was in the air for some time, but it took men of C. P. E. Bach and Haydn's stature to give ultimate authority to an emerging concept.

by the suite. Since it was largely Beethoven who was responsible for this innovation, I am inclined to believe that it was a concession he was prepared to give his audiences in exchange for first movements of tougher intellectual fibre. As early as Op. 2, he was producing first movements of considerable length that demanded concentration of a high order from listener and player alike—this at a time when most music was still exceedingly trivial and listened to with little respect. To throw in an extra dance movement (or scherzo) may well have struck Beethoven as sound psychology at the least. The four-movement sonata set a new fashion, but increasingly, the seriousness of purpose established in the first movement began to spread to the other movements as well. Their entertaining function receded into the past; the slow movement, once a sort of song without words, increasingly became the vehicle for profound, tragic or musico-philosophical thoughts; the scherzo, once a soufflé, was liable to become a storm, and the finale, so often an exuberant delight in the hands of Mozart or Haydn, more and more assumed the manner of an apotheosis. The heroic sonata was born, ironically enough at the very moment that the form began to disintegrate.

The very word 'heroic' has a whiff of romanticism about it, and the comparatively rapid decline of the sonata coincides with the emergence of the Romantic Movement in the second quarter of the nineteenth century. Beethoven's contribution to the development of the sonata was two-fold; he enlarged it and then destroyed it, a statement which I shall elaborate considerably in a later chapter. Innumerable pages have been written in the past by writers determined to prove Beethoven's mastery of the integration of irreconcilable ideas in his late works; it is as though they were apologizing for his eccentricity in thus perversely avoiding the road to academic respectability. The easier explanation seems to have escaped them—that he was not integrating the irreconcilable, but presiding over the *dis*integration of the sonata form. (Hence Benjamin Britten's percipient remark, 'It was Beethoven who started the rot . . .') What were the forms that replaced it? Ballades, Rhapsodies, the Caprice, Intermezzo,

Scherzo (in Chopin's sense) and the unashamedly literary or descriptive piece based on some non-musical inspiration—Night Pieces, Kreisleriana, Fantasy, St. Francis walking on the waters, Apparitions, Legend. In such a climate, the sonata could scarcely be expected to flourish, depending as it did on the calculated balance of phrase against phrase, on the concentrated development of a limited number of ideas, and on a belief in pure musical values. Surrounded as it was by a certain aura, the sonata continued to exist; it was a form to which a composer would pay homage, a guarantee of respectability that was always acceptable to the musical establishment. But with the slow collapse of tonality in music, one of the greatest strengths of sonata form was destroyed; new disciplines took over, and we have now reached a period when few composers are really concerned with a structure that is no longer relevant to the contemporary language, even though in the past, it proved to be the most adaptable and comprehensive form of all time.

Now, while it is perfectly acceptable for a sonata to be descriptive (and many of the early church sonatas were), it is much more likely to be abstract, concerned with purely musical ideas treated in a purely musical way. Much has been written about sonata form, and indeed it is important to have an idea of what it is. My complaint about conventional analysis is that it is so obsessed with anatomy that it takes no account of function. Even the most serious-minded medical student would be unlikely to say to his beloved, 'What a beautiful epidermis you have'. The language of anatomy and the language of love are not the same; nor does it make me love a passage in a Beethoven sonata more to know that a sharpened tonic note is changed enharmonically from D♯ to E♭ thereby becoming the minor third of a C minor triad. Technical jargon gives a feeling of intellectual superiority to its exponent, but it is no guarantee of sensibility.[1]

Essentially, sonata form is the framework for a musical adven-

---

[1] A choice example I came across recently: 'our understanding of the shape of Chopin's E flat Prelude is genuinely widened if we see it not merely as A B A Coda, but as a single amphibrach in which the accent is itself an iambic group'. Is it?

ture; if the journey is cerebral rather than physical it need be no less absorbing. The ensuing chapters might be said to be route-maps, intended to draw your attention to worthwhile landmarks on the way. I had originally meant to introduce a note of variety by exploring sonatas for two instruments as well as those for piano solo; but the piano literature is so vast that it really demanded a volume to itself. Equally, it would pay scant respect to the wealth of wonderful violin sonatas were I to select two or three and shuffle them into a sort of bargain basement at the end of the book. If I did succeed in choosing three violin sonatas, how should I then eliminate those for cello or clarinet? My choice therefore has been made on one ground and one alone, my deep love of the music which we are now equipped to explore.

## CHAPTER XXII

# HAYDN

## Sonata in E♮ Major
## No. 49 in Collected edition, but also known as Op. 66

Composed 1789–90. Published 1791. Dedicated to Marianne
von Genzinger.

1. Allegro (non troppo). 2. Adagio cantabile. 3. Tempo di
Minuetto [*sic*].

CONSIDERING THEIR NUMBER, the Haydn sonatas are still
curiously neglected. One would expect them to be the
happy hunting ground of any reasonably competent amateur
pianist, yet, surprisingly, only two or three of the fifty or so that
are available seem to have found general acceptance. I have
chosen this sonata rather than the 'big' E Flat[1] precisely because
it is the sort of music that tends to be under-estimated. Even
to identify the piece is something of a problem; as well as being
Op. 66 and No. 49, it is No. 3 in the first volume of the Peters
edition edited by Martienssen, as it is in the Hansen (Parlow)
edition. It also certainly exists in various volumes of selected
sonatas, few of which have any great pretensions to authenticity
with regard to matters of phrasing and the like. An unsympathetic
ear could easily dismiss the opening phrases as trite, over-sym-
metrical, and having a singularly unappealing left hand accompaniment that can sound more like grunts than harmony. (We must
remember the enormous difference in weight of tone between
Haydn's instrument and a modern grand piano.)

---

[1] Composed 1798; No. 1 in the Peters edition.

**Ex.1**

The last four notes of the example above show the start of
a phrase that exactly matches the first, except that it is based
on the dominant instead of the tonic. It is easy enough to dismiss this as being altogether too tidy and predictable, but we
must first remember that symmetry was much valued in the
eighteenth century. Haydn spent most of his creative life in
dwellings of the utmost splendour, serving one of the richest
princes in Europe. Wherever he looked, he would have been
aware of the symmetrical balance so favoured by architects
of the time; visual and musical terms even become interchangeable when we speak of the 'harmonious' perfection of a building,
and it is hardly surprising that Haydn subscribed to the commonly
held belief that a sense of order bred spiritual satisfaction. Part
of his genius lies in his skilful exploitation of symmetry, knowing
the exact moment when to foil our expectation by introducing
something unexpected. The true function of this opening phrase
is to say, 'Here is the key of E flat major; kindly remember it,
as it is important that you should realize when I decide to wander
into other keys'. It is a message which is to be found at the start
of nearly every classical sonata. Time after time, we find that the
opening theme of a work is designed to establish a tonal centre;
to take two of the best known examples (not in sonatas admittedly),
the two hammer blows that begin Beethoven's Eroica symphony,
or the torrent of notes that pour from the soloist's fingers at the
start of the Emperor concerto are both ways of saying exactly
the same thing that Haydn states with such elegance in this sonata.
The chords in the Eroica are abrupt and uncompromising; the
opening cadenza of the Emperor is grandiloquent; Haydn's
opening phrase is beautifully poised, unassuming but gracious.

Having made the point, having established the feel of E flat major beyond doubt, he starts the first journey away from 'home' with a phrase that rises, terrace-like, in easy stages.

Ex. 2

The progression is beautifully sustained, leading us in due course to a complete halt on a chord that is clearly destined to bring us to the dominant key of B flat. The stage is set for the appearance of the second subject, and if Haydn had been the sort of person to accept orthodox procedures without question, he would certainly have introduced his second subject here. (The example begins with the 'halt' chord, which is marked with a pause.)

Ex. 3

Since I composed this myself, I must not be too scathing about it. Suffice it to say that Haydn avoids such an obvious plan, preferring to catch us unawares by suddenly reverting to the opening pattern of the sonata—a move that is roughly equivalent to landing on the head of a snake in 'Snakes and Ladders,' and having to go back and start all over again. One would think that this was surprise enough; but having caught us off our guard, he follows up his advantage with another, more subtle surprise. Ex. 4 shows Haydn's double twist, starting from the same point as Ex. 3.

Ex. 4

surprise No. 1,
leading us to expect:

The little descending scale in Ex. 4 may seem unimportant enough; but seen in relation to Ex. 1 it represents a significant new departure. 'Why, what's this?' Haydn seems to say, and turning it upside down, promptly finds a use for it. The apparent irrelevance is transformed into the second subject; the surprise has been justified.

Ex. 5

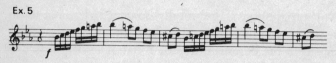

The music chatters along happily enough until our attention is caught by a near-operatic duet between a very deep bass and a very high soprano, both parts being played in turn by the right hand.

Ex. 6

Each 'voice' has the phrase twice, the second version being the more elaborate. A descending sequence of two-note chords flits down the keyboard, only to land on a very unexpected chord indeed.

Ex. 7

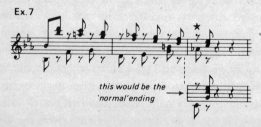

this would be the 'normal' ending →

Composition consists partly of moments of discovery; not everything in a movement is planned from the start, and I strongly suspect that Haydn was led to the chord marked ★ by chance, even though such diversions have now been safely catalogued in harmony textbooks as 'interrupted cadences'. At any rate, the effect of this interruption is remarkable, a stunned and incredulous silence as though the composer was thinking to himself, 'What am I going to do now?' Eight times he repeats the chord, as though questioning its validity, before he sees a way out of the impasse and bursts through to the required destination of B flat major, the dominant key in which the Exposition must properly end. Here, to save space, are the bare bones.

Ex. 8

Safely arrived at the goal of B♭, he wraps it up with a throw-away phrase that seems little more than a convention.

Ex. 9

At this point, the end of the Exposition, the composer would traditionally draw a thick double line across the music, a 'double-bar', and expect the performer to play the whole of the music a second time. It was a way of establishing the importance of the material, and of fixing both the proportions of the movement and the order of events in our minds. If a Development section lies ahead, it is as well that we should have a clear idea of what is likely to be developed, and repetition enables us to have a better chance of storing the music in our memories.

Now I have already suggested that this sonata is a very good example of the sort of music that audiences are all too ready to take for granted. There is a tendency to sit back, listening to what might easily be dismissed as tinkling eighteenth-century piano writing, while secretly we are longing for the time when the soloist will get on to some meatier stuff—a nice lash-up of Liszt perhaps. The whole purpose of this chapter is to show how superficial and misguided such a view is, for once we realize how cleverly Haydn avoids anything trite or predictable, the sonata is revealed as a work of genius. The very opening notes of the development are a striking instance of what I mean.

The normal procedure, to judge by far the greater bulk of sonatas of this period, would be to begin the Development with a reference to Ex. 1, though it would be stated in the dominant key, since that key has now been firmly established. In other words, the betting must heavily favour the supposition that the next notes we are going to hear will be these:

**Ex.10**

The composer might well carry on from here by taking a different turn, but the link with the opening of the sonata will have been established. If by any chance, the composer decides *not* to refer to the opening theme, the next likelihood is that he will choose another idea of established importance, but even this is fairly unusual. I very much doubt though if any listener of Haydn's day, or of any other day for that matter, would have succeeded in guessing what Haydn's decision was to be. Scorning every one of the main themes, he seizes on the most insignificant musical object (subject is altogether too pretentious a word for it); it is Ex. 9, the little tag with which he had rounded off the exposition. This bobtail of a theme is now exposed to the full expertise of a great composer. Time and again he unfolds it, now in the right hand, now in the left, spinning intricate counterpoint with consummate ease.

**Ex.11**

*(a derivation)*

Not only is it marvellously unexpected; it also gives us a completely new texture in the music, quite unlike the sound of anything in the exposition. For half a page, he plays tag with this pattern until at last he tires of the game. Only then does he allow Ex. 1 to re-appear; even so, it is in its secondary form (Ex. 4), and for the first time it is in a minor key. The whole natural momentum of the movement has been disturbed by the inspired interruption that Ex. 11 represents, and quite a storm now builds up, angry scales based on Ex. 5 and modulating into all sorts of unexpected directions. You will remember that I said that the real function of Ex. 1 was to say, 'Here is the key of E♭ major'. I think there is considerable support for this view, when we realize that the entire development section only contains one brief reference to Ex. 1, and that in a somewhat disguised form.

At the heart of the movement is a passage of sheer magic; like Ex. 11, it is a brilliant extension of what at first seems a relatively unimportant idea. Haydn suddenly becomes fascinated by the repeated-note pattern shown at the bottom of Ex. 8 (p. 28). Like a conjurer producing objects out of thin air, up here, down there, from his elbow, from his knee, from the back of his neck, Haydn now culls this fragment from different areas of the keyboard, never predictable, and yet, because of its rhythmical symmetry, perfectly satisfying.

Ex.12

In the process of this game, he gets further and further away from home, until he lands up in the key of G♭ major, one which is fairly far removed from the tonic (E♭), since it is based on a note which beyond all others cancels out the 'major' character of E♭. (The chord of E♭ major consists of the notes E♭, G and B♭; to change this to the minor, one simply alters the G to a G♭. If, in the context of a composition basically in E♭ major, one reinforces the

G♭ by building a solid G♭ harmony on top of it, one has struck a pretty destructive blow against the original tonality.) The way Haydn extricates himself from this situation is delightful; with a series of strong off-beat accents, he elbows his way through a thicket of harmony until he reaches a crisis chord.

**Ex.13**

The music is still in a state of considerable tension; but it is very much on the threshold of C minor, and C minor is the relative minor of E♭ major, our 'home' key. It is a simple matter for Haydn to change the B♮ in the last harmony of the previous example to a B♭, and having done so, the way home is clear. (See the first part of Ex. 14.)

Now a less inspired composer, assuming he had got this far, would probably have been quite content to plunge straight back into the Recapitulation; as Ex. 14 shows, it's a perfectly satisfactory move.

**Ex.14**

etc. as in Ex. 1

It is precisely at such moments that a composer of genius proves his superiority. Realizing the inherent danger of too much symmetry, Haydn now disrupts the entire rhythmical structure; first he combines the principal elements of Exx. 1 and 12 into the three-beats-in-a-bar pattern that has been observed all the way through the sonata:

The next step is to foreshorten this, compressing it into units of two beats:

then, and this really is a master-stroke, he eliminates the beat entirely, extending the music into a long ribbon of notes that is intended to be played with complete freedom.

Now any music student will be able to label this passage accurately as a *cadenza*; but unless one appreciates its function, one might just as well call it a kidney or an umbrella. By destroying all rhythmic symmetry in this way, Haydn has created a feeling of 'dis'-order; consequently, when he now does embark on his recapitulation, we have a wonderful sense of things falling back into their rightful place. A monarch cannot be restored to the throne unless he has first been deposed, and the skirmish of Ex. 17 serves to give us the greater reassurance that all's right with the world once Ex. 1 takes over again.

The recapitulation is an admirable demonstration of how many subtle and significant changes a composer can make, while appearing to carry on much as before. The 'terrace' phrase (Ex. 2), is considerably extended and modulates through several new keys; all the business of the 'halt' and the misleading return to Ex. 1 is jettisoned; as for the operatic duet, only one phrase from the soprano remains—the bass has apparently gone to try his luck elsewhere. There is a similar interruption to the one in Ex. 7, but it is followed by a delightful example of Haydn's humour when he makes the pianist seem to be afflicted with a nasty rash of wrong notes, as though, like one of my earliest piano teachers, he was playing the piano with gloves on. The entire procedure of Ex. 8 is followed out, and the movement seems all set to finish tidily and neatly with a repeat of Ex. 9. There follows the most beguiling section of all. Technically known as a coda, it gives a touch of humanity to the movement that I find irresistible. Like a small boy searching for any excuse to put off the evil moment of going upstairs to bed, Haydn takes Ex. 9 and seems to say, 'You wouldn't mind me playing this just once more, would you?'. He spins it out a little, coming to rest on this chord,

which ensures that he has got us hooked. He then tries the 'terrace' phrase in the left hand (for the first time), builds up to quite a climax, breaks off into a silence, and then seems about to settle for a quiet ending. But no. Once again, Ex. 9 begs for another chance, and again—and again—until, having teased us almost beyond bearing, Haydn seems to pull the pianist away from the keyboard by brute force, overshooting the mark by a couple of notes as he does so.

Ex. 18

What an ending to a movement that is packed with invention, despite its seemingly conventional facade.

I have spent a long time analysing this first movement as there is so much to be learned from it; by comparison to the language of Chopin or Liszt, Haydn employs a very limited musical vocabulary; his structures seem at first glance to be conventional to the

point of artifice; yet, as I have tried to show, he reveals extraordinary skill in avoiding the obvious, and his use of form is far more
often a means of taking us by surprise than allowing us to predict
what is going to happen next.

The slow movement is one of the most elaborate that he ever
wrote for solo keyboard, a piece that shows an intensely romantic
side to his nature that he is seldom credited with. The many embellishments may at first seem no more than pretty gestures; but while
they are integral to the style, they cannot conceal the depth of
feeling that lies beneath. Passages like this resemble Mozart at his
most tragic;

Ex. 19

In terms of the vocabulary of the eighteenth century this is
pregnant with emotion—the rarely used key of B♭ minor, the
broken phrases full of catches in the breath that are near to tears,
the throbbing accompaniment, the constant use of harmonic
tension, every bar beginning with a dissonance. As to the middle
section of the movement, it is even more remarkable. Too lengthy
to quote here, it employs the most extreme resources Haydn
could devise, the hands crossed and using the entire span of his
keyboard, modulations into 'extreme' keys, and the passionate
reiteration of one phrase that he piles ever higher, continually

increasing the harmonic tension beneath. The final gesture is a leap of five octaves, from the topmost note of the piano as it was in his day to the very lowest. In performance, I like to play these two consecutive notes with the same hand, so as to emphasize the enormous gulf between them. Something of its effect on a contemporary audience can still be felt if we play first the top and then the bottom note of a modern piano. It seems an awfully long way!

Even more elaborate versions of the opening material follow; but the decorations seem always designed to enhance the expressive qualities of the music. One strange event is worth mentioning; towards the end of the movement there are two sudden loud chords which pianists often find difficult to make convincing.

Ex. 20

Once again I draw attention to the danger of assuming that labelling a musical event necessarily means understanding it. The chord at the beginning of the second bar of this example is certainly an interrupted cadence, since the 'expected' chord is B♭ major, and Haydn denies this expectation by giving us G minor instead. But what interests me is not the event, but its repercussions. Just as the interruption at the end of Ex. 7 caused a long silence, and then an eightfold repetition of the chord—either incredulous, confirming, or a bit of both—so now the interruption causes a strong reaction. It is a reaction that can be interpreted in several ways. The unthinking player just accepts that Haydn asked that the two following chords should be played loud, plays them loud, and leaves it at that. I prefer one of two explanations. Either Haydn is saying to himself, 'I must resist the temptation to digress again, pull myself together, and stay in B♭ until the end,' which means that one plays the chords as a sort of corrective; or—and this

is a rather more fanciful explanation which appeals to me—
the music *itself* is reacting on Haydn's subconscious against the
violence done to its natural inclinations. It is difficult to explain,
but every composer will know what I mean when I say that
music is capable of assuming a certain power of its own, much as
the characters in a novel may develop personal traits that were no
part of the author's original intention. The composer may create
the idea in the first place, but once created, it works back on his
imagination, even to the point of making positive demands.
A cadence is the most rudimentary example of this. If I play this

chord, or commit it to paper, 🎼 I have created a situation

which demands to be satisfied. It is not I who makes the demand,
but the music itself. I have merely put four circles onto a framework of five lines, and experience has taught me that they are
symbols for a particular sound. If I move the symbols around to

this position, 🎼 I satisfy the demand. But if this second chord

is the one I begin with, there is no demand; the chord is satisfied
to exist in its own right.

The first chord is a bit like saying, 'I killed the ——', and
breaking off. It is not a group of words that can readily be left
incomplete. 'I killed him' may not be an everyday statement,
but it does not create the same demand of 'what' or 'who' that
the first phrase does.

Now once it is accepted that music has this power to create
its own demands, my interpretation of the two chords in Ex. 20
becomes less fanciful. It is as though the music itself is saying to
Haydn, 'Why did you do that to me? Why did you stop me from
going to the B♭ chord I wanted to reach?' A sceptic will laugh at
this, saying that it was Haydn's decision to interrupt the cadence,
and that he needn't have done it. I grant that the interruption was
the work of the mind, a conscious act on Haydn's part. My contention is that deep in the subconscious, where the creative springs
have their source, there was a reaction which then led to another
conscious decision on Haydn's part whose motive he probably

didn't realize, the decision to have a silence followed by two loud chords. This would mean that the performer should interpret them as protest chords, protests against the violation of a natural law. As if to confirm this view, there is another interrupted cadence nine bars later; it too is followed by a silence, and then a sudden loud chord which shows the way back to B♮ major.

The third movement of the sonata is a Minuet, though of a rather capricious kind. It is full of delightfully personal touches of craftsmanship, small things for the most part, but none the less significant for that, since in their sum they make for quality. There is one intriguing episode in E♭ minor which anticipates almost exactly the famous modulation that has caused audiences such untold joy in Beethoven's Seventh Symphony.

Ex. 21

If we transpose Haydn's music into A minor it will make the similarity easier to realize. Ex. 22 shows Haydn's melodic line in the right hand, and Beethoven's bare bones lying beneath.

Ex. 22

The link can only be one of pure coincidence, but a comparison of the two treatments of a similar harmonic scheme makes a nice study in the changing language of music.

I have stayed with Haydn long enough; let us move on to Mozart, to whose father Haydn once said, 'I declare to you on my honour that I consider your son the greatest composer I have ever heard; he has taste, and possesses the most consummate knowledge of the art of composition'. Something of that art we shall see in the course of the next chapter.

## CHAPTER XXIII

# MOZART
## Sonata in C Minor K.457

Normally coupled with the Fantasia in the same key, K.475, although the sonata was completed on 14 October 1784, while the Fantasia was finished on 20 May of the following year. The two works were published together with Mozart's sanction, and dedicated to his pupil, Therese von Trattner, the second wife of a publisher and printer. It was designated as Op. XI, which must rank as one of the most misleading pieces of information ever committed to print.

1. Allegro. 2. Adagio. 3. Allegro assai, though the first edition gives Molto allegro, agitato.

IT WOULD be less surprising if the gap of five years that separates this sonata from the one we have just been exploring were slanted in the other direction, for the Mozart sonata seems to stand so much nearer to Beethoven in spirit and in its sheer physical demands. For all its many delights, the Haydn must count as essentially a lightweight composition, even when one takes the remarkable slow movement into account. With this sonata by Mozart we move onto a different plane; all three movements show Mozart at the very height of his powers, strong, turbulent, bold, inventive, tender, lyrical, impassioned—not the sort of adjectives that anyone with only a superficial regard for Mozart would readily associate with him. We know from his recital programmes that Beethoven played this work; indeed, as we shall see, the slow movement of Beethoven's Pathétique sonata contains a phrase so close to Mozart that it could well be a direct crib. (Not necessarily culpable in those days; such borrowings were often regarded as a compliment, and Mozart himself took phrases from other composers on several occasions.) 'Beethovenisme d'avant la lettre' was one critical verdict on this sonata, and more than any other Mozart sonata it seems to lead us directly to the world of Beethoven.

The key of C minor is a warning sign; it was a key Mozart reserved for works of special pathos and tragedy, works which reveal the inner despair that the conventions of a society notable for a pose of insincerity forced him to conceal from all save his most intimate friends. For what it says, the first movement is strangely brief, with an ending so suppressed that it is almost as if Mozart had put a hand over his mouth to stop himself from saying too much. Perhaps it was for this reason that he subsequently added as prelude the marvellous 'Fantaisie',[1] a work packed with emotions so powerful and varied that they run the risk of overshadowing the sonata itself.

On the face of it, two sonatas from the same historical period could scarcely begin more differently than the Haydn E flat that we have just been examining and this severe but passionate work. Yet it is worth saying that from a structural point of view, both sonatas begin with identical opening gambits. The message, 'Here is the key of . . .' remains the same, however different the terms in which it is expressed. Where Haydn is elegant and almost casual, Mozart is alternately severe and poignant. But the balance of tonic and dominant harmony—those words again!— remains the same.

Fig. 1

[1] See preliminary note at head of chapter.

The bone structure is the same, but it is the outer flesh that changes the expression; on Mozart's musical 'face' we see the ravages of despair.

Ex. 23

To be strictly accurate, the chords in bars 4 and 7 are not pure dominant harmony; but by implication, the root of the harmony is dominant, and what has happened is that the chord has been twisted out of true by emotional stress. Smugly to label it a diminished seventh, which is its academic name, takes altogether too isolated a view. Mozart's use of the musical vocabulary is so subtle that he can make a single note sound like a dissonance.

In a bar like this for instance, one 'hears' the chord of E♭ against the first note of the melody, even though he is not so crude as to state it bluntly:

So here, in Ex. 23 bar 4, the *implied* harmony is almost Wagnerian

in its intensity.

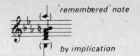

Similarly, the true anguish in bars such as those marked with
a ⌐────────┐ can best be shown to our dissonance-hardened ears
by taking out the ties; with the resistance offered by the G in the
bass, the effect is extraordinary.

Ex. 24

It is easy enough to dismiss these as 'suspensions'; my concern
is for the listener to sense and share the pain that caused Mozart
to write them.

He continues, keeping the same tension for several more
bars; then, stark and unsupported, the opening phrase of Ex. 23
returns, stripped of its darker resonance before being plunged
once more into the bass, this time against an angry torrent in the
right hand. A new tune appears in the relative major key of E♭;
although outwardly calmer, it still betrays an inner agitation as
surely as one of Mozart's operatic heroines caught in a compro-
mising situation. At last, her fluttering heart is stilled, and the
true second subject appears,[1] as operatic in lay-out as the duet we
encountered in Haydn's first movement (see Ex. 6). The human
voice was seldom far from Mozart's inner ear, and the essentially
vocal nature of this passage is only surprising because of the
extremely pianistic style of the rest of the movement.

Ex. 25

[1] Because the dominant of a minor key lacks conviction as a true major, the second
subject of a movement in a minor key is normally in the relative major.

The phrasing is revealing here, with the last two notes in bars 1 and 5 specifically *not* marked with a slur; our 'soprano' is still a little disturbed, while the 'baritone' is all smoothness. Just as it seems that Mozart has forgotten all care in the excitement of writing an imaginary operatic ensemble, there is a violent interruption. Thunderous triplets in F minor tax the resources of Mozart's fortepiano to the limit. The former agitation returns, intensified by another vocal trick, short three-note phrases that seem to gasp for air.

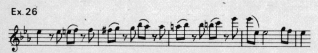

This agitation is sustained right to the end of the exposition, in whose final bars we find something that is interesting for two reasons. The opening phrase of Ex. 23 is made to overlap itself:

but if we forget about shapes for a moment, and think about performance, we find a subtle detail that shows how punctilious Mozart could be. In the second bar of Ex. 27, it is unthinkable that the rising octaves in the left hand should suddenly be emasculated on the last beat; yet Mozart has written *p*. That this only refers to the right hand is confirmed a couple of bars later, when he gives a further indication of *p* in the left hand. With the much wider range of tone we have become accustomed to on a modern piano, these directions are difficult to observe convincingly; but at least we should be able to accept that Mozart could contemplate the simultaneous projection of two contrary emotions, the strong, heroic octaves, and their frail antithesis. Such a conflict truly bears the hallmark of romanticism.

The development is short and concentrated, preoccupied almost entirely with one idea. The transposition of the opening phrase into the major, as shown at the end of Ex. 27, might suggest a more optimistic turn of events. But this is no true C major, however bravely it may set out. In a flash, Mozart reveals an alternative interpretation of the notes, treating them rather as the dominant of F minor, into whose turbulence he now plunges. We hear just a passing snatch of the theme that had preceded the second subject, and then the storm breaks. Six times, the strong opening phrase beats its way through raging triplet figuration,[1] until at last it cracks. The last two notes break away, and drift down into the abyss.

Ex. 28

In performance, it is essential to isolate the pairs of notes in bars 3 and 4 from the following chords in the left hand. Nothing is more likely to diminish the dramatic pathos of this inspired moment than to hear suggestions of a gavotte.

Ex. 29

Mozart's phrase is no dance; it is the disintegration of a noble idea, the classic hero come to grief, and nobody who understands what is happening can fail to be moved.

At the start of the recapitulation which follows the pause at the end of Ex. 28, we would do well to remember a profound truth about sonata form that is seldom mentioned. Though the notes we now hear are identical with the opening phrase (Ex. 23), our frame of mind is very different. Our emotions have been mightily played upon; we have been purged, and finally cast down. Therefore when we hear these notes again, they acquire a new heroism, the girding-up of the loins after defeat, the deter-

[1] Also, see Ex. 116.

mination to prevail. Properly presented, there should be no sense of
*déjà vu* (or *déjà entendu*), for we are hearing this phrase as we have
never heard it before.

Like all great composers, Mozart still has a fair number of new
developments in store for us in his recapitulation. He finds a more
complex way of interlocking the first phrase than the one revealed
in Ex. 27, and then introduces a completely new theme, one of the
most perfect moments of the entire movement, for in such a context we hardly expect to find anything so tender.

Ex. 30

But, as that last chord shows, we are not let off the rack for
long, and when the second subject reappears, it is in the minor,
with all the emotional change that that implies. The music continues on its tormented way, though again, moments of tenderness are interpolated in unexpected places. The greatest surprise
is still to come, the coda, in which, after the most forbiddingly
austere presentation of the opening phrase of Ex. 23, Mozart
ends with a striking demonstration of his genius. He takes what in
ordinary hands would be a cliché:

Ex. 31

conventional enough, but Mozart puts a *forte* on the fourth
beat of bars 1, 2, 4 and 5, and on those beats alone. It gives an
extraordinary limping effect; the movement sinks to its death
like a wounded animal, and, with a last gasp, peters out into silence.
In theatrical terms, it is one of the most dramatic 'curtains' Mozart
ever devised.

As with the Haydn sonata of the preceding chapter, we now find an immensely long slow movement, covering the widest range of emotion. Not surprisingly it is in the relative major key of E♭; one of the most valuable things about classical key relationships is their long-term effect. In the exposition of the first movement, the only moments of release from tension were when the music moved into E♭, though the emotional force of the movement was such that these passages were seldom left undisturbed for long. Nevertheless, they did hold out the prospect of happier things; when, therefore, the second movement allows us positively to luxuriate in E♭ major, it is as though we have finally reached the promised land.

Ex. 32

Again Mozart's instructions are revealing—the rarely used *sotto voce* (literally 'beneath the voice', or as one might say, 'in hushed tones'), the *f* in bar 2 which is totally free from aggression, but rather has the nobility of horns. The *p* in the second half of bar 2 warns us against taking the first three notes too loud, and emphasizes the delicacy of the embroidery.

In the eighth bar a new theme appears, and again one is struck by the operatic nature of the writing. We could be in the Countess's boudoir in the second act of Figaro and indeed, there are remarkably close parallels between this movement and *Porgi amor*; differences of notation need not blind us to such similarities of expression.

Ex. 33

FIGARO: ACT II., Opening Aria

SONATA: K.457. II bars 8-9

FIGARO: idem.

la - - scia al - men mo - rir

SONATA: bars 11-12

FIGARO: idem. (orchestral part)

8<sup>va</sup> bassa

SONATA: bar 14

The moral to be learned from these resemblances is that the pianist in such a movement must always strive to achieve the expressive nuance of a singer; however elaborate the embellishments may be, they are essentially vocal in character. On the rare occasions when Mozart's thought becomes entirely pianistic, the style of writing makes the change abundantly clear. There are some notable instances of extreme heroic gestures, sweeping scales that certainly could not be sung.

Ex. 34

Yet even this could be achieved in operatic terms. Are not the scales themselves a way of conveying the sort of dominance we might expect from a heroine, eyes ablaze, her arm extended in peremptory command?

Ex. 35

But if it is constructive to compare this movement with Mozart's operatic style, it is equally intriguing to examine the link I have already mentioned between it and Beethoven's Pathétique sonata. The central section of the movement, (bars 24–41), is built upon a new theme of great tenderness and nobility. The key is initially A♭ major, but later, after the dramas of Ex. 34, Mozart moves into the more remote world of G♭ major, giving the theme a new colour. It is the first version however that seems to have planted itself in Beethoven's mind.

Ex.36

*(Notice the subtle imitation of the melody suggested
by the arrowed notes in the L.H.)*

Now this is a work of Mozart's maturity, while the Pathétique
was composed when Beethoven was about twenty-eight—the
exact date is not certain. A note by note comparison of the two
slow movements would need an inordinate number of music
examples in a chapter of this nature, when both works are so
easily obtainable. It is a study worth making though, there
being no doubt that Mozart emerges as much the more powerful
figure. The Pathétique slow movement is a 'song without words'
of extraordinary beauty; admittedly it has tragic overtones,
and one central climax that generates considerable tension.
Starting from essentially the same melodic root, albeit in the
twenty-fourth bar of the movement, Mozart covers a far wider
range of emotion, gives us much more variety of figuration,
modulates with greater freedom, and stretches the whole
resources of the language of his time to a degree that makes
us realize what a wealth of passion lurks behind this elegant
Baroque facade. A movement that had started in serene beauty
erupts into drama, and it is partly because of the considerable
loss of tonal stability during the central section that Mozart
feels the need to take quite a time in re-establishing a feeling of
security at the end. The last few bars are like a lingering farewell;
one senses a feeling of nostalgia, almost, as Mozart echoes Othello's
forlorn cry,

> O now for ever
> Farewell the tranquil mind, farewell content.

The validity of this possibly over-romantic view is confirmed
by the entire third movement which is almost neurotic in its

intensity. There is scarcely a phrase which does not hint at a soul in torment. Mozart at this stage still kept his troubles largely to himself; the success of the operas sustained him, though he was very much aware of the fickleness of public taste. The creative daemon can be a cruel master though, consuming those on whom it battens. He must have known he was burning himself out, and in September 1784, the month before he wrote this sonata, he became seriously ill with rheumatic fever. For four successive days he suffered fearful attacks of colic with violent vomiting. (In the course of another illness, he was blind for nine days, a traumatic experience.) His was a frail body, and the incessant demands he made on it, composing, playing, travelling, must have taken a heavy toll.

Although the final movement begins quietly there are two clear indications of emotional tension—syncopation and dissonance.

Ex.37

The phrase is repeated an octave lower with a new twist to melody and harmony alike; then the control snaps, and the music breaks into an angry protest.

Ex.38

The 'spread' chords in the right hand give an impression of being ripped from the keyboard at this speed, while the octave

* But see note concerning the tempo of this movement on p. 306.

leaps in the bass are far from characteristic. It is about as near to an open expression of rage as Mozart ever allows himself to go, except where he has a text in justification, a Dies Irae perhaps or an operatic quarrel. There is a silence that a courageous performer can hold for an incredibly long time, and then a forlorn little phrase of the utmost pathos. Was the sheer impotence of man against the blows of fate ever more cogently or economically expressed? Again Ex. 38 bursts out in anger, again there is the silence, again the unwilling surrender. There follows a single chord, designed at any rate to drag us out of despair into the more tolerable world of Eb major. But even with the emergence of a new and more lyrical theme the relief is of short duration; it soon becomes distorted by chromaticisms that erode any confidence we might have gained about staying in a major key.

Ex.39

accpt. 8va bassa                                    loco

Every attempt to lessen the tension is frustrated; phrases are chopped into fragments, intervals distorted, quiet passages are violently interrupted by sudden accents, the music covers the entire range of the keyboard. Yet, despite the explosive force of the movement (and explosive is the word used by no less an authority than Einstein), Mozart's instinctive command of classical proportions manages to contain the essentially romantic qualities of the music. The movement is perfectly open to analysis as a textbook example of Rondo form.

Bars 1–45      Principal subject in ternary form.
Bars 46–102    Episode in a related key, though if we are to regard the movement as *Sonata* Rondo-form, bars 46–58 would presumably be the Second Subject, and bars 59–102 the Episode.
Bars 103–141   Repetition of principal subject.
Bars 142–145   Mozart being difficult.

Bars 146–166   New Episode in subdominant, followed by repetition in dominant minor.

Bars 167–220   Transposed version of first Episode, now in tonic minor.

Bars 221–231   Repetition of principal subject.

Bars 232–248   Mozart failing his diploma.

Bars 249–274   Repetition of second and third parts of principal subject.

Bars 275–286   Repetition of part of material of second Episode.

Bars 287–end   Final coda.

I concede that if one cannot think of anything better to do with a piece of music, this is a way of passing the time, although what it has to do with *understanding* is past my comprehension. One could construct a composition of absolutely no value that would fit the same ground-plan to perfection; but would that prove that Mozart's music was valueless? Of course not. Therefore the ground-plan in itself is meaningless unless one understands its function as well.

It is a cage within whose confines Mozart has contained fiery and rebellious ideas; it is a strong cage, reinforced by tradition. Mozart's classical self accepts the cage, admitting its usefulness as a discipline; but his romantic self beats against the bars, crying out to be let free. It was that romantic self that felt the need to write a Fantasia as a prologue to this sonata, a prologue which might be interpreted as an assertion of freedom. Had he managed to escape completely from the bonds of convention, he would have ended *Don Giovanni* with the main protagonist's descent into Hell;[1] as it was, Mozart made a concession to the taste of the time, a taste which, to a certain degree, he was willing to respect, for he acknowledged the classical virtues of order and restraint. It is in a sonata such as this that we can see intimations of the direction Mozart might have taken had he lived another ten years. He died, leaving Prometheus still in chains. It was Beethoven who was to assume the role of Hercules in breaking them apart.

---

[1] As Verdi or Berlioz would certainly have done.

## CHAPTER XXIV

# AN INTRODUCTION TO BEETHOVEN'S PIANO SONATAS

THE THIRTY-TWO piano sonatas of Beethoven are his most significant biography, worth more than all the thousands of pages that have been written about him. In them we see not the events of life outside, as we do in most biographies, but the infinitely more important life within. In the sonatas, written clearly for us all to hear, lie the stages of a great composer's development from youth to maturity, a journey which paradoxically began with the complete confidence of a young man, knowing he had the stuff of genius within, and ended in loneliness, cut off from the world by a barrier of silence, pushing bravely but sometimes gropingly into a new era. Beethoven has been described as a cautious revolutionary, but there is certainly no doubt that he changed the entire course of music. The first and last sonatas seem to belong to different worlds, and I doubt if any other composer in history, apart from Stravinsky, so transformed his own musical language.

Hindsight can be dangerous when it comes to interpretative decisions. The very name of Beethoven is surrounded by such an aura that it is easy for us to read too much into the early works, forcing us to fit them to our preconception of what Beethoven ought to sound like in the light of what we know his ultimate achievement to have been. But used discerningly, hindsight can also be very revealing, and the main purpose of this chapter is to trace links that show how Beethoven was continually enlarging his resources rather than radically changing them. Though his nature may have become more surly as the embittering effect of deafness made itself felt, he still remained the same man. The optimistic hopes of the brilliant youth may have become clouded by disease and poverty; but just as we can detect the style of a painter like Van Gogh from his early imitative studies to his last strange masterpieces, so we can find fascinating intimations of mature Beethoven in some of the most taken-for-granted pages of his youth:

Much as an archaeologist uncovers the various layers that conceal a number of civilizations, so now I want to penetrate Beethoven's subconscious so deeply that we find the very sources of his invention; such an exploration must start at the end, at the top layer so to speak; let us begin then with a phrase which shows Beethoven at the summit of his powers in the longest and most complex of all the sonatas, Op. 106, the Hammerklavier.[1] It begins with a gesture of tremendous force.

Ex.40

The most notable features here are the catapult-like spring of the very first two notes in the left hand, the strength of the rhythm, the silences between the phrases, and lastly, the pairing off of the final two chords of each phrase. In best Sherlock Holmes mood, let me concentrate, my dear Watson, on these last two chords. If I lengthen the first chord in bars 2 and 4, I get this.

Ex.41

Turn back more than twenty years to 1796, and we find Beethoven beginning his sonata in E♭, Op. 7, with this theme.

[1] Despite its rather emotive sound, the word Hammerklavier simply means 'piano'.

Ex.42

Exciting though this is as a sonata, it is still a very formal piece, with the influence of Haydn in particular clearly to be seen. The left hand here is an unadventurous formula, the chords sit down contentedly enough on the first beats, and in common with most young composers, Beethoven likes to keep the music moving along in case we should lose interest.

Let us now turn to Op. 22, which is not only in the same key as the Hammerklavier, but has several other remarkable similarities as we shall discover. Beethoven has already hit on a much more arresting opening rhythm.

Ex.43

If we make a comparatively small alteration to that, changing the little four-note group [♪♪♪♪] to a three-note pattern slanted in the opposite direction, we arrive at this:

Ex.44

Repeat the first note a couple more times, and even Dr Watson at his most imperceptive could see that this is not all that far removed from the opening phrases of the Hammerklavier.

Without bending the evidence too far then, it can be established that these three sonatas, Opp. 7, 22 and 106, are all saying the same thing in their opening bars, even though the musical vocabulary shows substantially more complexity as Beethoven progresses. In Op. 7, the language is essentially conventional and derivative; Op. 22 shows him finding his way to a much greater individuality of expression—the gaps between the phrases, the alert, vital quality of the rhythm, the restraint implied by the instruction *p*, giving an especially arresting character to what might otherwise be a slightly trivial idea. But both these early sonatas are the music of mortals; in the Hammerklavier he is like a god armed with supernatural weapons, and he commands our attention with the authority of a god.

It would be stupid to discount the importance of the actual development of the piano in the evolution of Beethoven's mature style. We still find it hard to accept that the instrument he used as a young man (when it seems that he was a prodigious player) was not far removed from a harpsichord in sheer weight of sound, having about a quarter of the tonal resources of a modern concert grand.[1] Even if as a young composer his vision had contemplated anything so immense in stature as Op. 106, he would never have committed the notes to paper, since they would have merely sounded ineffective and puny on the only pianos that were available. It is a mistake to assume that the sheer size of a work is somehow related to the age of the composer; the stature of Beethoven's earlier sonatas was very much dictated by the limitations of his keyboard. Brahms, as a young man, had the instruments he needed, and his only three piano sonatas, Opp. 1, 2 and 5, are all conceived on a gigantic scale.

Let us return to the Hammerklavier, picking up with the very next phrase.

[1] For a more detailed discussion of this, see Chapter One of *Talking about Concertos*.

**Ex.45**

It makes a smooth contrast to the smash-and-grab effect of the opening bars (Ex. 40); it is clearly melodic, yet not in the least vocal in conception, as the themes that we found in the Haydn or Mozart sonatas were. Yet again, we can find a very similar texture in Op. 22, only a fleeting similarity perhaps, but worth mentioning.

**Ex.46**

The two textures are almost identical, but the thought in the later sonata is so much more varied, and the danger of a mechanical sequence of textbook modulations is avoided.

Now one of the most striking passages in Op. 22 is the second subject, a martial phrase totally lacking in those feminine attributes which are normally regarded as the essential quality of Second Subjects.

**Ex.47**

The unusual thing about this is the consistent use of thirds[1] in both hands; it is a texture you would never find in the keyboard music of Haydn or Mozart. Turn to the Hammerklavier and we

---

[1] A third is a two-note chord (or an interval) whose notes are three semitones apart (minor third) or four semitones apart (major third).

find another instance of the same technique; but where in Op. 22, the two hands march together in parallel, in the later work they go their separate ways, thus adding considerably to the musical interest.

Ex. 48

Beethoven's mature technique no longer allows him to employ the slightly over-simple version of Op. 22; but equally, that simplicity was strong enough for 1799, when it was written.

If this chapter seems to be over-concerned with 'coming events casting their shadow before', it is because the differences between late and early Beethoven are so self-evident that it is a more instructive exercise to pursue the similarities. The enormous changes that he brought about in matters of form have tended to blind us to the remarkable continuity of his language. Certainly it too changed substantially, but whereas his approach to sonata form was ultimately to be destructive (since it ceased to serve any useful purpose), his treatment of what might be termed the basic language of music was to enrich and to extend, but never to destroy. We find similar accompanying figures in works that are twenty years apart; his careful plotting of surprise, his capriciousness of invention, his bluntness, and his ability to think in large paragraphs are constant factors that did not change. Let us pursue the matter a little further.

The exposition of the Hammerklavier ends with three giant steps, struck with all the power the soloist can command.

Ex. 49

Those last two phrases are like dim recollections of the opening theme (Ex. 40), which indeed Beethoven has now left so far behind that we are in danger of forgetting it. They call us back to it like off-stage trumpets, and despite the huge span of the movement the classic convention of repeating the exposition needs to be observed. All the same, one can scarcely imagine a more arresting way of giving the utmost drama to a long-established custom. What does he do the second time round?

Ex.50

(reinforced by L.H. as before)

Here there is a double surprise; first, the striking change from B flat to B natural on the third note; second, the totally unexpected duplication of the three hammer-like blows at a point when we have been conditioned to expect a distant horn-call.

Some eighteen years earlier, Beethoven had written a sonata in D major (Op. 10 No. 3) whose first subject ends with an identical pattern.

Ex.51

There is no doubt that the three rising notes are meant to be every bit as emphatic, nor that their purpose is to catch our attention. But in the earlier sonata, the gesture is largely wasted, leading as it does to a pleasant enough tune whose texture is virtually identical to a multitude of passages in Mozart or Haydn. The exploitation of surprise in the later sonata is typical of Beethoven's maturity; the same three steps now lead us to mystery and suspense.

A comparison of slow movements can be equally revealing. In Op. 22, which really does seem to have been a direct ancestor of several of the later works, we find Beethoven beginning in a fairly conventional mood.

The world of Mozart is not very far away; the accompaniment is a convention of the time, used almost as frequently as the more flexible version Mozart preferred . The tune is elaborately decorated, and even the wide leaps that appear later are frequently found in Mozart's vocal writing. The harmony to begin with is the soul of orthodoxy, although there are admittedly moments in this movement when Beethoven produces chords that anticipate Debussy.

Yet astonishing though these harmonies are, they are 'explained' by their resolution (the subsequent chord), and they are still enclosed within an essentially eighteenth-century fabric. If then we deduce a formula from this music, we can say that it consists of repeated chords in the left hand and a decorated melody in the right. Even as late as Op.110, Beethoven still clung to this some-what pedestrian formula. The difference lies in the expressive power with which he uses it. In the entire piano literature there can be few passages as profound in their expression of grief as this, and yet the 'formula' is identical.

Ex.54

What an infinitely more individual voice speaks to us here. The slight artificiality of utterance is thrown off entirely; instead, we find an expression so intimate and personal that I feel myself an intruder into Beethoven's privacy when I play it.

The pace of change in our own century has been frightening; there are many people still about who were born before man had learned to fly an aeroplane; in the span of a single lifetime, we have progressed from the first clumsy attempts of the Wright brothers to the Apollo missions to the moon. But the nineteenth century was not exactly stagnant. Had Liszt been born two years earlier he would have been a living link between Haydn and Stravinsky[1]—a gulf that seems like centuries. It was Beethoven more than anybody else who brought about a complete change of view as to what music was capable of expressing. The truly 'classical' composer serves music as something greater than himself, much as a priest serves his God; the 'romantic' composer uses music as a form of self-projection, a public expression of personal emotion. Across the span of the thirty-two piano sonatas, we can observe this change of attitude taking place, and it seems likely that Beethoven's deafness may well have accelerated the process. By being driven ever further into himself, deprived of social contact, it was inevitable that he should increasingly regard music as a means of *self*-expression as opposed to mere expression. In doing so, he opened the door to the Romantic Movement; inheriting the mantle of Haydn and Mozart, he not only reworked the fabric, but changed its entire function. The slow movement of Op. 106 contains clear anticipations of the language of Chopin and Brahms, just as surely as the early sonatas are sometimes unashamedly derivative from Beethoven's great predecessors. In a book of this

[1] Haydn died 1809: Liszt 1811–86: Stravinsky 1882–1971.

size, I cannot discuss more than a very few of the sonatas, but I hope that this introduction has done something to demolish the 'Three-period' theory which has had altogether too long a run. It is the sort of neat, cataloguing approach that appeals to tidy minds—first period, up to 1800 when he was still showing some in-debtedness to the past, second period, 1800–15 during which he began to forge a much more personal style, and lastly, the period from 1815 up to his death in 1827 when he moved out into a world of his own. There is some truth in the theory, but like most such generalizations it can lead to misleading conclusions. I prefer the view I have attempted to convey in this brief introduction, a view that shows the course of Beet-hoven's creative life as an inevitable, almost pre-destined journey. It was a search for a language, the right language to express thoughts and emotions that were certainly dormant in him from his middle twenties. The links I have traced between early and late works may reveal differences of technique; but they also show a similarity of purpose. A man may set his heart on Everest while he is still tackling his first few rock-climbs. Beet-hoven first planned to set Schiller's 'Ode to Joy' to music when he was in his early twenties; it took him the experience of writing eight symphonies to discover how to do it to his satisfaction. Whereas Mozart and Haydn, Bach and Handel were able to write with astonishing fluency because the techniques they had learned were entirely suited to their needs, Beethoven found composition a constant struggle. His sketch-books reveal agonies of indecision; how *could* he express such new concepts of music with a language inherited from his forbears? As a young man, Beethoven did not lack technique; he had all the facility one could wish for. But it was a technique that was no use for climbing his particular mountain. The sketch-books are the clearest evidence of his dissatisfaction with an existing language, of his arduous search for something more adequate. The view of his ultimate destination was inevitably obscure, but the journey began sooner than people realize.[1]

[1] For the full understanding of the following chapters I would recommend keeping a copy of the Beethoven sonatas to hand, the least cumbersome being the *Lea Pocket Scores* (P.O. Box 138, New York 32).

## CHAPTER XXV

# BEETHOVEN
## Sonata in E♭ Major Op. 31 No. 3

Composed in 1802. Unusually, there is no dedication. Op. 31 Nos. 1 and 2 were first published in 1803 in an edition called *Répertoire des clavecinistes*. A subsequent edition corrected by Beethoven then appeared, still as *Deux sonates, Op. 31, Édition très correcte*. This was published by Simrock, simultaneously with an edition from Cappi of Vienna, still giving only the first two sonatas, but labelling them Op. 29. This sonata first appeared on its own without an opus number, Edition Nägeli, in 1804. In 1805, Cappi brought out all three sonatas in one volume, though they were still erroneously called Op. 29.

1. Allegro. 2. SCHERZO: Allegretto vivace. 3. MENUETTO: Moderato e grazioso. 4. Presto con fuoco.

THE IMAGE OF Beethoven as a frowning giant wrestling with intractable material is so commonly held that I thought it essential to include at least one sonata that would show him in a good humour. There is a wider choice than one would at first imagine. Rather surprisingly, the really dramatic sonatas are in the minority; individual movements may stand out, but the only sonatas I would classify as essentially 'tigerish' would be Nos. 5, 8, 17, 21, 23, 29 and, *hors de concours*, the first movement of 32. Their impact is such that we tend to forget how often Beethoven shows quite a genial face to the world. I think the reason for this lies partly in his complete avoidance of sentimentality; slow movements may be lyrical, deeply felt, poetic or tragic, but they are never saccharine. He knows exactly when to tauten the harmony by a touch of dissonance, or to dispel with a sudden shock any tendency to drift into a vague reverie.

I have sometimes called this sonata 'The Case of the Missing First Subject'. It is a facetious title, but it serves to draw attention to one of the most characteristic aspects of the sonata, its avoidance of the obvious. Time and again, Beethoven lures us into carefully prepared traps, only to show a schoolboyish glee at having fooled us once more. When one remembers that 1802 was the year of the famous *Heiligenstadt Testament*,[1] it is almost impossible to imagine how a man could drag himself out of such a pit of despair to write music that radiates humour from every page. Perhaps Ries gives us a clue when, describing the onset of Beethoven's deafness, he says, 'When occasionally he seemed to be merry it was generally to the extreme of boisterousness; but this happened seldom'. Beethoven was near to suicide; to quote part of the *Testament*:

> ... but little more and I would have put an end to my life—only art it was that withheld me, ah it seemed impossible to leave the world until I had produced all that I felt called upon to produce, and so I endured this wretched existence—truly wretched, an excitable body which a sudden change can throw from the best into the worst state—Patience—it is said I must now choose for my guide, I have done so, I hope my determination will remain firm to endure it ... [etc.]

The near incoherence of the prose is striking confirmation of Beethoven's extremity of despair. It is at such times that the creative artist is most likely to turn to work for consolation. Human companionship could give him little solace; it only served to remind him of the rapidly encroaching deafness that was to isolate him from society. Op. 31 no. 2, the so-called Tempest sonata, is the music that most accurately reflects the agony of mind revealed in the *Testament*. This third sonata of the set is a marvellous demonstration of the resilience of the human spirit.

The sonata begins with an enigmatic harmony that could be in one of several keys. I have already underlined the importance of tonality in the whole concept of sonata form. Of the

---

[1] A historic document in which Beethoven expressed his despair at growing deaf and losing contact with humanity.

thirty-two piano sonatas, twenty-nine begin with themes that
define the home key unmistakably within the first two or three
bars. The first sonata to be even a mite ambiguous is No. 15, the
Pastoral in D, whose first three bars are a trap, designed to make us
imagine that the piece is in G—something like this perhaps:

Ex.55

but as soon as a C♯ appears in the fifth bar, Beethoven shows us
that he has been bluffing; the mild ambiguity is a refreshing
change from the normal clear definition of a tonal centre.

Now, three sonatas later, Beethoven makes much more conscious play with the idea of keeping us guessing. The opening
harmony of the sonata is in no key at all. The Germans call this
work *Die Frage*, or 'the Question', and the first notes certainly have
an interrogatory flavour.

Ex.56

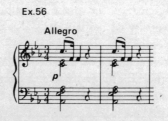

Even the repetition of the phrase suggests an air of disbelief,
as though Beethoven had found his hands playing the chord by
chance and then asked himself if he really meant it. When I stated
that this was in no key at all, it might seem a rather lunatic assertion;
but the fact is that this is the sort of transitional harmony that could
lead in several directions. For instance,

Ex.57

which would lead us into quite a serious movement in C minor. On the other hand we could treat the first bar as the beginning of a sequence, almost playful in nature, leading to something lyrical and charming.

Ex.58

This gives us the possibility of a gentle, undemanding sonata in B♭ major.

Beethoven, having proffered an enigma, soon clarifies it, removing all doubts as to the tonality of the piece. Indubitably and emphatically, the fourth bar of Ex. 59 establishes the key of E♭ major.

Ex.59

Having sat down so firmly in the fourth bar of Ex. 59 (actually bar 6 of the sonata), there is something very beguiling about the way the following bar seems to say, 'Now we can relax; we know where we are'. We have had a brief introduction; our location has been established; now, surely, we have every right to expect a nice, clearly identifiable First Subject.

Ex. 60

A splendid solution of impeccable orthodoxy—which is presumably why Beethoven rejected it. Instead, he goes wandering off into a vague little ascending scale, has another couple of bites at Ex. 56 (one of them with 'this week's deliberate mistake' inserted), states Ex. 59 even more firmly, and once again settles down with a sigh of relief onto the tonic chord of E♭. It's like the sort of scene one might find in *Alice in Wonderland*, a scene in which the heroine finds a mysterious little door (bar 1), taps on it gently (bar 2), laboriously pushes it open (bars 3–6) and goes through into a little courtyard marked E flat (bar 7). She climbs a staircase out of the courtyard (bars 8–9) and at the top of the stairs finds a mysterious little door (bar 10), taps on it (bar 11), pushes it open (bars 12–15) only to find herself in another identical courtyard marked E flat (bar 16). Needless to say, I am not suggesting for one moment that Beethoven is actually describing any such events; but there is a parallel in the way he 'discovers' E♭ major twice, and each time by the same rather curious route.

The well-informed listener sits back, confident that now, at least, a recognizable First Subject will emerge. What happens? Some casual flicks of a duster across the keyboard, mere snippets of phrases—related it is true to Ex. 56, but scarcely having enough substance to be regarded as a theme at all.

Ex. 61

If this sonata can be said to have a first subject in the textbook sense of the word, that is it, in its entirety. Everything that precedes Ex. 61 is unquestionably an introduction, and what now follows is equally clearly a Bridge Passage. I defy even Perry Mason to detect so much as another bar of first subject, hence my facetious title.

The bridge passage behaves with complete predictability. It *sounds* like a bridge passage, chattering on like a professor giving a breathless definition of the difference between a scale and a broken chord.

Ex.62

Bridge passages are destined to take us from the tonic to the dominant, and this one does so in exemplary fashion. At last, we feel we have something we can hang on to, something that seems to be behaving as it should. It is precisely at such moments that Beethoven is most likely to catch us off our guard. At the very instant we are confident that the second subject is going to emerge, he plunges us back to square one. No wonder there is an air of depression about the place.

Ex.63

Now this sort of thing is really upsetting; here is Beethoven, apparently getting all soulful ('not a dry eye in the house' by the end of the phrase), and then suddenly, thump, bang, crash, thud, four nasty shocks, each specifically marked with an individual $f$ in case the pianist should attempt to soften the blow.

If one is sufficiently determined to force Beethoven into his popular role of Titan, it is possible to take all this quite seriously, to shed tears during the middle of Ex. 63 and then interpret those four rude blows as a cry of protest against destiny or something equally inspiring. That I reject such an interpretation is not due to any inherent frivolity on my part, but to my firm conviction that all the evidence goes against it. So surprising a gesture cannot be taken out of context; we have seen what happened before; the more important question is what happens after.

All sweetness and light, Beethoven suddenly produces an enchanting second subject, a tune that must certainly be classed as one of the happiest he ever wrote. 'It's all right, I didn't mean to hurt you', he seems to be saying, and smiles so charmingly that we forgive the box on the ears he has just given us.

Ex.64

We need to make a cut to the recapitulation for confirmation of my view. It begins exactly as before, the same repetition of the ♪♪♪ figure, the same embellishment of E♭, the same relaxation followed by the little rising scale, the same duplication of each stage. There is a tiny change of detail in the repetition of Ex. 61, but otherwise everything is identical. The bridge passage (Ex. 62), sets out on the same journey, even appearing to modulate into the dominant. Then comes the stroke of genius.

Ex.65

The whole of Ex. 63 is thrown away—no sad return to square one, no expressive tears, no poignant harmony. Only the irrelevance is preserved, the thumps that had so rudely interrupted our sympathetic response. But their function is now to be like stepping stones that carry us triumphantly to the second subject; what had seemed so out of place is now seen to be very much *in* place, and Beethoven can say with a wink, 'I knew all along I'd find a use for these'. I just cannot accept that had the expressive phrases of Ex. 63 really been intended to be as profound as they at first appear, Beethoven would have been content to eliminate them entirely, not only here but from the rest of the movement as well.

This inevitable diversion has interrupted the continuity of our exploration of the moment, but it is often necessary to glance across several pages before we can understand the whys and wherefores. Let us return to the exposition, where the genial nature of the music seems to me to be amply confirmed by a number of signs of what the immortal W. S. Gilbert would have called 'innocent merriment'. There is a little scale passage of sorts, in which the pianist is expected to cram far too many notes into a bar for comfort, there is a second version of Ex. 64 that seems positively to chuckle, and some mock-angry trills that dissolve into a fountain-like arpeggio that could well have the traditional ping-pong ball bobbing on top of it, waiting to be shot down by an expert marksman. Just near the end of the exposition, Beethoven makes fun of the conventional trill that so often brings the orchestra in at the conclusion of the cadenza in a concerto. The pianist has a couple of tries at establishing a dominant seventh, makes a boss-shot in the left hand (x), puts it right, and flushed with triumph, at last manages to arrive at the long-delayed B♭.

Ex.66

The development begins with Ex. 56 unaltered. One could almost say that the fact that there is no surprise is a surprise in itself. Beethoven then takes the chord progression of Ex. 59, thickens its texture, and moves it outwards with an air of menace towards C minor. By way of experiment, I am now going to effect a marriage between this sonata and the seventh symphony. There is one passage in the symphony notable for an almost overpowering intensity, an effect that is unforgettable in its starkness. It comes in the last movement.

Ex. 67

Now this idea is merely an inversion of the opening figure of this sonata; but here it is treated with genuine ferocity. Let us transplant something of the kind into the context of the sonata.

Ex. 68

My reason for combining elements from these two very different works is to establish a difference of emotional intensity. Without further comment let us see what Beethoven actually did in the sonata.

Ex.69

I tread on dangerous ground here, so let me underline that my conclusions are designed not to diminish Beethoven's stature, but to make him altogether more lovable. One does not have to be ultra-perceptive to realize that the last four bars of Ex. 69 represent a sort of disintegration; the disruption of the rhythm, the almost random appearances of the ♩♪♪ figure in different areas of the keyboard are both signs of deliberate chaos. The problem is to decide just how seriously it should be taken. I cannot believe that if Beethoven had wished to inspire genuine awe, he would not have used larger resources, similar to the ones I have suggested in Ex. 68. Disintegration there may be, but I believe it is nearer to the classic domestic defence of 'It came to pieces in me 'ands!' than to the splitting of the atom. Looked at as bucolic humour it makes sense, and is entirely characteristic of known aspects of Beethoven's behaviour. Treat it as a serious crisis, and it sadly lacks resource.

The twinkle in the eye as Beethoven immediately restores Ex. 61 (this time in F major), would seem to support my view. He may have knocked the music about a bit, as he did at the end of Ex. 63, but once again the aftermath reveals that it was all in good fun. In the coda there is one delightful moment when pairs of chords advance a step—another step—another—and another, like a child's game. I have heard performances of this work that imposed a deadly seriousness on the entire first movement; they seemed to me a travesty, a denial of all the implications of the notes. There is little surprise that a man so afflicted as Beethoven should be able to write tragic music; what a much greater triumph of the human spirit is revealed when, in one of his darkest hours, he could write something that bubbles over with wit and humour as this delightful sonata does.

The high spirits continue in the Scherzo,[1] which a little surprisingly comes second. Its character, Vivace (lively), is qualified by a warning not to take it too fast. (Allegretto is slower than Allegro.) It is the sort of movement that only Beethoven could have written, full of a rough humour that treads the borderline of slapstick. Let us begin by imagining the theme in a less individual guise.

**Ex.70**

Charming though this is, it is relatively characterless. Beethoven's treatment is vastly more original, nudging the tune on its way with strong accents in the places where you would least expect them. It isn't often that I allow myself actually to visualize an extra-musical image which is not sanctioned by the composer, but I find it difficult here to resist the idea of being seated in a pony-cart while Beethoven, holding the reins, occasionally digs me in the ribs as he guffaws at some rather school-boyish joke.

**Ex.71**

The phrase comes twice, being rounded off with a sprightly 'A-men to that'. And now the music goes on tiptoe, its air of stealth being very similar to that of children sneaking up on Grandpa as he is enjoying an afternoon snooze in the garden. The trill should sound like a suppressed giggle.

[1] Unusually in 2/4 time instead of the almost invariable 3/4.

Ex.72

L.H. doubles up an 8va below

We now have a delightful example of musical wit. Beethoven appears to have got stuck on the dominant of F minor (C). How to get back home again seems to be the problem; now in fact it's no real problem at all. The two keys of A♭ major and F minor are closely related, as we have seen on p. 20. But Beethoven makes a bit of a mystery about it for reasons that we shall discover later in the movement. For the time being, he comes to a complete halt, ponders awhile, tries the semitone above C (D♭), and with an air of triumph shows that it's just the thing he's looking for to get him back home again.

Ex.73

Back trots the first theme, just as before. There's the same little 'A-men', and the same tiptoe phrase (Ex. 72), although this time it's an octave higher. Once again, Beethoven appears to get stuck on the note C. So what are we expecting? A repetition of Ex. 73 of course; Beethoven's rather overdone bewilderment about how to extricate himself from the situation at the end of Ex. 72 has drawn our attention to the point. We remember it, and we remember the earlier solution. What we expect and what we are given are two very different things though; at the quietest moment, indeed after what seems a quite measurable silence, he suddenly bangs down two very loud chords of F major (Ex. 75). The children have let off a firework under Grandpa's deckchair, and the reaction is a frenzy of activity; other isolated explosions follow, but we do not need the word scherzo to tell us that this is all a huge joke. The notes themselves make that clear.

The movement continues with many incidental delights, not the least of which is the descending scale that spans more than four octaves before it finally brings us exhausted back to Ex. 71. But the most subtle and purely musical joke is still to come. Once again, it can only be appreciated in the context of the movement as a whole, and not as an isolated event. Beethoven prepares it very carefully by duplicating the events described in Exx. 71 and 72. Again he goes through the same procedure of repeating the whole section, again he arrives for the second time at that C. Two possibilities seem to be available; either he can give us the D♭ above very quietly, like this:

**Ex. 74**

or we can stand clear for the explosion.

**Ex. 75**

Unpredictable as ever, Beethoven combines the two ideas, and gives us two D flats, very loud. There follows the double-twist that lifts it out of the realms of clowning into high art. Up to this moment, the D♭ has always been used as a pivot that would swing us back into A♭ major (see Ex. 73, bars 3–5). Now, and it is the only time that it happens, the D♭ in its new explosive form shoots us into the totally unexpected key of G♭ major.

**Ex. 76**

The practical joke is made to serve an intellectual purpose. The sudden crash that Haydn had amused himself with in the slow movement of the Surprise symphony, is here given a new function, one which is purely musical in its effect. After these shocks, the end of the movement is sheer delight, a tiptoe exit that makes something new out of the oldest cliché in music.

The third movement is something of a throwback, a Menuetto, the last that Beethoven was to use in a major piano work. (The 'Tempo di Menuetto' movement in the little G major sonata, Op. 49 No. 2 is not in fact a minuet at all, but a rondo; anyway, it is an adaptation of an earlier composition.) It shows Beethoven in his most beguiling mood, with a beautiful singing tune presented in terms of the utmost simplicity. The only touch of pathos is introduced by an occasional C♭ (x), though its effect is nearer to the sweeter pangs of love than any real despair.

Ex.77

The implied harmony in this passage is echoed in the second part of the unusual Trio (or middle section of a minuet), which is based on a pattern of what can only be described as sedate skips. It is this Trio that Saint-Saëns used as the basis of a two-piano work called 'Variations on a theme of Beethoven', its combination of simplicity and easily remembered landmarks serving his purpose admirably. The movement ends with a brief Coda, based on the principal feature of Ex. 77, though this time there is something nearer to genuine pathos in its presentation.

Any possible tinge of sorrow is instantly dispelled by the galloping finale, a movement that takes off like a potential Derby-winner and only slackens its pace once—unnervingly near to the winning-post I may say. Czerny tells of an incident in the summer of 1802 when Beethoven saw a rider gallop past

the windows of the house in the country where he was staying.
The regular beat of the horse's hooves supposedly gave him the
idea for the finale of Op. 31 No. 2.

**Ex.78**

The indications Allegretto and *p* make this into a very leisurely
gallop, and I can't help wondering if Czerny's recollection was
not at fault; it seems much more likely that the music inspired by
the incident was the finale of this sonata. It was inevitable that
it should acquire the nickname of *La Chasse* or the Hunt. The
suggestion of pounding hooves and hunting horns is irresistible.

**Ex.79**

Superficially, there are resemblances between this and the
second movement of Op. 109, although the later work has
much greater variety, and considerably more seriousness of
purpose. There is one comparison worth making though for
the indications it gives of Beethoven's greater awareness of
craftsmanship as he grew more mature. In this finale we find one
passage in which he repeats the same note a number of times.
The harmony beneath remains virtually unaltered.

**Ex.80**

In Op. 109 we find a rather similar idea of repeated notes,
but now with a much more interesting treatment.

Ex. 81

Op.109
II.

However, it is only fair to say that much of the exhilaration that we derive from listening to the last movement of Op. 31 No. 3 is caused by the non-stop drive of the rhythm and the elemental appeal of the harmony.

The central section of the movement has some quite impressive modulations, but again I think there is a danger, in the light of our knowledge of late Beethoven, that we may be tempted to make the teacup a sight too large for this particular storm. Here is that 'extreme boisterousness' of which Ries spoke, and Beethoven plays a cruel joke on the pianist on the final page when prodigiously rapid crossing of the hands is called for. Twice in the last few bars the music comes to an abrupt halt, like a horse being urged towards a jump only to refuse at the very last stride. A little wistfully, Beethoven turns away and then, suddenly resolved, dashes off the last few bars.

Now I can well imagine that my rather frivolous approach to this sonata may cause some exasperation to many sincere lovers of Beethoven's music. If I have committed what seem to be heresies, let me defend them by saying this. We know from the evidence of Beethoven's associates that he was given to outbursts of boisterous humour; their musical manifestation is evident in many individual movements, bagatelles, the scherzos of the symphonies, and of course in parts of the quartets. In its more obvious forms, this humour is unmistakable; this sonata shows humour of a more subtle kind. So much stress has been laid on the near-divine quality of Beethoven that we tend to feel something almost sacrilegious in treating him as a human being. Yet he was the greater man for being able to laugh as well as weep; surely he would want us to share his moods rather than to deify him.

## CHAPTER XXVI

# BEETHOVEN

## Opp. 57 and 111—a comparison

Op. 57 in F minor. (The Appassionata.) Date uncertain, though sketches appear as early as 1804. Published February 1807 by Bureau des Arts et d'Industrie in Vienna; dedicated to Count Franz von Brunswick, brother to the Countesses Therese and Josephine with both of whom Beethoven was enamoured, and either of whom might be the unknown woman who never received the three impassioned love letters that Beethoven wrote, but then concealed in a secret drawer.[1] The nickname, Appassionata, was supplied by the publisher Cranz, who was also responsible for calling Op. 28 the Pastoral.

1. Allegro assai. 2 Andante con moto. (Variations), leading to 3. Allegro ma non troppo—ultimately Presto.

Op. 111 in C minor. The final sonata. Composed January 1822; first published April 1823, Schlesinger, Berlin and Paris. Dedicated to his patron and beloved pupil, the Archduke Rudolph of Austria, although according to Grove the dedication was added by the publisher. Only two important piano works written after this were the Diabelli Variations and the Bagatelles Op. 126.

1. Maestoso, leading to Allegro con brio e appassionato.
2. Arietta; Adagio molto, semplice e cantabile. (Actually a set of variations.)

There is no third movement.

ALTHOUGH, as we have seen, Op. 31 begins with a chord that is enigmatic and non-committal, it was not destined to establish a precedent. Each one of the remaining sonatas begins

[1] See *Letters of Beethoven*, trans. Emily Anderson, No. 373 Vol. 1, Macmillan, and other sources.

with a theme which establishes the tonic key without possibility of doubt, all, that is, save for Op. 111, whose opening phrase is cast in a truly heroic mould. It begins with a magnificent gesture.

Ex. 82

One feels that Beethoven positively resents the limitations imposed on him by the pianist only having two hands; a chord such as the one marked with a bridge ⌐——⌐ covers a span of more than three octaves, yet one senses that ideally, Beethoven would like it to be played as one huge chord.

Now the opening harmony, xx, is what is known as a diminished seventh, and it is a chord that has a special function in music. It invariably has implications of drama, even melodrama. When, in the days of the silent cinema, the pianist was called upon to accompany moments of villany—('In vain Mabel struggled in his clutches; blackhearted Rudolph clasped her in his arms and dragged her screaming to the foot of the stairs')—he would inevitably use diminished sevenths by the handful. Over the years this particular chord must have accompanied more attempted rapes than any other harmony. Why should this be so? Why should great composers and pit pianists alike use this chord to convey drama? What intrinsic quality does it have that makes it so different from any other?

To a composer of the pre-Wagner era, the diminished seventh was a cross-roads chord; it represents a moment of choice, when a number of roads lie open before him and he must decide which one to take. A diminished seventh is a modulating device of great flexibility, as the chart below demonstrates.

Fig. 2

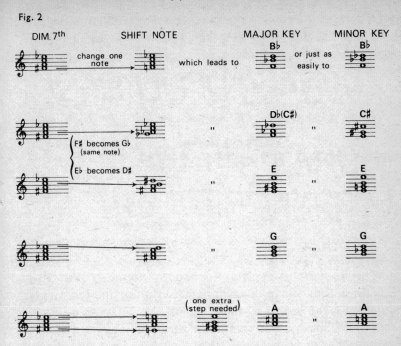

The single chord in the left-hand column opens the door to ten different keys shown in the two right-hand columns. Small wonder that Samuel Butler described it as 'the Clapham Junction of music'. The moment that a composer uses such a chord he poses a question to the listener: 'Which road shall I take to put an end to this suspense?' Suspense, then, is the factor that is shared by the awe-inspiring opening of Op. 111 or the inane accompaniment to Mabel's tribulations at the foot of the stairs.

The introduction to this sonata is like a cross-roads itself, a mountain pass, overcast with black clouds shot through with lightning. Above all, though, is this suggestion of seeking the way out—which path is the right one? Which chord will ultimately resolve the torment and confusion which the opening phrases convey so eloquently? Surely this sequence is a search, even to the moment of decision at the end.

Ex. 83

(Will it be Ab? No: Eb minor? No: Db? No:

Perhaps Ab No: Bb minor? No — HERE is the dominant of C minor,
after all? it is decided.)

That final chord resolves our doubts; Beethoven may drag
out the suspense still further, which indeed he does most movingly,
but it was the first of all those tentative explorations of key to
have established a clear dominant harmony. Where there is a
dominant, a tonic will surely follow in due course, and after so
dark a prologue, it must inevitably be C minor. As a prologue,
its purpose is remarkably similar to the first page of the Pathétique
sonata, Op. 13; both introductions set the scene for tragedy,
both lead into movements of great turbulence and intensity.
Few comparisons give us a clearer idea of how vast a change
had come over the language in the space of twenty-five years.

Logically we might expect the Appassionata to have been
written half-way between these two works, but curiously enough
it comes much sooner after the Pathétique than one would imagine.
Op. 13 dates from 1798; it was a mere six years after this that
the first sketches of Op. 57 appear. Its composition must have been
an almost frightening experience for Beethoven. He had unleashed
forces that were nearly beyond his control, and it's scarcely
surprising that he took a couple of years to find how to handle
them.

The first essential difference between the start of Op. 111 and the start of the Appassionata is that the earlier work, for all its essentially romantic character, still observes the time-honoured convention of beginning with a clear indication of tonality. In this it is no different from Op. 2 No. 1, the first of the thirty-two sonatas.

Ex. 84

Here we have an arpeggio of F minor stated in crisp, classical terms in a language that was essentially the same as Haydn's—indeed, the sonata is dedicated to Haydn. The Appassionata also begins with an arpeggio in F minor.

Ex. 85

The same arpeggio maybe, but what a difference these dark evocative tones convey. The wide spacing of the hands, the more varied rhythm, the almost imperceptible merging into harmony, the trill that dissolves the phrase into silence—the whole treatment is infinitely more Romantic. Yet it still acknowledges the classical need for the clear definition of tonality at the start of a work. Beethoven's technique, based on the traditional precepts of key-relationships, tells him to use a theme that establishes the tonal centre of F minor; but his emotional inclination is towards something much more mysterious. That air of mystery he now attains by immediately repeating the phrase in G♭ major, only a slight

★ I once heard Cortot describe this as 'The moon rising through the trees. . . .' No comment!

change of pitch, but an enormous change in other respects. Not
only is the immediate denial of the carefully established key of
F minor disturbing, but the release of tension involved in shifting
from minor to major has its effect as well. He retraces his steps,
back to F minor, building suspense with ominous drum-beats
in the left hand. It is the hush before the storm. The music, which
up to this point has seemed to be veiled in mist, is suddenly torn
apart, first by a vivid lightning flash, and then by thunderous
chords.

**Ex. 86**

This is a passage which is extremely difficult to bring off
convincingly in performance, the alternations of soft–loud–
soft–loud being so rapid, and the *fortissimo* chords tending to make
the pianist sound as though he is merely having a tantrum.
This indeed could be a legitimate interpretation of Beethoven's
intentions. As I see it, he is beating his head against a wall here,
which is frustrating at the best of times. What he is really trying to
do, although he is unaware of it, is to make the journey from Op. 2
No. 1 to Op. 111 by a quicker route than natural development
would allow. The goal is there, but as yet indistinctly seen. Time
and again in this sonata, we can see intimations of things to come;
nor are they only later developments in his own music. The noble
romanticism of the second subject of Op. 57 bears more than a suggestion of Schumann.

**Ex. 87**

As for this marvellously turbulent passage:

**Ex. 88**

surely it sows the seeds of the finale of Chopin's sonata in B minor.

**Ex. 89**

They may not look all that similar on paper, but the emotional content is very close, and the actual 'feel' in the hand is a likeness which any player must appreciate.

The start of the Appassionata is curiously elusive and fragmentary; by comparison, Op. 111 is as strong as a rock. From its Homeric introduction emerges an immensely arresting theme,[1] the more dramatic for the roll of thunder which precedes it.

**Ex. 90**

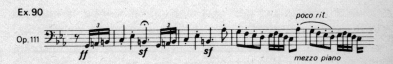

Now curiously enough, Beethoven had had a premonition of this shape in the Appassionata. The very last section of the finale is a frenzied dance based on this pattern. (I quote its second appearance.)

---

[1] It had first appeared in the sketch-books some twenty years earlier, in the key of F♯ minor, as part of a violin sonata.

Ex. 91

The relationship is fairly easy to spot, in spite of differences of notation and key. The differences between the two works become most marked when we see how Beethoven continues from such similar beginnings. In the Appassionata we find what in my opinion is the one unsatisfactory part of the composition. Even in masterly hands, I find this ending something of an anti-climax, a little too near to the traditional Gipsy Dance that appears so often in the less probable nineteenth-century operas.

In Op. 111, those same notes are used as the seed from which the most wonderful developments spring. The music is no less tigerish in its intensity, but gains immeasurably from its greater intellectual power. Although the first movement is extremely economical in themes, there is a remarkable freedom about it. It far transcends the bounds of normal sonata form, having elements of fugue, fantasy and inspired improvisation in it. Yet it can also at a stretch be analysed in terms of normal first and second subjects if you wish.

As in so many of the late works, the thing most calculated to confuse the listener is the sudden changes of mood that are so characteristic. Beethoven demands a very rapid and flexible response from his audience; the music is torn apart by conflicting emotions. The person who is unable to adjust quickly enough tends to give up and turn to a nice quiet nocturne or waltz; at least one knows where one is. In this movement, which is like a sort of musical equivalent to *King Lear*, there is much that is stormy, but also there are moments of great pathos.

Ex. 92

Here again we have a fascinating instance of the two-way process of composition that I have discussed already on pp. 303–4. The chords in Ex. 92 have 'softer' implications about them, not just in terms of volume but emotion; driven by the storm though he is, Beethoven clutches at them in passing, and automatically, because they are chords of that particular quality, the tension is diminished. It is a moment every real composer knows, when the music takes on a life of its own, and goes in a direction one hadn't bargained for. There is something terrifying about the way in which this moment of compassion is obliterated by a great cascade of notes that seem to come tearing out of the sky, sweeping all before them.

In the development, Beethoven tries to cage his tiger. Usually, the development section implies a loosening-up, an expansion of material. After such a tempest as we have ridden out here, he tries instead to compress, to impose the disciplines of strict form and counterpoint on the unruly material we have heard so far. He takes Ex. 90, the principal theme of the allegro, and binds it tight with academic cords. Ex. 93 shows the framework, leaving out the inessentials.

Ex. 93

Within ten bars, things have got out of hand again. I am convinced that Beethoven originally planned a longer section of controlled counterpoint here, but the gesture proves as ineffectual as a single professor trying to quell a student riot. Any suggestion of fugal treatment is swept away by sheer force. The hammer-blows of Ex. 90 strike again and again until the immense central climax is reached.

Surprisingly, the movement ends quietly, perhaps in preparation for the unearthly serenity of the second movement, perhaps because the driving force finally burns itself out. Certainly there is a strange effect of disintegration towards the end as Ex. 90 breaks into fragments.

Ex.94

This last phrase, in conjunction with its swift moving left hand, is an uncanny anticipation of the dying fall that comes so near the end of Chopin's Revolutionary study. But where Chopin flings the music into one last gesture of defiance, Beethoven's movement sinks at last into an uneasy rest. It is interesting that the first movement of Op. 57 ends the same way—with disintegration, followed by an unexpected descent into darkness.

The motive may well be the same in both sonatas, for in each case, from the storm-racked turbulence of the first movement we are suddenly translated into a world of extraordinary peace. Both movements are sets of variations, both are in a major key, both have themes of notable stillness, though in Op. 57, Beethoven cautions the performer against adopting too slow a tempo. The theme in Op. 57 is more a sequence of harmonies than a melody; had he been so inclined, Beethoven might have thought of it as a sort of Chaconne, though it would then have required three beats in a bar instead of two. There is a tendency for occasional movements in the bass to attract our attention, and I think this is proof that Beethoven did not want us to become too absorbed in the melodic aspect of the music. The variations throughout are designed to stress the harmonic nature of the theme.

In a rather earlier period, there had been a great vogue for a type of variation known as 'doubles'. Handel's Harmonious Blacksmith is a good example, with each variation sticking to the same harmonic framework, but with a progressively increasing number of notes allotted to each beat. Theoretically, the theme is in units of one beat; in the first variation you divide each unit by two; variation two has three notes per beat; next we find four notes to a beat, then six, and eight for the last, thus bringing the house down with an increasingly dazzling display of virtuosity.

These two slow movements are both very elaborate examples of this long-established technique. The Op. 57 movement is less varied in mood, but this, no doubt, is because there is still a vigorous third movement to come. The variations are also somewhat more strict in their adherence to the original theme, but that is largely the result of concentrating on the elaboration of harmony rather than the extension of melody. It is here that the movements begin to differ.

A composer of variations may decide on several courses of action; he may choose to adhere strictly to the original framework, as for instance Brahms does in his Variations on a theme by Handel for the greater part of the work. He may take one small aspect of the theme and develop it freely in its own right, as Rachmaninoff does in the famous D♭ Variation XVIII of his Paganini Rhapsody. He may concentrate on a rhythm, a sequence of chords, a technical trick such as constructing a canon, or even introduce a totally extra-musical idea as Elgar does in the Enigma variations. Beethoven's technique in Op. 111 is a remarkable instance of musical growth. The theme itself is a mere sixteen bars long, though, as was the usual custom, both halves are repeated. Yet although the music continues to evolve with this limitation very much in mind, one has a feeling of an immense span unfolding. The 'units' in the Diabelli variations for instance remain very clear cut for the most part, even though Beethoven's ingenuity in dealing with a trite little idea is staggering. But in this sonata, apart from one frenetic outburst whose savage syncopations give a strangely demonic quality, the rest of the movement remains extraordinarily still, even though the page is black with notes. It is a style of writing that occurs quite often in late Beethoven, when he marries a broad slow-moving tune to an accompaniment of great activity. Demi-semi-quavers and trills make the music glitter with their abundance; listening, I remember the Biblical phrase about the Spirit of God moving over the waters, water in constant, rippling movement, reflecting the light of a million stars, teeming with life and creation, yet contained in one all-embracing and infinite intelligence.

## CHAPTER XXVII

# TOWARDS SCHUMANN

## Some thoughts on Beethoven's Sonata in A Major Op. 101

Sonata No. 28 in A major, Op. 101. Finished early in 1816. Published 1817 by Steiner of Vienna. Dedicated to the Baroness Dorothea von Ertmann, herself an accomplished pianist. Beethoven admired her playing enough to give her the nickname, 'Cecilia', after the patron Saint of music. Despite his contempt for patronage, some of his truest friends were aristocrats; it is said that when the Baroness was demented with grief over the death of one of her children, Beethoven saved her reason by playing to her.

It was for this sonata, not Op. 106, that he first invented the term Hammerklavier, in preference to the Italian word Pianoforte. His nationalistic fervour briefly extended to instructions about tempo and style of playing, but he was soon to revert to Italian again.

FACTS HAVE THEIR PLACE in the field of scholarship, and, since my own mind is singularly empty of them, I am grateful to the many excellent scholars who have consigned facts to print; and on whose store of knowledge I am entirely dependant when it comes to matters of dates, places and the like. But sometimes convictions are better than facts; sometimes it is more important to believe than to know. It is in this spirit that I say that I am quite sure that I know which Beethoven sonata Schumann loved the most, even though I haven't a word of documentary evidence to prove it. If I was a scholar, and had the sort of conscientious dedication that goes with a scholarly mind, I would settle down to a happy couple of years' research through the whole of Schumann's writings (which were considerable) in order to find some confirmation of my belief. Curiously enough, I don't really care all that much whether such confirmation exists or not; I would go further and say that it doesn't even matter to me if Schumann wrote somewhere that his favourite Beethoven sonata was a different one altogether, since my reason for being interested is not to prove a small historical fact but to demonstrate a large artistic truth. This truth is that there is one sonata of Beethoven's in which we can find so many anticipations of Schumann's mature style that I am utterly fascinated by it. It is almost as if, by one of those miraculous shifts in time so favoured by writers of science fiction, Beethoven had been able to peer into the future and look at some of Schumann's music. (One fact here by the way, confirmed by a quick look in a book of reference—Schumann was seventeen when Beethoven died in 1827, so there is no chance that Beethoven could have seen any of his music.)

Now, it is one of the main contentions of this book that Beethoven grew increasingly dissatisfied with sonata form towards the end of his life. All the late sonatas seem to be moving towards something far more rhapsodic, more loosely constructed. (The slow movement of the Hammerklavier sonata even moves into what might be called the Mahlerian time-scale.) He expressed this discontent in several ways: one, as in the first movement of Op. 109, was to preserve solely the 'idea' of contrast that was originally exemplified by first and second subjects, but to pursue it to an extreme—contrast of tempo, emotional content, style of writing, contrast of opposites too violent to be acceptable in a normal sonata form context. Another way was to jettison even contrast, to make a whole movement more unified so that while there would be some variety of theme, the essential mood would remain constant. Both movements of Op. 78, the finale of Op. 90 and the first movement of this sonata, Op. 101, are the clearest instances of this trend; it begins to move the sonata as a form much nearer to what, for want of a better term, might be called Mood Music. Considerations of sentiment begin to govern considerations of intellect. The third, and most unkind, way of

expressing his frustration was to write thoroughly unpianistic
music that allowed its intellectual demands to override all thought
of practicality. The Hammerklavier is the supreme example—
as is the Grosse Fuge in the quartet repertoire—but the last movement of this twenty-eighth sonata is vastly inconsiderate to the
pianist.

If Beethoven allowed his feelings for the Baroness Dorothea
to be expressed in the first movement of Op. 101, they must have
been tender indeed, for the music begins in the most meltingly
beautiful fashion.

Ex. 95

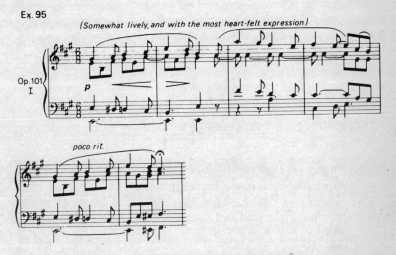

I have put his indications of performance into English, since,
if he was so determined to play a nationalist game, I don't see
why I shouldn't be allowed to play as well. But it is interesting
as an indication of his dread of sentimentality that even here,
when he asks for 'heartfelt expression' (*innigsten Empfindung*),
he should feel the need to qualify it by the seemingly contradictory
*Etwas lebhaft*, or 'somewhat lively'. One suspects that had these
notes actually been written by Schumann, he would not have
betrayed such qualms.

The music continues in this lyrical and tender mood. The
rare indications of *f* seem to call for the full tone of a string

orchestra rather than an aggressive impact. The wide-spaced harmony is one significant pointer to the full romantic style of Schumann or Brahms. The spacing of a chord is one of its most important attributes. As the keyboard itself acquired a wider compass, composers tended to open out the harmony. The so-called Alberti bass that occurs so frequently in Haydn and Mozart, was merely extended to cover a wider range of the

keyboard in Chopin's hands. The effect is

richer, since the notes have a greater variety of colour. When Stravinsky began his Symphony of Psalms with this version of the chord of E minor:

he was simply taking a remarkably fresh look at the familiar notes E G B which had been in use for centuries.

The spacing of Beethoven's harmony is a study in itself. When, for instance, he transposes the opening melody of the slow movement of Op. 13 up an octave, he realizes the need to compensate for the relative thinness of the middle range of the keyboard. If you try playing the first phrase an octave higher with exactly the same lay-out as when it first appears, you will hear what I mean. So far as I am aware, the interval of a tenth simply does not exist in the piano music of Haydn and Mozart, yet Beethoven uses it as early as Op. 2 No. 3 (bar 56). (I don't count the 'scrambled' tenths in the first movement of Op. 2 No. 2—they are the result of counterpoint, not harmony.) What in my opinion is the single most beautiful chord that Beethoven ever committed to paper is to be found in the first movement of Op. 109. It is instructive to compare it with another magical chord, the one that begins the fourth piano concerto. Here they are, side by side.

If the words Classical and Romantic have any significance with regard to taste, one could say that these two chords, each perfect in its own right, epitomize the difference. It is the use of tenths however which gives the second chord its particularly romantic quality, the F♯ → A♯ and then the A♯ → C♯. Schumann, the German Romantic *par excellence*, constantly exploits chords of the tenth. Look in bars 3 and 4 of Ex. 95, and you will find the melody itself stated in tenths. As I have suggested, the whole language of the sonata is moving towards Schumann.

One of Schumann's most notable idiosyncrasies is an obsession with tied notes, notes held over silently from a previous beat. Here is a typical passage from his magnificent Fantasy in C, Op. 17.

With a prodigious amount of sniffing and nodding of the head, it's perfectly feasible for the pianist to show an audience where the beats actually lie, although they are all silent. Equally, it's possible to disregard the subtle implications of Schumann's notation and produce a sound like this, which, theoretically, has exactly the same note values.

Ex. 97

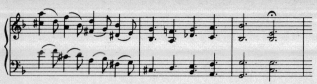

I feel that the slight disorientation of the beat that Schumann conveys by his way of writing is an indication of 'beatless-ness', a deliberately contrived effect of anti-rhythm, totally different from what we normally think of as syncopation. If Ex. 96 seems perverse in its notation, Ex. 97 is downright dull. Schumann's version also carries some implications of a slight emotional tension, a quickening of the heartbeat which is difficult to bring off, but worth trying for. At the very least, his notation could be said to convey 'Don't just play the notes—do *something*!'

In Beethoven's Op. 101 we find exactly the same technique, employed, I would surmise, for just the same purpose. Here is the rhythm only (alike in both hands), of one passage.

L.H. drops out

Again the same effect of 'beatless-ness', giving a beautifully spontaneous feel to the occasional wisp of melody that emerges from what an orchestral musician would regard as 'viola territory'.

Ex. 98

Op. 101    *(pp)*

(Notice the very subtle difference between the two left hand melodies, the first one with its dipping quavers on the second beat, the second aiming more directly at its peak.) For Beethoven to use this rhythm was very unusual; he seems, as I have suggested, to have hit upon one of the hallmarks of Schumann's style. I stress Schumann at the expense of the other Romantics simply because it was a trick he used much more frequently than his contemporaries. For instance, when Chopin began his F major Ballade, he did *not* choose to start like this,

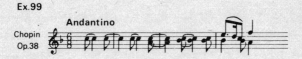

but used the more normal rhythm, without ties.

I should be making out a poor case if this was the only evidence I was to produce in support of my argument that this sonata is not only a gateway to Romanticism, but to Schumann in particular. There is a stronger link to be established in the next movement. This is as unique in Beethoven's output as the first movement is, though in a different way. It's a March of immense vigour, characterized by an obsessional use of one rhythm.

This driving rhythm continues relentlessly for more than two-thirds of the entire movement. Now anybody who has even read through a fair sample of Schumann's work, however ineptly, will recognize this as one of his most typical rhythms. To quote three examples, the final movement of the Etudes Symphoniques:

Kreisleriana, No. 5:

Ex.102

or the second movement of the Op. 17 Fantasy:

Ex.103

In each of these examples, the rhythm shown is a persistent and outstanding feature, continuing for long stretches at a time. This is the point—not the rhythm itself, but the persistence with which it is pursued. I know of no other movement in Beethoven that employs so similar a technique of composition.[1] There are other Schumann tricks too, the piling of entries on top of each other, the way that phrases interlock, the crossing of hands, all perhaps best revealed in this climax.

Ex.104

Op.101

The instruction *dolce* (sweetly), when the left hand is suddenly

[1] I refer to piano music. The Grosse Fuge comes to mind as another example of dotted rhythm. The 'Turkish March' section of the Ninth Symphony also has a surprisingly Schumannesque quality, but is scarcely a fair comparison.

projected into the pianistic stratosphere is typical of Beethoven's inhumanity to man, when it comes to questions of practicality. But the whole 'feel' of this passage in the hand is astonishingly close to Schumann in texture.

At this point, the impatient reader may well be muttering, 'So what?' I've made the point, but is the point worth making? My justification for devoting a chapter to it is that I am always fascinated by the inevitability of certain developments in music. There *is* a sort of pre-destination at work; for instance, like it or not, the twentieth century had to come; its course was pre-ordained from the moment that Schoenberg discovered that he could not outdo Wagner on his own ground. It is like those endless 'begat' chapters in the Bible—'and Haydn begat Beethoven, and Beethoven begat Brahms, and Liszt begat Bartók, and Wagner begat Schoenberg, and Schoenberg begat Berg', and so on. But it isn't often that one can put a finger so surely on an actual work that links two composers so widely differing in their fundamental approach to music. Essentially, Schumann and Beethoven belonged to two completely different worlds united only by the Germanic tie. Schumann was far more drawn to a literary or pictorial conception of music's function; atmosphere and emotion were much higher priorities with him than structure. His admiration for Beethoven was enormous, but his natural inclination was to use very different forms. When, therefore, I lay so much stress on the Schumann-like qualities of Op. 101, it is not my intention to suggest that Schumann copied it or was even consciously influenced by it. What concerns me is not Schumann looking back, but Beethoven looking forward. If one says flatly that Beethoven's life-work was to bridge the gulf between Haydn and the mid-nineteenth-century Romantics, it is an over-simplification, suggesting that the gulf was one of time alone. It was not; it was an immense change of outlook involving the rejection of the classical aesthetic, and the acceptance of a more personal, involved approach to composition. The whole of the next chapter is devoted to the work that best symbolizes that journey.

## CHAPTER XXVIII

# BEETHOVEN

## Op. 110 in A♭ Major

Composed in December 1821, the penultimate sonata, and the only complete work to be written in that year, the rest of his time being devoted to the Missa Solemnis[1] and the Ninth Symphony. The sonata bears no dedication, although at one time Beethoven appears to have considered dedicating it to his pupil Ries, or to a Frau Brentano.[2] In the event, it was published by Schlesinger in 1822. Beethoven claimed (to his friend Anton Schindler) that he had written the last three sonatas 'in a single breath', in order to quiet the apprehension of his friends about his mental condition, which was growing ever more eccentric. But this was a downright lie, since Op. 109 clearly belongs to 1820, and was actually published before work on Op. 110 had begun.

1. Moderato cantabile molto espressivo. 2. Allegro molto. 3. Adagio ma non troppo—Recitativo—several rapid changes of tempo over a few bars—Adagio, ma non troppo (Arioso dolente). 3(a). Fuga; allegro, ma non troppo—return to the tempo of the Arioso—return to tempo of Fuga—a gradual increase of speed to the end.

THE LANGUAGE OF MUSIC, like any other language, is capable of expressing things simply or obscurely; but since few people are capable of 'thinking' in musical abstractions, the average listener tends to enjoy most those pieces that have the power to suggest things outside music. Tchaikovsky's symphonies are easier to listen to than those of Beethoven

---

[1] By then more than a year overdue for the occasion for which it was supposed to be written.

[2] Mother of Maximiliana, dedicatee of Op. 109.

because they are more likely to bring imaginary pictures into the mind; a cavalry charge, a gipsy dance, a vast expanse of woods and lakes, the dead ashes of burned love-letters, death, love, darkness, loneliness. While I'm all for identification with the music, I cannot help deprecating this response, except when it is sanctioned by the composer. Yet there exists a great demand to know what a work *means*, to unravel the secrets in some way. Precisely because we find the emotional content of music easier to grasp than its intellectual aspects, we fall back on the prop of analysis, feeling that some sort of illumination should follow, once we know that the nice bit on the clarinet is the recapitulation of the second subject in the tonic key. It was Mendelssohn who said, 'The thoughts which are expressed to me by music . . . are not too indefinite to be put into words, but on the contrary, too definite'. This slightly enigmatic remark makes sense once we accept that the musical language exists in its own right, and that it is as foolish to expect it to speak to us in verbal concepts, as it would be to play a tune to the grocer over the telephone and expect him to translate it into an order for the week's provisions.

Before we examine this sonata in detail, let us look at one phrase. It is by no means new in Beethoven's work; as early as Op. 10 No. 1, the piano sonata in C minor, we find this fragment.

Ex. 105

The same shape occurs in a rather smoother guise in the String Quartet, Op. 18 No. 5.

Ex. 106

Two years later, in 1802, it emerged from Beethoven's subconscious in yet another form, as part of the Violin Sonata, Op. 30 No. 3;

Ex.107

while in 1808, it reappeared yet again in the Trio, Op. 70 No. 2.

Ex.108

The only thing remarkable about these resemblances is not their similarity but the completely different ways in which they evolve. There can be little doubt though that the most perfect version of this useful and versatile pattern is to be found starting in the fifth bar of this sonata.

Ex.109

The accompaniment Beethoven gives us to this exquisite arch of melody would seem at first glance to be a cliché of unbelievable banality. Can the mature master really be satisfied with this relic of childhood days?

Ex.110

How are we to accept the same basis that 'Chopsticks' is built on, in a work which all authorities agree to be one of the most sublime ever written for piano?

In explanation, I would turn back to verbal language. One of the most profound and moving lines in the whole of English literature is made up of words of the utmost simplicity:

To be or not to be . . .

It would be hard to invent a phrase that said more with

less effort; it is not 'better' to say, 'To exist or to stop existing', or, 'TheproblemisthatIcan'tdecidewhethertogoonmaking theseawfuldecisionsortoputanendtoitallbydoingmyselfin'.    The simplicity of utterance lends dignity to the thought expressed; so here, Beethoven, by daring to be simple, succeeds in being profound.

Despite its confusing, indeterminate number of movements, there is an overwhelming unity about Op. 110, a unity which Beethoven achieves in a number of subtle ways, as we shall see. We can afford to make a very detailed study of this sonata, since it might literally be described as the 'work of a lifetime'. To my mind, it sums up the whole purpose of Beethoven's life; in this one work, we find a perfect symbol of his journey from Classicism to Romanticism, terms which I use not to indicate two periods of time, but rather attitudes of mind.

The work begins with a serene phrase which Beethoven specifically asks us to play 'lovingly'. Yet as early as the third bar, it hesitates, coming to rest on a trill before continuing into Ex. 109. It must rank with the start of the Fourth Piano Concerto as one of the most poetic openings of all time.

Ex.111

Moderato cantabile molto espressivo

p con amabilità

These brief opening bars are much more than a mere prologue, more even than a first subject; they are, as we shall discover, the source from which many later events are to spring.

The music goes on its way, lyrical, sustained and tranquil in spirit. Suddenly, and to our perplexity, Beethoven embarks on a whole series of glistening arpeggios. What place do these digital exercises have in such a meditation?

Ex.112

The clue is to be found in 112a, which shows us that these are far from digital exercises, but a variation on Ex. 111. On a modern piano it demands extreme delicacy of touch to achieve the filigree effect that must be neither too clouded nor too sparkling. Meantime, the left hand sketches in suggestions of harmony, mere props for the fragile structure above. The figures climb higher, up to the topmost note of Beethoven's piano, the high C. From this improbable peak, where sound has begun to lose substance, an almost languorous melody drifts down, its shape growing more definite as it descends. No sooner has it coalesced into actual chords than it begins to climb again, the feeling of ascent being intensified by the now-spread chords, which seem to be reaching out towards the unattainable. It is Beethoven's masterly way of disguising the fact that he has already overshot the note that he now wishes us to feel is the summit. He is aiming for the top B♭, a tone lower than the previous high C. But the approach is so skilfully done, with descending trills in the left hand widening the gap between the hands, that we have no sense of anticlimax.

Ex.113

This last dramatic plunge downwards through more than two octaves is another way of emphasizing the climactic nature of the top B♭; the music seems literally to have broken apart. Three more brief ascents bring us indeed to the top C, now attained in such a way as to seem the real climax of the movement so far. The music gently unwinds and settles down into a dominant harmony that has every appearance of leading us to a traditional double-bar, with the consequent repeat of the opening exposition.

Ex.114

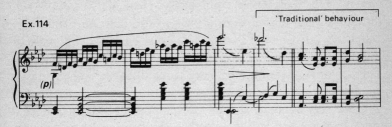

Beethoven has grown impatient with such traditions by now, and in Opp. 101, 109 and 110 he abandons them. It is perhaps significant that these three sonatas all have first movements of an unusually lyrical nature; in the more demanding first movements of Opp. 106 and 111, he still preserves the custom of repeating the exposition.

What he actually does in Op. 110 is to shift the bass down to D♭ at the same time as the top line, effectively destroying any suggestion that the D♭ is merely a rather feeble dominant seventh, and giving it the strength to move us into a new key, F minor. This change is underlined by a crescendo that goes against the grain; just as the pianist's instincts cry out to play with even more sentiment, Beethoven forces him to push on. (Ex. 115 picks up from bar 3 of Ex. 114.)

Ex.115

Suddenly, as though Beethoven realizes how contrary he is being by forcing this music to go against its nature, he relents, and the rest of the remarkably short development is all meditative, an oft-repeated contemplation of the opening phrase of the sonata, tinged with melancholy and subtly changing direction till, through several related keys, it brings us back to A♭ major.

In the world of tonal music, there is a deep underlying sense of 'rightness', a feeling of proportion that is akin to architecture. There's some interesting evidence to be discovered about this if we compare the development section of this Beethoven sonata with the very different sounding development of Mozart's K.457. (See Chapter XXIII.) Where Beethoven is contemplative, Mozart is turbulent; but both in essence are disguising a sequence of *harmonies* by presenting them as *melodies*. On the face of it, the emotional content and melodic outline of these two examples could not be much further apart.

Ex.116
Mozart K.457

Beethoven Op.110

Yet once we look at these bars as alternations of harmony, they begin to seem extraordinarily alike; the details may differ, but the procedure, and the sort of logic that governs it, is virtually the same. Here, first, is a sort of ground-plan:

Fig. 3

| Mozart: | F minor | Dominant of G minor | G minor | Dominant of C minor | C minor | Dominant of C minor |
|---|---|---|---|---|---|---|
| Beethoven: | F minor | Dominant of F minor | F minor | Dominant of D♭ major | D♭ major | Dominant of D♭ major |

Using the most similar placings for these harmonies on the keyboard, we would find something like this:

Ex.117
Mozart:

Beethoven:

The resemblances are obvious when presented in this skeletonic form. My only reason for revealing them is to show the instinctive sense of harmonic balance that seems to have been developed in the classical composer, even when he was writing in an impassioned vein. Poles apart emotionally, the two sonatas both have developments of exceptional concentration, devoted virtually to one idea; both are also concerned with tonic-dominant relationships, the 'twist' being to turn to an unexpected new dominant from time to time so as to be able to move forward to a new tonal centre.

By these gradual steps, Beethoven gently steers us back to A♭ major; this time, the opening phrase is accompanied by the exercise-like figure which had seemed so curious an interruption when it first appeared as Ex. 112; its function is now made plain. The movement proceeds without drama, its outlines remarkably clear and orthodox. One problem occurs when Beethoven finds himself climbing to a non-existent note. Owing to a necessary transposition, he is driven towards a top C♯ instead of the top C he had reached earlier. Since such a note did not exist on any piano of his time,[1] he was compelled suddenly to plunge the music down an octave; ineptly performed, it can sound a bit clumsy, though in the right hands it has the effect of enriching the texture. The only other point that demands attention is a slight darkening of the mood in the very final bars of the movement.

Ex. 118

The repercussions of this phrase are destined to extend further than we think.

The scherzo that follows is an example of Beethoven at his most terse; at first glance, the music seems almost naive in its

[1] We now have an entire octave more than Beethoven's piano had in its upper register.

simplicity, and it's quite possible to imagine a piece suitable for a child beginner, with a melody on these lines.

Ex.119

From such fundamentals Beethoven builds a movement of tremendous nervous energy. One gets the impression of explosive forces barely held under control. Brutal syncopations knock the music off course; attempts to introduce sentiment are roughly dashed aside; a strange urgency imbues the movement with a character that the relative scarcity of notes hardly suggests on the printed page. Strangest of all is the central section, a whole series of rapid descending figures, each of which begins with a violent accent at the top of the keyboard and then, unexpectedly, slithers down hastily but quietly. It is like a climber perched on a cliff-face clutching desperately at a handhold that is almost out of reach; each time, the strain is more than exhausted fingertips can manage, and he slides a little further towards the fatal drop. The left hand, precarious in rhythm, does nothing to steady the music; it is a disturbing symbol of impotence, and being impotent, it dies away to nothingness.

Bowing to convention, Beethoven re-starts the movement, even allowing himself the luxury of a *ritenuto* on one dying fall; but again, the moment of pathos is shouted down. We are all ready for a violent ending, Beethoven seeming to be in his most unforgiving mood. But even this angry music is made to disintegrate; the movement ends with a curious collapse, the isolated chords all off the beat save for the final one, which brings an unexpected softness as it turns into the major. It is another symptom of Beethoven's wish to impose unity on the whole sonata; the traditionally clear-cut barriers between the movements are replaced by something much less defined. The scherzo emerges almost stealthily from the first movement, and then dissolves into the third. It is hardly a movement in its own right any more, but a fleeting episode that is over before we have fully adjusted to its premptory and abrupt demand.

We now stand on the threshold of the most revealing piece that Beethoven ever wrote. The first movement might be described as the apotheosis of classicism. Its beauties are gentle and lyrical, but they also have a sense of serene detachment—Olympian would be a misleading word, suggesting a more grandiose concept, yet there is something of Pallas Athene in its still, calm beauty. Like the Fourth Piano Concerto, it makes its mark by reticence; it is the music of a poet rather than a warrior. The scherzo impatiently brushes these abstractions aside, sparing little time for pleasantries; like most revolutions, it finds it easier to destroy than to rebuild, though its final bars acknowledge its impotence. Here is a situation then in which the classical concept has achieved perfection, which, in more cynical terms, is a way of saying 'a dead end'. Perfection cannot be surpassed. The scherzo lets in the 'Red Guards', but all they can do is to wreak havoc. Beethoven now turns his eyes inward, and in doing so, unbares his soul to us.

It takes courage for a performer to treat music with a proper mixture of authority and freedom. One must of course try to be true to the text, but that is only a beginning; what is also needed is a personal touch, though not so personal as to become eccentric or perverse. There can be few passages in the whole of Beethoven's compositions in which there are more detailed instructions than he now gives us. There is a paradox here since, in essence, what he is asking for is an abnormal freedom from conventional restraint; by giving us such an unusual number of exhortations, he tends to make us try to be even more punctilious than usual in observing them, and this can be an inhibiting factor. One must realize then that these are not rigid demarcations, but indications of flexibility of the most sensitive kind. Just to show how liberally the page has been scattered with *words* as opposed to notes, here is a reduction to chart form.

Bar 1. Adagio, ma non troppo. Una corda.

Bar 4. Recitativo. Piu adagio. Andante. Cresc.

Bar 5. Adagio. Sempre tenuto. Tutte le corde. Dimin. Ritardando. Cantabile. Una corda.

Bar 6. Meno adagio. Cresc. Adagio. ten. dimin. smorzando.

Bar 7. Adagio, ma non troppo. *p.* tutte le corde.

Bar 8. Cresc. Dim.

Bar 9. (Klagender gesang) Arioso dolente. *p.*

In the space of nine bars, Beethoven uses no less than forty-four words or abbreviations, which must be something of a record; this alone should be evidence that something exceptional is taking place. Because the music has now become so intensely personal, it matters far more to him that he should not be misunderstood. In the early days, one indication of tempo would be enough for a whole movement because the music spoke for *itself* (i.e. it was based on the Classical concept). Here, the indications are far more numerous because it speaks for *him*—the hallmark of Romanticism by my definition.[1] The passage is so unique that I quote it in full.

Ex.120

The earliest anticipation of this degree of freedom in his piano music is to be found in the first movement of Op. 31 No. 2 in D minor. There too, Beethoven has several changes of tempo, even more marked in contrast, as well as recitative passages which have a very vocal quality about them.

Ex. 121

But profound though their effect may be, these are simply alternating sections of widely contrasted material, for which precedents may be discovered in innumerable compositions of the seventeenth and eighteenth centuries. What is so very different in the Op. 110 example is the enormous effort Beethoven has made to convey considerable freedom of tempo within a basically slow passage. He is demanding a flexibility that must seem to be spontaneous, a refinement of interpretation that musical notation has always been ill-equipped to indicate.

As to the repeated As (Ex. 120, bar 5), I shall not add to the enormous amount of speculation that has already been put down on paper as to precisely what Beethoven meant. As long as the effect is deeply expressive, I think it is perfectly acceptable to treat the passage freely, even to the extent of playing a few more notes if one feels moved to do so.

Once Beethoven has opened the door to his inner self, which I believe is the true function of Ex. 120, he reveals a profound grief, the more touching for its lack of rhetoric. The slow, pulsating harmonies are for the most part simple, only occasionally tinged with dissonance. One feels, without blasphemy, that here truly was 'a man of sorrows, acquainted with grief'. Not only was he acquainted with grief; he had become reconciled to it, and if there is one lesson to be learned from the late works of Beethoven it is that those passages that seem most violent in protest are railing, not against any personal despair, but against the inadequacy of his musical resources. It was the conflict with the material that he found so frustrating; the inner grief he could cope with, since it could be sublimated into musical terms. This brief *arioso*[1] is a perfect instance of such a sublimation. It ends with a gesture which, while in no way denying grief, seems to accept it without a trace of bitterness.

Ex.122

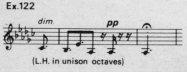

(L.H. in unison octaves)

[1] The melody is a more straightforward version of Ex. 126.

Beethoven's religious beliefs veered towards what we would think of as Humanism, although at times he was willing to accept orthodoxy. He was familiar with Eastern mysticism, and kept framed on his desk a significant phrase that he had copied out in his own hand.

I am that which is. I am all that was, that is, and that shall be.

Where a truly religious person would turn to the Bible for consolation in time of sorrow, I think it more probable that Beethoven would have looked for solace in music itself. I suspect that in his eyes, music was an aspect of divinity, an aspect he could comprehend more readily than anything the Church could offer. I do not think it too far-fetched, then, to suggest that at the end of the *arioso*, having exposed almost too openly his innermost feelings, he should seek consolation in the purest musical form, the fugue. It is as though he were to say to himself, 'This delving within hurts too much; let me return to the impersonal, detached world of classicism.' For subject, he chooses a pattern of such purity and serenity that it might have been carved in marble.

Ex.123

This grave and beautiful theme is a distillation of the essence of the very opening phrase of the sonata. Omit the first note of Ex. 111, and we find the melody consists of rising steps, A♭—D♭—B♭—E♭; this pattern has not only been the sole content of the development section, but has also been hinted at in Ex. 118— the first time that Beethoven plants the idea of reducing the theme to a succession of rising fourths. (You can see it in the lower part of the right hand.) The mere fact that it now eschews the sensuous garments of harmony is a symbol of purification. Moreover, the fugue is notable for its control. For the greater part, it is quiet and restrained; any tendency towards loudness is soon suppressed.

There is one fascinating moment which is worth mentioning, although I willingly admit that my interpretation is open to challenge. The first time that Beethoven admits a *f* into the texture is at the fourth entry of the subject.

Ex.124

Now Beethoven is being at his most pedantic in matters of notation here, as the awkwardness of the 'tails-up and tails-down' in the right hand shows. He is determined to keep the counterpoint absolutely clear. The point that intrigues me, though, stems from the duplication of the mark *f* in *both* hands in the first bar of Ex. 124.[1] It lasts for these four bars only, and then the indication *diminuendo* brings us back to a long continuation, all kept at a low level of sound. When at last a crescendo does begin, it too dissolves rapidly, the music being reduced to two slender lines of counterpoint in the right hand. Then comes the moment that intrigues me so, a massive entry of the fugue subject in octaves, touched with additional drama by being put in the minor for the first time.

Ex.125

[1] See *Ur-text*, published by Henle.

The conventional view is to regard this bass entry as the sort of thing that happens so often in a Bach organ fugue, the subject appearing on the pedals with majestic effect. A close look at the copy reveals a possibly significant difference between this and the earlier octave entry of Ex. 124. There, as I pointed out, Beethoven took the trouble to write *f* in both hands; here there is only the one *ff*, which directly contradicts the *p* of the preceding bar. We have seen how Mozart can employ conflicts between *f* and *p* in Ex. 27. There is no reason therefore why Beethoven should not do the same thing, and for the same reason—to contrast the frailty of the right-hand part with the strength of the bass. If this reading is correct (and I personally am very drawn to it), it gives an extraordinary quality to this moment, as though the 'temple' were being rocked by an earthquake. It is not long before the fugue recedes into its initial calm. Soon, a final crescendo leads us to what appears to be a triumphant conclusion. But no; at the very moment when victory seems to be in our grasp, the music loses all confidence, comes to a halt on a chord that is far from final, and then sinks despondently back into the minor key. Could disillusionment be more graphically expressed? It is the cry of despair; the hoped-for consolation has failed to materialize, and he must sink even deeper into the abyss. Once again the haunting theme of the *arioso* returns, this time broken by little silences that give an increased pathos to an already grief-stricken melody.

Ex.126

The music disintegrates, the pattern of Ex. 122 being repeated, but with each note now isolated from its neighbours. There follows one of the strangest passages Beethoven ever wrote, the chord of G major repeated no fewer than ten times, constantly growing in intensity, but always preserving this sense of isolation. The silences outnumber the chords; they are like great gulping breaths, the gasps of a dying man. I find this passage very near to Berlioz in spirit, in its combination of a rather naïve imagery with an intensely dramatic idea. Naturally, there are other ways of interpreting it, but none that accounts for its unique effect quite so convincingly.

At this, the darkest hour of all, what can Beethoven do but again seek for consolation in the purest form of music? He returns to the fugue in an even more cerebral form, the subject inverted, the shape seen as in a mirror.

Ex.127

(p)

There are times in a man's life when work is one of the only cures for some great personal grief—the loss of a dearly loved one, the collapse of some cherished hope. The sheer self-discipline involved is a salutary corrective to self-pity; so now, I feel, does Beethoven brace himself with still more intellectual a challenge. The result is little short of miraculous, for in due course, as we shall see, the theme is transformed.

Imagine a great dam containing a vast reservoir; as we watch, small trickles of water begin to percolate between the huge stones that make up the face of the dam. Even after the first dislodgements, the great arc still stays in place, but as the trickles become a torrent, the weight of water suddenly overwhelms us, sweeping everything away from its path. In my analogy, the dam is the inherent restraint of Classicism, the water is the emotional tide of Romanticism. Seen in these terms, this passage, symbolizing the ultimate collapse of an entire musical era, is awe-inspiring.

The first cracks in the facade appear with this phrase:

Ex.128

the fact that this is what is called a diminution of the subject (i.e. the theme of the fugue quickened) lends weight to my theory that Beethoven is becoming more and more intellectual, trying to contain the inner force by every means in his power. Simultaneously with these disruptive phrases, we also find the fugue subject in augmentation, notes twice as slow.

Ex.129

The rhythm grows more and more chaotic, so that all continuity of pulse is destroyed; for some few bars, every single first beat is suppressed, as though the very foundations were being swept away.

At this point, Beethoven has a tricky problem of notation. He wants the music to be gaining in impetus the whole time—he has even asked for that in words; but as the trickle increases to a flood, as more and more notes crowd into a bar, the actual pulse must be slowed to accommodate them. He therefore says, 'Meno Allegro' or 'less quickly' at the very point that the music sounds as though it is growing quicker. It is the exact equivalent of a change of gear.

Ex.130

'Chaos . .'                                        'change of gear'

Although it is my belief that this movement is the perfect

symbol of the Revolution that Beethoven accomplished, it can easily be seen that it is being brought about in an entirely Evolutionary manner. The pattern at this 'Meno Allegro' may look very different from the serene fugue subject, but it is so closely related as to be virtually identical. Only two notes have been omitted (**xx**).

Ex.131

As if to emphasize the essential continuity of the music, Beethoven manages to keep the fugue subject going in one way or another. Even the inverted form of Ex. 127 reappears, distorted it is true by the flying pieces of fugal material that seem almost to be attacking it, but still there.

Ex. 132

After all the turbulence, the safe haven of A♭ major is reached at last, and the fugue subject boldly reappears in the bass, free of distortion.

We now come to the crux of the matter, on which my entire view of this sonata must stand or fall. Naturally, every previous analysis of this work has pointed out the triumphant emergence of the fugue subject; some go so far as to use some such phrase as 'the fugue subject transformed'. This seems to me to miss the point completely. Suppose that only one page of this sonata had been preserved, the last page; suppose even that we had no more than these few bars:

Ex.133

ten thousand scholars could look at that through microscopes for a decade, and not one of them would be so foolish as to suggest it might be part of a fugue. There is nothing remotely 'fugal' about the writing; fugues are contrapuntal, and there is no counterpoint here, only a striding melody over a turbulent accompaniment. It is not the triumphant emergence of the fugue subject; it is the triumphant emergence of a *rhapsody*. The shackles of classicism have been severed; the new freedom is embraced with fervour, just as surely as in the ninth symphony, Beethoven rejects the material of the first three movements, saying 'Not with these tones . . .' and welcomes something completely new.

Compare the ending of this sonata with the closing pages of the mighty fugue that is the culmination of the Brahms–Handel Variations, and you will see at once what I mean. Even though Brahms introduces massive chords, the music remains essentially fugal in character. The whole point of Op. 110 seems to me that only by pushing beyond the limitations of classical form (as represented by the fugue) does Beethoven find the release from suffering that he has searched for for so long. That this release happens to contain the same elements as the previous music is a glorious affirmation that the solution to man's problems lies within himself.

# CHAPTER XXIX

# A WORD ON CRITICISM

THE VIEWPOINT put forward in the previous chapter is a very personal one, supported by an intuitive approach to the notes themselves rather than by any documentary evidence. It is, I hope, nearer the mark than the critic who wrote on 11 September 1806:

> Recently there was given the overture to Beethoven's opera, 'Fidelio', and all impartial musicians and music lovers were in perfect agreement that never was anything as incoherent, shrill, chaotic, and ear-splitting produced in music. The most piercing dissonances clash in a really atrocious harmony, and a few puny ideas only increase the disagreeable and deafening effect.[1]

Nor can I agree with a contemporary verdict on his Second Symphony, which described it as 'a crass monster, a hideously wounded dragon that refuses to expire, and, though bleeding in the finale, furiously beats about with its tail erect'.[1] All the same, there is something of value in these reactions, grotesque though they may seem to us today. We may think of the Moonlight sonata as a Beautiful Work, but Beethoven certainly wanted us to be electrified by the finale. Suppose that I had been a reasonably conservative listener in Beethoven's time, and had been given the job of writing a criticism of Op. 27 No. 2 in C♯ minor for a daily paper. Following the examples I have just quoted, I suspect that I could have written something like this.

> Herr Beethoven's latest composition reverses all expectation by commencing with an *adagio*, a procedure which is scarcely

[1] Both quotations are culled from Nicholas Slonimsky: *Lexicon of Musical Invective*: Coleman-Ross, 1953.

to be recommended since it revealed a total lack of contrast in ideas, and none of the considered musical argument which we have come to expect as proper in a work dignified by the name of Sonata. The monotonous repetition of triplets throughout the entire movement, some of them revealing almost laughable faults in harmony, could only produce a feeling of *ennui* in the listener. The second movement was a pleasing enough trifle, though somewhat too brief to make any lasting effect. As for the finale, it proved to be an hysterical jangling of notes which was impossible to grasp at a single hearing, nor was it likely to encourage one to undergo the experience a second time. If Herr Beethoven can do no better than to assault the keyboard in this brutal manner, he would be advised to apprentice himself to a blacksmith, preferably an harmonious one.

I would like at this point to suggest a paradox. Although such a hypothetical criticism strikes us as outrageous today, it is right in a way. The reaction seems all wrong, and yet it is nearer to the truth, nearer even to what Beethoven sub-consciously wanted, than our own tendency to sit back and wallow in the beauties of an accepted masterpiece. It merely draws the wrong conclusions from the evidence. In fact, we *ought* to be aware of the monotony of the triplets in the first movement, not as a means of producing *ennui*, but as a deliberate calculation on Beethoven's part. He knows that we are expecting contrast, so he witholds it. We should be aware of the alleged 'faults' in the harmony, for they are Beethoven's way of expressing pain, of giving profundity to a movement that might otherwise have been merely pretty. We should notice the economy and reticence of the second movement, and we should certainly respond to the terrifying impact of the finale, which is not a series of clearly articulated arpeggios from a primer on piano technique, but the musical equivalent of a volcano in eruption.

Now to watch a volcano on film is an awe-inspiring and thrilling sight; to run from it as it destroys your home is a nightmare. It is part of the creative artist's job to enable us to experience emotions at every level. As total human beings we may expect to find occasional moments of exaltation, a reasonable portion of happiness, a fair amount of boredom, stabs of pain—physical and emotional—and deep troughs of despair. They come to us all in varying degrees, even though we may not have the artist's ability to crystallize them and translate them into a durable form. A great sonata is like a life compressed; in it we may find the emotion of a lifetime, although obviously not in any chronological order. But what of quality; how do we recognize greatness and what is it?

Relatively, the grief of a seven-year-old child when its adored puppy is run over is as great as the heartbreak of a woman whose lover is killed in a war. The child recovers more quickly because, however sharp the pain at the time, it doesn't actually go so deep. There is a similarity in music. A third-rate composer can simulate grief perfectly well, but in the long run, it is only the grief of a seven-year-old. Beethoven's pain was the pain of an adult, an adult moreover who had suffered so much that he was able to transcend the personal and become universal. It is the Christian belief that Christ carries the burden of our sins; I do not consider it blasphemous to say that Bach, Mozart and Beethoven carry the burden of our sorrows. I certainly feel so when I hear or play something like the *Arioso* from Op. 110.

What is hard to accept is that for all its emotional profundity, there is not one note, not one chord, that has not been precisely chosen by Beethoven. The music seems to speak spontaneously, and yet it is full of artifice. How conscientiously he writes down every smallest rest, the calculated gaps in the melodic line that are like suppressed tears, the disturbing elements in the harmony that are like a stab of pain. To imagine that this emotion that Beethoven shares with us is not harnessed throughout by intellectual control is to be completely deluded about the true nature of composition. But we do not need to be consciously aware of what a cynic might call the 'tricks of the trade' to respond to the emotion, because by now the language of Beethoven has become sufficiently familiar for us to be able to get the message, even though we may not appreciate the subtlety or daring with which it is expressed. The composer himself uses craftsmanship in varying degrees, sometimes taking intuitive short-cuts, sometimes labouring mightily, sometimes falling back on sheer technical expertise.

I am not suggesting for one moment that Beethoven was consciously aware of the sort of scenario I have suggested for Op. 110. I believe my interpretation of the evidence is valid, or I would not have put it forward; but it is only valid in the light of our knowledge of the whole corpus of Beethoven's work, and of what came afterwards. (Even so, there is some confirmation in his treatment of the finale of the ninth symphony, as I have already pointed out.)

My real reason for including this short essay is to draw attention to the danger attendant on familiarity. It is said to breed contempt, though I cannot believe that anybody who professes contempt for Beethoven has the remotest claim to familiarity with his works. There is a risk, however, that we may come to take them for granted, paying lip-service to their greatness, while secretly feeling that their impact has become somewhat dulled. It is here that my view of a constantly evolving language can help to preserve the freshness that these works had when first we heard them, for the simple reason that we cannot have heard them all at once. When our knowledge of Beethoven is wide enough to be able to trace a link, however tenuous, between the first and last sonatas, using the Appassionata as the central point, we find an added interest in every work. We see the man developing as we might watch one of our own family develop. Few composers have exciting lives; they are too busy writing notes on paper to have time for adventures. They live through their music, and music is a magical time machine that enables us to share their triumphs and disasters in astonishingly vivid terms. By all means let us search for the heart of the matter, but not if it means that our own hearts cease to be involved. Better to hate Beethoven than to remain aloof . . .

## CHAPTER XXX

# SCHUBERT

## The last great trilogy

Sonata in C minor. D.958.
1. Allegro. 2. Adagio. 3. Menuetto. 4. Allegro.

Sonata in A major. D. 959.
1. Allegro. 2. Adantino. 3. Scherzo: Allegro vivace. 4. Rondo:
Allegretto.

Sonata in B♭ major. D.960.
1. Molto Moderato. 2. Andante sostenuto. 3. Scherzo: Allegro
vivace con delicatezza. 4. Allegro ma non troppo.

First published by Diabelli in 1838, in an edition dedicated
(by the publisher) to Schumann. Schubert had intended to
dedicate the three sonatas to Hummel; but as Hummel died
in 1837, Diabelli, always an opportunist, decided to change
the dedication.

B Y NOW, it is fairly general knowledge that Mozart wrote
his last three symphonies in one extraordinary creative
outburst of six or seven weeks; another equally remarkable
achievement has not been mentioned so frequently. In September
1828, Schubert, who had received nothing like as much acclaim
as Mozart during his lifetime, wrote three massive sonatas for
piano whose total length must exceed the duration of Mozart's
three final symphonies by a substantial margin. I realize that this in
itself is not necessarily a significant yardstick; we do not measure
music by the foot or the minute, nor are long works automatically
better than short ones. But Schubert's last three sonatas, which he

specifically labelled 'Drei grosse Sonaten', are to his total compositions for piano what Opp. 109, 110 and 111 are to Beethoven's.
If the comparison is not wholly fair, it is because Schubert was
able to learn a great deal more from Beethoven than Beethoven
could from his predecessors. Although Haydn, Mozart and
even lesser figures like Clementi unquestionably contributed a
good deal to Beethoven as a young man, he was to move increasingly into a world of his own. Schubert, who outlived Beethoven
only by a year and a half,[1] was able to benefit from his example.
Not having any pretensions to being a concert pianist himself,[2]
it is impossible for us to judge how well Schubert knew the
Beethoven sonatas in terms of actual playing. Did he, as one
would expect, read them through at the keyboard whenever
he could obtain copies? Could he even afford to buy them?
Certainly he revered Beethoven above all other composers, and,
in his humility, would have felt that to be interred next to his idol
was an honour he could never deserve. Those loving friends who
saw to it that he was buried in an adjacent grave were paying him
the greatest compliment they could. It was an ironic one, for
Schubert had found all too little fame in his lifetime, except in
his successful partnership with the singer Vogl. An English
musical dictionary published in 1827 devotes more space to
Beethoven than to any other composer of the time; Schubert
is not even mentioned, so little was the outside world aware
of his genius.

Two men could hardly ever have worked more differently
at the same craft; Beethoven's melodies were often the result
of months, even years, of patient endeavour, changing a rhythm
here, an interval there, beginning sometimes from commonplace
banalities that one is surprised to find him even bothering to
write down. Schubert had so natural a melodic gift that he could
write as many as three complete songs in a day; his 'sketches' of a
movement are often little less than a hastily scribbled rough copy
in which it is clear from the handwriting that his pen could

[1] Beethoven: 1770–1827. Schubert: 1797–1828.
[2] Mozart, Beethoven, Chopin, Liszt, Brahms, Rachmaninoff, **Bartók**—to name only a
few—were all successful as concert players.

scarcely keep up with his thoughts. When one speaks of his prodigious facility, it was not of an academic, trained kind, such as we find in Mozart, Haydn or Bach. The contrapuntal feats that astonish us in Bach's Musical Offering or in the finale of the Jupiter symphony do not come naturally; they are a sort of musical sleight-of-hand, acquired by years of practice, and by having what one might term a musical crossword-puzzle mentality. The fact that the crosswords happen also to be poetry is one of the miracles of music. Schubert's facility was more horizontal than vertical, by which I mean that his first impulse was to travel across the page in pursuit of a melody; some of his most inspired twists of harmony have an almost accidental air to them, and I tend to think that they were indeed happy discoveries of the moment rather than carefully planned.

Not even his most ardent admirer would seriously maintain that the complete piano sonatas of Schubert are as significant a contribution to the literature of the piano as those of Beethoven. It is no accident that the most played keyboard works of Schubert are the Impromptus, Moments Musicaux, the Wanderer Fantasy, and the F minor Fantasy for piano duet. Had he been born some twenty years later and grown up alongside Schumann and Chopin, I suspect that he might have written far fewer sonatas, and occupied himself with shorter forms to which his essentially lyrical gift was more suited. The overall perfection of the songs is something to marvel at; but with the example of Beethoven before him, he obviously felt a tremendous urge to write symphonies and sonatas. It was by accepting their challenge that he himself would be accepted. However beautiful the songs were, audiences of the time could scarcely estimate them as highly as we do today, since they could have realized neither the sheer magnitude of his achievement nor its historical importance. Here then is one of the ironies of musical history, a composer perfectly equipped by nature to write miniatures, drawn compulsively towards the very peaks which presented the greatest perils. Mahler and Schubert have much in common in this respect.

The use of the word 'miniature' may seem both derogatory

and provocative. Schubert's major works are far from concise; could a miniaturist conceive such compositions as the great C major symphony or the Octet, both of them immensely long, though unquestionable masterpieces? The answer obviously must be 'yes', or he would not have written them; but they are saved by the virtue of the unteachable qualities of genius. Sonata form was not the natural medium for Schubert to use; for instance, when he was still young he devised what seems at first glance to be a highly ingenious approach to the Recapitulation. Instead of beginning again in the tonic key, he would start in what is called the sub-dominant, the key a fifth lower. While this gives a deceptive air of surprise to the re-entry of the first subject, it is actually a lazy short-cut, as this little plan reveals.

| NORMAL FORM | SCHUBERT'S DEVICE |
|---|---|
| *Exposition* | |
| 1st subject. TONIC. Bridge modulates to 2nd subject. DOMINANT | 1st subject. TONIC. Bridge modulates to 2nd subject. DOMINANT |
| *Recapitulation* | |
| 1st subject. TONIC. Bridge modified to stay in TONIC for 2nd subject (i.e. different from Exposition) | 1st subject. SUB-DOMINANT. Bridge does identical modulation up a 5th which brings us back to TONIC for 2nd subject (i.e. same as Exposition) |

In other words, all Schubert had to do when he got to the start of his recapitulation was to copy his exposition exactly, merely transposing the first subject down a fifth. It's a clever idea, but it defeats the dramatic function of the Recapitulation and minimizes the necessity for any new invention. It is evidence that he misunderstood the true function of the form. Later, when he acquired a maturer view, he was to make a much more important contribution; having a remarkable flair for modulation into unexpected and remote keys, he decided to break the unwritten law that second subjects must always be in the dominant (or the relative major if the sonata happened to be in a minor key). With the complete conviction that only true genius can bring to unorthodoxy, he would introduce his second subject material in a totally foreign key. This was true invention, whereas his earlier device had been little more than an ingenious trick.

In the last year of his life, the year of these sonatas, Schubert must have become aware of some deficiences in his technical equipment; he even tried to take a formal course of counterpoint with a renowned teacher called Sechter. Death deprived him of the chance, but his several attempts at writing fugues show that he was very much in earnest. A great deal of his music existed in a vacuum; he never heard any of his mature orchestral music for the simple reason that it was not performed in his lifetime. The first five symphonies were written by the time that he was eighteen; as Donald Tovey has pointed out with devastating logic, 'Every work Schubert left us is an early work'. Had Beethoven died at the same age, he would have written only one symphony, three piano concertos, the Op. 18 set of quartets and the first fifteen piano sonatas (up to Op. 28). Seen in this perspective, whose achievement was the greater?

Let us turn to the subject in hand. There is no doubt that Schubert intended these last three piano sonatas to be a trilogy, since they are numbered 1, 2 and 3 in his own hand. I marvel that even Schubert, with all his facility, was able to compose the three works in one month. Yet, when we look at them closely, there are quite a few points of resemblance between them, as though the ideas that were churning round in his mind had become so enmeshed with each other that try as he might, he could not disentangle them. Is there perhaps a more subtle explanation? Did Schubert envisage deliberate links between the three works, so that they would in effect become one gigantic sonata, each 'movement' of which was a complete sonata in itself? I don't want to labour the point, and indeed it may not be worth making; but once I had realized that the three sonatas were written in so short a period, my attitude towards them changed. Similarities between the openings of the first two sonatas, between the finales of the first and third, between the slow movements of the second and third, and even more notably between the beautiful coda to the first movement of No. 2 and the still more beautiful coda to the slow movement of No. 3, begin to add up to something more than just coincidence. The similarities of construction are probably less significant, since each one might be said to be typical of Schubert's way of manipulating the form.

I have already suggested that Schubert was drawn towards writing sonatas because of his admiration for Beethoven. This is particularly apparent in the first sonata of this unique trilogy, the one in C minor. It begins with a theme of immense power, its massive quality partly derived from the fact that the bass stays solidly rooted on the tonic for so long, while the melody reaches out further and further from the starting point.

Ex.134

Now it is impossible not to be aware of the very close resemblance between this theme and the one with which Beethoven begins his thirty-two Variations in C minor. No doubt the tribute was unconscious, but it underlines Schubert's assumption of a Beethoven posture, to say the least.

Ex.135

* Legend has it that years after writing these variations, Beethoven heard them being practised by a girl student. Failing to recognize the work, he asked who had composed it; on being told it was his own, he expressed dismay, saying, 'Such nonsense by me? O Beethoven, what an ass you were!'

Was Brahms also tapping the same source when he conceived the mighty Passacaglia that comprises the last movement of his Fourth Symphony?

Ex. 136

Brahms: Op. 98. IV

* Try a G♯ here and the resemblance becomes more striking.

The greater richness of harmony reflects the age in which Brahms lived, but there can be no doubting the similarity of musical intent that exists in these three examples. To place Schubert thus as a link between Beethoven and Brahms is only proper, since it would be fair to say that Brahms was even more influenced by Schubert than he was by Beethoven.

It is interesting that both Beethoven and Brahms used this framework as the basis for a massive set of variations. Schubert too is aware of the enormous possibilities such a strong harmonic sequence offers. After a couple of descending scales that also recall moments in Beethoven (the finale of the Pathétique and the first movement of Op. 90), he sets out on a direct variation of Ex. 134.

Ex. 137

Such discipline proved foreign to his temperament however, and this is as far as he can go without launching into a new, lyrical extension. The song-writer takes over from the musical architect, and the dramatic tension goes out of the movement. This struggle between the two aspects of Schubert's personality is fascinating to watch; his aspirations are so frequently at odds with his inclinations. He is certainly aware of the hazards involved; the second subject, full of felicities of harmony, is lovingly explored at some length. Then, as if to prove his ability to accept the intellectual challenge of sonata form, he subjects it to a rigorous

treatment, putting it into the minor and disguising its gentle
outline with rather choppy figuration.

The development is remarkable. At first hearing, it seems to
have little to do with the exposition, and one is tempted to dismiss
it as irrelevant rambling, touched with inspiration it is true, but
lacking the compactness of argument we have come to expect in a
sonata. In fact, it is an admirable example of Schubert's inventive
genius. Rambling is scarcely the right word to describe music that
occupies itself entirely with one idea for a page and a half. What
worries us is that the idea seems to have no relationship to what has
gone before. Here is this new theme he seems to be so taken with
(Ex. 138):

Ex.138                          138a

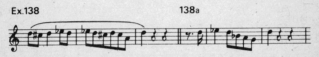

Its most noticeable feature is the 'narrowness' of the intervals.
Now the opening theme, Ex. 134, is also concerned with narrow
intervals; its culmination (not quoted in Ex. 134) is a pattern which
I have shown, conveniently transposed, in Ex. 138a. Marry
elements of Ex. 137 and 138a, and one can begin to see that Ex. 138
is far from irrelevant. It is not so much a development of a theme
as its 'descendant'. Here then is the clue that shows us that Schubert
was far from incompetent in his handling of large forms. We will
find the same technique being employed in all three sonatas; it
is a precursor of that 'transformation' of themes which was to
became the favourite practice of composers such as Berlioz,
Liszt and Tchaikovsky. In Schubert's hands, the device is used
less obviously; but once we see how subtly he uses what might be
called a process of melodic evolution, passages that seemed diffuse
and irrelevant are seen to be very much to the point.

I have already touched on the similarities that exist between
these sonatas. Even though there is a world of difference between
the mood of the C minor sonata and its successor in A major,
the rhythmic resemblance is strong. Compare bars 4–6 of Ex. 134
with this next example and you will see what I mean.

Ex.139

Similarities of modulation are easier to sense than to demonstrate. Here, for instance, is a quite remarkable passage from the finale of the C minor sonata. It shows Schubert at his most ingenious; if, to our ears, he seems to indulge in a sequence too many, we must remember how fantastically swift the changes of key must have seemed to a listener in 1828; it takes time to take in the formula that the composer has devised.

Ex.140

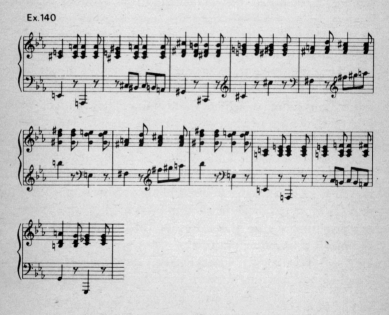

If we turn to the thirty-second bar of the A major sonata, we find a sequence which is nearly as unusual. The constitution of the harmonies is curiously similar, and if we merely change the rhythm to the characteristic ♩ ♪♩ ♪ of the previous example, the resemblance becomes much clearer.

Ex.141

(D. 959. I)

Another instance of this sort of cross-fertilization of harmony can be traced from the A major sonata to the glorious B♭ sonata which follows it. Since we are concerned with harmony, I will reduce the music to its fundamentals. Notice that in the first example, from D.959, the 'shift' note in the harmony is to be found at the top; in D.960, the 'shift' note is at first in the bass, but the technique is so similar that one passage seems to be a mirror of the other.

Ex.142

(D. 959. I)

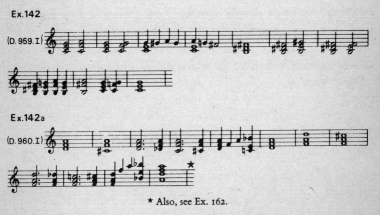

Ex.142a

(D. 960. I)

★ Also, see Ex. 162.

At the end of the first movement of D.959, the A major sonata, Schubert has a coda of extraordinary beauty; for the first and only time, the proud opening subject (which he has completely neglected during the development) is seen as though from afar, wrapped in a romantic haze that changes its entire character. This, coupled with some modulations that only he could have conceived, provides us with one of the most memorable phrases in the whole movement.

Ex.143

(D.959.I)

The effect of the delicately placed bass-notes, like a softly plucked
'cello, is unforgettable; the writing breathes a serenity that
few other composers could ever achieve. Yet if we turn to the
slow movement of the B♭ sonata, D.960, we find a passage that
not only excels this in sheer beauty, but seems to be derived directly
from it. If I change Schubert's notation by doubling the note-
values—it need not affect the sound at all—the likeness is easier to
see with the eye.

Ex.144

(D. 960)

The textures are virtually identical. The later sonata shows a
rather more complex treatment, but that is only to be expected,

since it is the main substance of the movement and not the inspired afterthought that it seems to be in D.959.

The sublime melody of the slow movement of D.960 appears complete in every detail in Schubert's 'rough' sketch; but the central section of the movement was recast entirely. He hit upon a fairly close approximation to the final version, but laid it out so that the contrasting theme in A major was given to the left hand.

**Ex.145**

The accompanying figure in the right hand was a little too fussy, and for all his haste in committing these sonatas to paper, Schubert had enough critical faculty to be able to make an extensive revision of this section. The version we now know has a far greater nobility than his first draft.

Mention of his critical faculty leads me to a fascinating demonstration of how a composer can have second thoughts. The finale of the A major sonata is a Rondo, based on a theme of immediate appeal.

**Ex.146**

(D. 959. IV)

A version of this tune appears in far more than embryonic form in an earlier sonata (D.537) written in March 1817. Schubert presumably felt that anything more than ten years old must already have been consigned to oblivion. He therefore resuscitated the melody, altering it as he saw fit, not, I am convinced, to disguise it, but to show what experience could teach. Here now is the earlier version, and a close comparison of the two is instructive. (The tune is in octaves throughout.)

**Ex.147**

(D. 537. II)

Allegretto quasi andantino

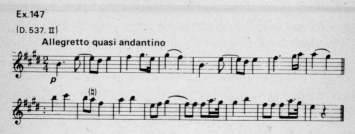

Both are beguiling, but there is no doubt that the later version (Ex. 146) shows a far greater awareness of craftsmanship.

The B♭ Sonata, one of the supreme masterpieces of the whole piano literature, is the one in which Schubert most successfully comes to terms with his own natural genius. It is almost as though he had said, 'Why must I try to measure my strength against Beethoven; let me be content to be myself'. Since his instinct drew him most readily to song, the sonata is the most lyrical ever written. To cavil at its length is to show a churlish ingratitude, for even Schubert was never more generous with melody than he is here. Over an accompaniment of remarkable simplicity, he extends a first subject whose serene character is enhanced by its tendency to move step by step, with the minimum of wide intervals.

**Ex.148**

(D. 960. I)

Molto moderato

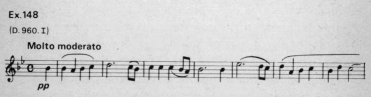

There follows a touch which instantly gives the stamp of romanticism to this otherwise rather classical melody, a low, distant trill that might well have been suggested by thunder heard far away in the mountains on a fine autumn day. There is a silence, as though the contemplation of a perfect landscape had indeed been momentarily disturbed; then, unaffected by the remote possibility of storms ahead, the song continues. Once more there is a distant rumble of thunder at the end of the phrase, but it is quickly integrated into an accompanying figure, and the melody goes on its way.

Now the problem of using a broad melodic span of this nature as a first subject is that it is hard to develop something that is already so complete. The very word 'develop' presupposes the idea of extension, of starting with a small unit, and causing it to grow. For instance, if I were to take the notes Bb—A—Bb which appear in the first bar of Ex. 148, I could 'develop' them in the classical sense of the word, by doing something on these lines.

Ex.149

If the result of this little exercise has been to fuse elements from the finale of Mozart's Jupiter symphony with a significant theme from the opening bar of Brahms' second symphony, it is hardly surprising. Fragments such as this are the stock material of the composer bent on development; they are readily manipulated, flexible, and easy to recognize in disguised forms.[1] For Schubert to develop his melody in this way would inevitably mean sacrificing its very essence—the long line as opposed to the concise rhythm. No sonata that I have discussed so far in this book has so long an opening theme; the nearest to it is the Appassionata, but there, as we have seen, the purpose of the theme is fundamentally to suggest the *harmony* of F minor. Beethoven's Op. 110 also begins with an extended melody, but it falls into two clearly defined sections. Schubert's mature genius shows itself in his solution to the

[1] For a detailed analysis of Brahms' treatment of this very theme, see *Talking about Symphonies*, Chapter VII, pp. 103–109.

problem; instead of developing by the accumulation of fragments, he develops by modifying the shape of the initial tune. The starting-note, B♭, becomes the third note of the scale of G♭ major, a beautifully subtle twist which at once opens up new possibilities.

Ex.150

Here we have the hand of a master at work. The drift from melodic to harmonic thinking is barely perceptible. The four notes in the fifth bar bring the first suggestion of a chord as opposed to a line of melody; they are repeated two bars later, and then we are gently rocked into harmonic motion. There is none of the abruptness with which Beethoven changes the texture in Op. 110 (see Ex. 112); yet the function of the two passages is identical insofar as they lead us from an essentially song-like concept to a purely instrumental one. At the very moment when it seems as though things may be getting out of hand, Schubert restores order by bringing back the opening theme. It is the first *forte* of the movement.

As is so often the case, it is instructive to consider an alternative. Musical scholars have sometimes led us to believe that Schubert lacked discipline in composition, that he worked 'off the cuff' to such a degree that he was too easily led away from the matter in hand. It is an argument that has some substance, but in this sonata we are dealing not with the inspired ramblings of a teenage boy, but the work of a vastly experienced composer. By way of experiment, let us suppose that Schubert had got carried away by the excitement of these triplet chords. How easy it would have been to have digressed into something quite out of keeping with the movement as a whole.

Ex. 151

Schubert avoids such temptations; he uses the first bar of Ex. 151 as a pivot that enables him to slide effortlessly back into the home key of B♭ major; the theme emerges triumphant, but subtly changed by the fact that it now rests on a sustained dominant in the base instead of the original tonic. It prevents us from having too strong a sense of finality; sure enough, there are surprises just ahead. With a modulation of typical daring, he flings us into the totally unexpected tonality of F♯ minor.

At first glance one is tempted to dismiss this as shock for shock's sake. A little thought shows us how carefully Schubert has prepared the ground—or perhaps it would be fairer to say how surely his musical instincts led him. For fourteen bars, starting from the beginning of Ex. 150, the music has clearly been in G♭ major. Now the notation of the scale of G♭ *minor* is extremely cumbersome, so it is habitually written as F♯ minor—the same sounds, but considerably easier to read or write.[1]

G♭ minor harmonic          F♯ minor

[1] A key-signature for G♭ minor is theoretically impossible, but it's an amusing academic exercise to invent one. It would look like this:

Small wonder that composers, publishers and musicians prefer the three sharps that suffice for F♯ minor.

The point of this excursion into the heady delights of musical
theory is to show the justification for using F♯ minor as a key for
the second subject of a sonata in B♭ major. By all precedent, the
second subject should be in the dominant key of F major; but by
dividing his first subject into two clear sections, one based on B♭,
and the other based on G♭, Schubert has given us what feels like
*two* tonics to choose from. To put his second subject into the minor
version of this subsidiary tonic is an inspired way of getting the
best of both worlds. The new key is wildly remote from the true
tonic of B♭, but closely related to the subsidiary tonic, G♭.

Technical analysis of this type is as abhorrent to my nature
as fugues were to Schubert's, but there are occasions when one
has to show an awareness of the law, if only to reveal how cleverly
it has been broken.

The second subject material is full of riches, showing the same
process of melodic evolution that Schubert exploits so skilfully in
the opening pages. There comes a point, however, when he seems
in danger of drifting into the commonplace. Figures that have a
vague suggestion of students' exercises in piano technique begin to
monopolize the page.

Ex.152

In the hands of a great artist this can sound exquisite, but looked
at dispassionately, it must be admitted to be something of a
ready-made formula. How marvellous then that Schubert should
have found ways of making such familiar devices peculiarly
relevant to this sonata. The subconscious of a composer works in a
mysterious way, and I am convinced that Schubert himself was
unaware of what I am going to show you now; yet I am equally
sure that it is a valid example of the instinctive sense of balance in
matters of musical architecture which I have already commented
upon in earlier chapters. Here first is a small part of the second
subject material; it appears in two forms—first as simple chords,
one to each beat, and then in this more active rhythm.

Ex.153

Now wouldn't it seem the most natural thing in the world to balance such a phrase with an answer that gave a hint of the pattern without actually being a true mirror?

Ex.154

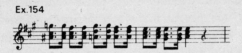

Apply a few touches of make-up:

Ex.154a

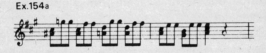

transpose into the key of the moment:

Ex.154b

and you have precisely the sort of figure that soon emerges from the misleadingly pedantic triplets of Ex. 152. It bears a suggestion of melody, while recognizing that in a primarily melodic movement, the ear needs some contrast. It is different in texture from any of the preceding sections, and yet, as I have shown, seems to have a sense of 'rightness' that only comes with the sure touch of genius.

A new, even more delightful example of this sureness of touch is to be found in a moment. Schubert is heading for the safe haven of the dominant in order to be able to bring his exposition to a proper conclusion. He has a problem though which would have appealed to Lewis Carroll. One can imagine the perplexed voice of Alice saying 'But how do you arrive

at somewhere you're already *at*?'. I spoke of Schubert heading
for the haven of the dominant; the fact is that he has already
arrived there at the start of Ex. 152. How then can he give
us a feeling of arrival? His solution is brilliant. Like a conjurer
who seems to be making the most awful mess of a trick, Schubert
begins a series of abortive journeys into other keys, even stopping
and starting as if he had lost all sense of direction. The effect of this
is to disorientate our feeling of any tonal security. The changes
are so swift, so unexpected, that when we finally do arrive back at
F major, we have virtually forgotten what it sounded like.
Presented here in simplified form, we can follow the stages of this
diversion which, like those devised by urban highway authorities,
takes us into the back streets, getting us thoroughly lost before
we finally find our bearings again. (Imagine the figuration of
Ex. 154b throughout.)

Ex.155

Bar 1 seems to be heading straight for F major; bar 2 turns
us right away to Ab major in bar 3, which at once gives way
to Eb major in a half-hearted sort of way; bar 4, after a non-
plussed silence, starts in Gb major, only to slide into an equally
unconvincing Db major; a diminished seventh in bar 6 puts
us momentarily into no-man's-land while at the same time
suggesting the dominant of Bb; bar 7 seems to confirm that
maybe we are going to Bb after all; bar 8 says, 'Goodness, look
here we are in F'.

After so eventful a journey, we need time to settle down,
and Schubert unfolds a radiant new tune, richly harmonized.

Ex.156

Once again we can see Schubert's evolutionary process at work. The most notable feature of the second subject has been a tune beginning like this:

Ex.157

Each time it has appeared, there has been a note of wistfulness in the surrounding harmony; in a sense, the melody remains unfulfilled until it reaches the version we find in Ex. 156. While it is presumably correct in textbook terms to label Ex. 156 a 'codetta', it is considerably more enlightening to see it as the apotheosis of the second subject.

This sonata is immensely long, but its proportions are nobly realized. Schubert is very much aware of the danger of losing our attention at this juncture. We have reached the dominant; we have been offered a delectable morsel of melody; it is the moment to tantalize us a little more. He repeats Ex. 156 an octave lower, rich as divided violas and 'cellos, then again catches us out by a sudden shift of key. So sudden that the music itself seems to take offence, for two angry chords cut short any tendency to drift too far afield. With a gesture of extraordinary grace, Schubert readmits us to the strangely elusive world of F major, and rounds off his exposition. The melting final phrase:

Ex.158

was a last-minute inspiration which only appears in his fair copy of the movement.

Because it is a sonata, Schubert seems to have felt that the exposition should be repeated, though few pianists share his view. But to have started once more after so quiet a conclusion would hardly have been effective; some change of mood was needed. He introduced a new, restless little figure, toyed mysteriously with the last three chords of Ex. 158, then suddenly startled his audience out of their wits with a great thunderclap, the only time that that distant rumble which had lent such an individual colour to the first theme is allowed to reveal its latent power.

With a typical stroke of magic, Schubert wafts us gently into C♯ minor[1] at the start of the development. Our ears have been sated perhaps with an overdose of B♭, E♭ and F; how like him then to move into a key in which these notes cannot really be said to appear. It opens the door to even remoter worlds, 'sharp' keys which have only been visited briefly, if at all, during the exposition.

There can be no finer example of Schubert's highly individual method of development than this movement. The music gives a deceptive impression of expansiveness, deceptive, because in its unique way it is every bit as concentrated as a Beethoven development. He begins by giving his opening theme a completely new face. Not only is it in the minor for the first time; it has an unforeseen variant, turning it in new directions.

Ex. 159

How subtle is the relationship between the opening notes of the melody and the apparently new continuation; how un-expected too, the process of compression by which Schubert is able to follow this immediately with a reference to Ex. 157,

[1] Also the key of the slow movement: cf. Mozart K.457, p. 46.

originally a remote contrast to the first subject, but now a close
neighbour. The fusion accomplished, Schubert is content for the
moment to leave it at that. He turns his attention to Ex. 152,
the triplet arpeggios. It is hard to uphold the accusation of long-
windedness so often levelled at Schubert in the face of such economy; three main subjects in the first fourteen bars of the development is hardly garrulous.

The ingenuity of his construction is remarkable. For some
time, he avoids any further reference to what we have presumed
to be the most important themes of the movement. The figuration
of Ex. 152 continues, continually changing its tonality, supported
by a bass which we can be forgiven for supposing to be no more
than a conventional prop.

Ex.160

A climax is reached in the key of Db major. The music descends
to a low Db, reiterated like a soft drum-beat. It is here that
Schubert plays his most unexpected card, a stroke of sheer genius
that truly shows he had no further need to look over his shoulder
to the towering figure of Beethoven for help. He takes the
unobtrusive bass from the first bar of Ex. 160 and transforms it into
a theme of the utmost importance.

Ex.161

With relentless inevitability, he builds this theme up, now
in the right hand, now in the left. Dissonances increase the tension,
the texture thickens, single notes become octaves, rhythms
clash. It is the exact centrepoint of the sonata, a summit from which,

on both sides, the landscape descends to the pleasant valleys
beneath. Few men, on climbing a mountain, would wish to
start the journey down at once. It is only natural to stand and gaze.
This is exactly what Schubert seems to do; the music becomes
curiously static, the harmonies having a strangely modal quality
(see Ex. 142a). In the far distance, we hear again that thunder-roll,
and it turns our minds once more to the opening theme. It too is
affected by the environment; the harmonies belong, one would
think, more to Grieg than to Schubert.

Ex.162

This whole central section is one of the marvels of music;
it dies away at last to nothingness—complete silence, the
memory of thunder still hanging in the air, yet with our hearts
filled with the peace of Nature at her most serene. If Beethoven's
Pastoral symphony is, as he claimed, 'more an impression of the
countryside than an actual painting', I make no apology for
making the same observation about this sonata. I am not inventing
Schubert's love of nature; here he is, in a letter to his brother,
dated 12 September 1825, describing the inner Salzburg valley.

To describe to you the loveliness of that valley is almost impossible. Think of a garden several miles in extent, with
countless castles and estates in it peeping through the trees; think
of a river winding through it in manifold twists and turns;
think of meadows and fields like so many carpets of the finest
colours, then of the many roads tied round them like ribbons;
and lastly avenues of enormous trees to walk in for hours, all
enclosed by ranges of the highest mountains as far as the eye
can reach, as though they were the guardians of this glorious
valley; think of all this and you will have a faint conception
of its inexpressible beauty.[1]

[1] Otto Erich Deutsch: *Schubert* (trans. Blom): J. M. Dent, 1946

Inexpressible? Perhaps if Schubert felt that words were inadequate, he may have used music, even without openly admitting it.

As if there were not beauty enough in the first movement, Schubert follows it with a serenade-like Andante that, so far as the piano can, matches the sustained perfection of the slow movement of the C major quintet. I cannot believe that any piano of his time can remotely have done justice to it, but the vision is there. The accompaniment sticks to one rhythm and shape, suggesting a softly-played guitar. The melody is like distant voices singing, moving in simple thirds as people do when they harmonize spontaneously. For all its appearance of simplicity, Schubert employs some wonderfully rich harmonies. Ex. 144 gives a tiny sample of a movement that needs no help from me in conveying its message. If there should ever come a day when the machines finally take over, when the composers abdicate all responsibility, when concert-music is pronounced dead, when man has at last grown artistically impotent—on that black day, let someone play this movement to the dying world; at least we would learn again what beauty is.

The Scherzo is a delight of a different kind, quicksilver and delicate, imbued with the wit that Schubert may have learned from Beethoven, but free from any suggestion of the rough, boisterous character that some people find offensive in Beethoven's music. Schubert exploits extreme registers in this movement, the tunes nearly all being conceived as dialogues, as though between a flute and a bassoon. As one might expect, the modulations are marvellously adroit, turning always in unexpected directions. The central Trio is a subtle example of the village-band joke.[1] All the lads are playing quietly except for

---

[1] I know most performers make it sound darkly spiritual, but I see no reason not to admit it to be as entertaining as the rest of the movement. It can still be great music.

old Joe on the tuba, whose isolated notes stand out like discreet farts at the vicarage.

Ex. 163

The joke is the funnier for being handled so erratically; the pattern of the explosive accents is inconsistent. Occasionally old Joe does manage to pop a note in just right, and we can sense that if only he had had a bit more time to practise or had bought a better instrument, all would be well.

It is unusual to find a sonata in which the only movement to be touched by pathos is the finale. (There are those who would say that the slow movement is sad; but if it is sadness, it is of that nostalgic kind which is a sort of self-indulgence. So much of it is in the major that I refuse to believe that it contains any hint of true grief, such as we found in Beethoven's Op. 110.) The last movement is characterized by a curious inability to stay in the major. Time after time Schubert tries to get into a major key, but it won't 'take'. The movement begins with a single octave G, like two orchestral horns, a note that commands our attention without violence. A little tune begins, Mozartean in style almost, touched with that same pathetic urgency that is so haunting at the start of Mozart's G minor symphony. It is clearly in C minor, even though, with typical deftness, Schubert turns it towards B♭ major.

Ex.164

That reappearance of the first note is more than just a repetition; it is a denial of Bb major. A few bars later, the music does seem to have established a successful hold on Bb, but again it is diverted, this time to G minor. Back comes the first little tune again, and as before, it reaches for Bb major. No sooner is the rightful key for the movement established for the third time than the music drops strangely into Ab major. This new tonality lasts for a matter of seconds before it too is sabotaged and pushed towards G minor; the crisis is averted, a clever twist taking us back to the elusive Bb. There is a flutter of unease, and the 'horn-call' pulls us away once more into C minor.

It would be laborious to analyse the whole movement in these terms, but I have done enough to draw attention to the curious ambivalence that prevails. Tunes have a habit of ending up in the 'wrong' key. One long sustained theme, whose smooth appearance is belied by the strange off-beat notes that accompany it in the bass, actually starts a phrase in F major and finishes it in D, which might be described as 'a proper turn-up'.

Ex.165

Nothing in this movement seems to behave predictably. The loudest storm emerges out of a total silence; the strongest, most dramatic theme is transformed into something gossamer, delicate as Titania dancing on a moonbeam; a passage that looks as though it is all storming heroics has to be played right against nature, making a continuous diminuendo where one wants to batter the keyboard. If ever a movement deserved the soubriquet Caprice, this is it. Even the ending revels in contradiction; Ex. 164 unfolds for the last time, ambiguous to the end; there is a silence: suddenly, without warning, we are swept away in a torrent of octaves. Is there a suggestion of impatience, of anger even? No: the movement ends joyously, its pathetic opening resolved at last.

I have tried to ride the uneasy precipice between technical jargon and fulsome rhapsody in this analysis; it is difficult to avoid either in a work which combines the mature skill of a craftsman with the divine instinct of an artist to such a degree. It *is* important to understand the intricacies of modulation and key-relationships in classical music, and there is no avoiding the issue. Analysis can only take us so far, and if the end-product of analysis is to make the music less appealing, it has failed utterly. In his *Essays and Lectures on Music*,[1] Donald Tovey has two brilliant chapters on Schubert, the second of which is highly technical, being full of those near-algebraical symbols ($\flat$VI, $\sharp$vi, etc.) that take music into the esoteric realms so dear to the academic mind. He devotes a good deal of space to this sonata, exposing its harmonic bones to the naked eye, if not to the untrained ear. But—and it is a big 'but'—he ends his chapter with what might be described as a perfect cadence when he says:

> Schubert's tonality is as wonderful as star clusters, and a verbal description of it as dull as a volume of astronomical tables. But I have often been grateful to a dull description that faithfully guides me to the places where great artistic experiences await me . . . .

Tovey had a scholarship to which I could never begin to

[1] Oxford University Press, 1949.

aspire, but even at his most professorial, he preserves a proper scepticism about the theoretician's approach. To give a detailed analysis of the last three sonatas of Schubert would need a book in itself—and a very dreary book it would be. I have tried to say enough to make you realize something of their wonder. Did ever a man spend four weeks of his life bequeathing so much pleasure to mankind?

## CHAPTER XXXI

# LISZT

## Sonata in B Minor

Composed 1852–3. Dedicated to Schumann. Surprisingly there is no opus number, but Liszt was haphazard and prolific with his compositions, which number over 700. A set of three early sonatas, written in 1825, was lost or destroyed, as was a sonata for piano duet written in the same year. His only other extant sonata is No. 7 of the second set of 'Années de Pèlerinage' (Italie) which is described as 'Après une lecture du Dante, Fantasia quasi Sonata'. It is too much a 'programme' work to be classified as a sonata in the accepted sense of the word.

To follow Schubert with Liszt may seem something of a stylistic gaffe, but there is more logic in it than first meets the eye. Liszt was a great admirer of Schubert's Wanderer Fantasy, a work which he transcribed with excellent taste, making it into a concerto by adding an orchestral part. Its form, which imposes unity on a long work by making some themes common to all four movements, impressed him enormously. (Berlioz had used the same idea, though in a rather more naïve way, in the Fantastic symphony.) It was to become a widely used device during the second half of the nineteenth century, appealing to composers as different in style as Tchaikovsky, César Franck, Wagner and Liszt himself. It can hardly be a coincidence that he should have made his transcription of the Wanderer Fantasy the year before he wrote this sonata. Schubert seems to have given him the clue he was seeking, and his subsequent solution to the problem of how to give sonata form a new look is one of the most significant landmarks in musical history.

Personal taste weighs very heavily in our assessment of a composer like Liszt; even his most ardent admirers would admit that he does flirt with danger at times, going very near the borderline of vulgarity. (Notice the diplomatically ambiguous nature of that phrase: one can be near a border on either side.) All the same, to dismiss the sonata as meretricious trash, as some critics are prone to do, is carrying prejudice too far. Written in his early forties, not long before he deserted the concert-platform, the sonata was not well received at the time, a fact which at once suggests that it was one of Liszt's best compositions. The truly first-rate seldom receives universal critical claim. One must take into account Liszt's position when he was at the height of his career. He was the 'lion' of the century and the leaders of society fought to have the privilege of welcoming him into their homes. Audiences were hungry for sensation at all costs, and Liszt's phenomenal virtuosity could supply it. For him to play an entirely simple piece was to deprive them of their meat and drink; to write a sonata without virtuosity entering into it would have been unthinkable to such a man. Under the circumstances, it is remarkable that he produced a work that is astonishingly inventive in its construction, and truly revolutionary in form. Despite his indebtedness to Schubert for the idea, Liszt was to employ a very different method. The cross references that we find in the Wanderer Fantasy are retrospective; in other words, a theme that has been thoroughly established in the first movement will appear as a reminiscence in the scherzo. Schubert himself probably took the idea from Beethoven's fifth symphony, where the scherzo theme makes a ghostly reappearance in the finale. (It is doubtful whether either Beethoven or Schubert would have known the relatively early symphony by Haydn in which that most inventive composer had already tried the experiment.) Liszt's approach was far more radical. In fact a much later composer, Sibelius, is usually given the credit for inventing the form that Liszt uses in this sonata, just as Debussy is usually credited with inventing the whole-tone scale—a device Liszt was using with assurance when the French composer was still a student.

The very first page proclaims the Revolution. Instead of

the long-established tradition of joining first and second subjects by a bridge passage, Liszt gives us three ideas, separated from one another by silences, and seemingly quite unrelated. It's as though a lecturer were to say, 'Tonight I am going to talk to you about horses, eggs and trees'. On the face of it, this doesn't look like a very promising evening, but by the end of it you have been convinced that horses live in trees and lay eggs. A work lasting nearly half an hour has been built from a few fragments; the apparently irreconcilable has been fused together; the insanity of the opening is revealed as a masterstroke. I doubt if there is any other work in musical history that is so concentrated in its use of material, apart from Bach's Musical Offering or the Art of Fugue. Since both of these are by way of being contrived demonstrations of particular and limited skills, they are hardly fair comparisons. In the whole sonata there are only five themes, which could all be jotted down on the back of a postcard and still leave room for a message to Mother.

The sonata begins unpromisingly with a couple of isolated notes followed by a slow descending scale. The two notes are repeated; the scale descends again, picking its way a little more carefully; two notes; silence.

Ex.166

We wait expectantly; suddenly, out of the blue, with the dramatic impact of a Nijinsky leaping onto the stage, theme no. 2 arrives.

Ex.167

Another silence; then, deep down in the most menacing register of the keyboard, comes a fateful knocking, a theme of extraordinary compressed energy.

Ex.168

A quick glance at these three examples shows that in effect, each one consists of a phrase that is stated twice, albeit with some modification. Liszt could hardly make things more compact, yet he is careful to impress these themes upon our minds by this repetition. He has preserved the idea that lay behind the classical convention of repeating the exposition, realizing that it still had a function; but he has reduced it to the barest minimum, and, by choosing themes of so clearly defined individuality, he has made it that much easier for the listener to retain them in his mind.

If we are to explore this sonata in detail, I am going to have to quote these three examples so often that it will be simpler to identify them by name. Let us call Ex. 166 the 'scales' theme, or I, Ex. 167 the 'octave' theme, or II and Ex. 168 the 'knocking' theme, or III. The ingenuity with which Liszt manipulates them, changing their emotional content and continually establishing new relationships between them, is something that gives me as much pleasure now as it did when I first heard the work as a student. There is no better way of discovering just how adaptable musical motifs can be than by observing Liszt at work.

After the very theatrical presentation of his three main ideas, there is a brief silence, as well there might be after such shock tactics. Out of this silence emerges a figure of great agitation:

Ex.169

*agitato*

Liszt repeats this several times, raising the pitch step by step in the sort of sequence that some critics would suggest (with some justification) to be a bit glib. The fact is that it is so effective a way of whipping up excitement that it has become a cliché, debased by overmuch use. In 1852 it was more than enough to set pulses racing. Morever, it is the first of the many transformations we are to experience. Sounding like a completely new idea, it actually proves to be derived from Ex. 167, the 'octave' theme. The stages are easy to see:

Ex.170

*(Ex.167, bars 5-6)*        = start of Ex.169

At the height of this first climax, the octave theme returns, harmonized for the first time with a full-blooded chord of E♭ major, while its descending tail streams out like a comet. More dramatically still, the knocking theme thunders out in the bass once more as the music settles for the first time into the tonic key of B minor. It is a moment to store in one's mind, for although this vast one-movement sonata is constructed on such original lines, it also pays considerable tribute to traditional form. Some twenty-five pages further on, a recapitulation in the classical sense is destined to appear. It starts at the point we have now reached; according to conventional analysis then, all that we have heard so far has been a prologue, an announcement of the *dramatis personae*. The exposition proper begins.

At once a battle is joined between the second and third themes.

II has its tail twisted to some purpose, III hammers away in opposition.

Ex.171

Again the sequences pile up until a summit is reached; down we plunge into a strange turbulence, the rhythm violently disturbed by agitated syncopations. For all its appearance of violent conflict, Liszt's concentration on the matter in hand is extraordinary. The innocent ear could be forgiven for assuming that here, at least, some new material is being used, but Ex. 172a proves how wrong we are.

Ex.172

Ex.172a

Out of all the excitement, the octave theme emerges triumphant; even here, Liszt finds a new way of presenting it, making the phrase overlap itself.

Ex.173

This develops into a tremendous passage in octaves, virtuoso music certainly, but evolved legitimately from what has gone before. It finally climbs down on to an A♮ which hammers away relentlessly. Two staccato bass-notes draw our attention to the left hand. A distorted version of the scale theme (I) appears, casting a shadow that makes us quickly forget the heroics of the previous page. Yet even this phrase must be used constructively. Liszt is preparing for a grand entrance, the first appearance of the fourth of the five themes that are all he allows himself in the whole of this sonata.[1] An enormous sense of expectancy is aroused by his ingenious treatment of I, which soon drags itself out of the sepulchral depths and quickens its step.

Ex.174

At last the Grande Dame appears, making a truly royal entrance. Pulsating chords flood our ears with harmony, and one can imagine the magisterial authority Liszt would have brought to such a passage. Of course it is theatrical, more than life-size; but it was written in an age when cynicism had not eroded belief in grandiloquence.

Ex.175

Grandioso

This noble theme, which I shall call IV, is dismantled by the composer after it has run its course; the four notes marked ⌐‾‾⌐ are the subject of a brief argument about tonality which ultimately comes to rest on a widespread, expressive chord which turns out

---

[1] By conventional analysis, it would presumably be termed the 'second' subject, though a more misleading term for the fourth main theme would be hard to find.

to be that old stand-by, a diminished seventh. From this moment of repose, the octave theme (II) reappears, utterly transformed.

There is an interesting point to be raised here about the whole question of musical 'language'. A purist, like Stravinsky, argues that music is something so complete in itself that to use words like 'grand', 'tempestuous', 'tender', 'sad', 'happy' to describe a theme is misleading. He has claimed that, 'by its nature, music is essentially powerless to express anything at all, whether a feeling, an attitude of mind, a psychological attitude, a natural pheno-menon, etc. . . . If music seems to express something, this is merely an illusion and not a reality. It is simply an additional attribute which, by tacit and inveterate agreement, we have lent it, thrust upon it, as a label, a convention.'[1] Harsh words from the composer of such vividly descriptive scores as Firebird or Petrushka.

In a way, this sonata, for all its romantic appearance, could be said to bear out Stravinsky's contention. It is almost irresistible to describe theme II as 'heroic', theme III as 'menacing' or theme IV as 'grandiloquent'. Indeed, I am positive that Liszt meant us to think of them in this way. But if I take a *word* like menacing, I cannot give it another meaning, any more than I am likely to make the words 'I love you' convincing by shouting them in anger. (I realize it is possible to imagine a situation in which a man, exasperated by a girl's indifference, might end by yelling, 'Can't you see that I love you!', but it is an unnatural interpretation of the words, affected by an accumulation of events leading up to the particular moment.) I myself have often argued that a musical phrase has a certain emotion built-in to it; to deny the emotional power of music is as foolish as it would be to suggest that a funeral march could be mistaken for a waltz. The fact remains (and this sonata gives a vivid demonstration of its validity) that while we may not be able to change the meaning of a word, we can certainly change the meaning of a musical pattern. Can I suggest a middle road, not so uncompromisingly dispassionate as Stravinsky's,

[1] See Eric Walter White: *Stravinsky*, p. 93: John Lehmann, 1947.

but equally not so governed by sentimentality as are the reactions of the listener who merely uses music as a sort of drug.

In the battle-scenes of his wonderful film version of *Henry V*, Laurence Olivier was clad in armour, riding a white horse. His stirring call of 'Cry God for Harry, England and Saint George!' was delivered at the top of his voice. That he wears doublet and hose and uses gentle tones when paying court to Katherine, the French Princess, does not mean that he is no longer the same man, but only that we are seeing a different aspect of the same man. Thus when we find theme II presented with all the expressive beauty of a Chopin nocturne, it does not mean that it is no longer the same theme. Liszt would be dismayed if we failed to realize that it was, since the idea of transforming the theme is fundamental to his concept. This leads us to the conclusion that it is not the theme itself, but its treatment or presentation that is decisive. Volume, tempo, instrumental timbre, harmonization and, regrettably, standards of performance all have a part to play in deciding our reaction—though a bad performance can only obscure the quality of greatness, not destroy it.

Notes in themselves are virtually meaningless; about the most you can say is that they are high or low, and even that is only relative; the lowest note on the flute is very high for a double bass. Even a sequence of notes as sacrosanct as the theme from the opening movement of the Moonlight sonata is far from absolute in meaning. Suppose that I present them in this way:

Ex.176

The notes are unaltered, yet nobody would suggest that the meaning had not changed. The emotional effect of a composition is due to a wide range of factors, of which melody is, surprisingly, far less important than we imagine. It seems a suitable moment to return to Liszt.

The new version of II, 'tenderized' as the tele-commercials might say, is a reverse application of the technique I have just demonstrated on Beethoven's Op. 27 No. 2. Liszt helps the imperceptive by reminding them of II, presenting it as a single line of unsupported melody, slow and quiet, but with its melodic outline unaltered. He has paved the way for a remarkable change of character:

Ex.177

A visual comparison with Ex. 167 reveals both the similarities and the differences. Tempting though it must have been for Liszt to dally in this dream-world, he soon reminds us that this is not a rhapsody but a sonata by re-introducing III, whose menace is only partly lessened by being played quietly. Yet this theme too, which one would have thought too powerful and compact to be susceptible to much alteration, is transformed.

Ex.178

The supporting harmonies have a faint suggestion of the famous A♭ Liebesträum, written a couple of years earlier,[1] but

[1] Actually a piano transcription of a song composed about 1845.

this could well have been the sort of private cross-reference between works that Schumann enjoyed making (namely Papillons-Carnaval), and the dedication to Schumann suggests the possibility that Liszt had some ulterior motive of an amicable kind. Needless to say the tune is beautifully laid-out for keyboard with some cunning division between the hands. A rising chromatic scale leads us to one of the most magical touches; theme II, having been both heroic and sentimental, now becomes delicate and capricious.

Ex. 179

Liszt toys with it for some time, the right hand meanwhile dazzling us with exquisitely wrought patterns that are typical of his keyboard mastery. Just at the moment when virtuosity is beginning to get the upper hand, Ex. 178 puts in an appearance, all sentiment cast aside. Even the most beautiful girl can have a temper, as Liszt would have been the first to know. A soft answer turneth away wrath however, and theme II duly gives it.

Ex. 180

Two finely spun candenzas bring us back to a much more dramatic mood, and theme II re-assumes its original heroic attitude, a new figure of brilliant ascending octaves in the left hand intensifying the contrast. For a couple of pages, the storm beats about our heads, although, for all the sound and fury, Liszt keeps an iron control on the material, everything being derived from II.

Sudden storms often bring sunshine in their wake, and so it is now when Liszt causes the music to dissolve into delicately shimmering figuration of the most decorative kind. Almost unbelievably, II is still present in yet another guise.

Ex.181

Having enjoyed himself with a dazzling display of keyboard writing that never loses sight of musical values, for all its glitter, he now brings back Ex. 178 in a still more dramatic version. It leads to one of the most technically daunting pages in the sonata, with fearsome skips in the left hand. At the climax, the scales theme, which has been absent for some time, re-appears in a form more violent than we would have suspected was possible from so reticent a beginning.

Ex.182

All the themes are being thrown together with increasing violence; II returns in its original form, though transposed into a different key; IV presents an entirely different face to the world, no longer a Grande Dame, but an Amazonian Queen ordering a slave to be executed. Despite the savage ferocity of these phrases, we gain the impression that the music is gradually losing momentum. Liszt, whose sense of overall proportion has never deserted him, is preparing the way for what, in effect, is a miniature slow movement. We are very near to the exact centre of the work; the composer is giving us a forcible reminder of the three main components before he bids them a temporary farewell. The knocking theme (III) returns twice in its original form, the first three notes of the octave theme are hurled at us in chunky chords before, remarkably, II and III are combined, a marriage which has not even been hinted at since they were first flung into violent opposition in Ex. 171.

Ex.183

At last, on the nineteenth page of a forty-page work, the only remaining theme of the five makes its long-delayed appearance. As I have said, it serves the function of a slow movement, yet this gives the misleading impression that the first four themes are now going to be put aside. For a time we might well imagine this to be the case as this new and very Wagnerian melody casts its spell.

Ex.184 = V

'Casts its spell' is right, for soon themes III and IV find themselves in this new environment, and are deeply affected by it. Some traces of the Amazonian severity that had so transformed IV still linger, but the general tone is lyrical, whether tender or passionate.

A sustained increase in tone brings us to the re-emergence of II, now plunging into unaccustomed depths, but in the end it is the new theme, V, that dominates this central section. Liszt's use of slow descending scales is particularly ravishing here, recalling something of the serene simplicity that we find in the slow movement of Beethoven's Emperor concerto—a work he must

have played many times. The slow movement, as we may legitimately think of it, ends with two solemn reminders of the scale
theme, (I), virtually unaltered from its original version apart from
a change of key. The music dies away to silence.

Counterpoint and fugue are not the first two words that
spring to mind when we think of Liszt; however, we should
remember his enormous admiration for Bach, and the magnificent
transcriptions he made of a number of Bach's organ works. He
was so gifted that he could turn his hand successfully to most
things, and he now has the sense to realize that our aural palate
is in danger of having been glutted by a surfeit of sweetness.
Something cerebral is needed by way of contrast. In a moment of
sheer inspiration, he embarks on a fugue, a muted, diabolical
sort of fugue, such as Mephistopheles might have given a lazy student
to practise as punishment for past sins. II and III are interwoven
with uncanny facility. It is more complicated to describe than
to witness; here, then, are some of the fusions of the two ideas.

Ex.185

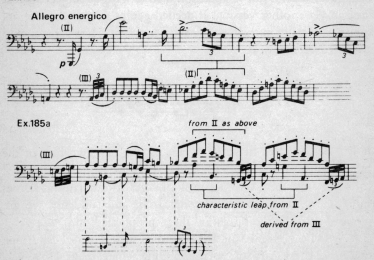

Ex.185a

Gradually out of this bustling counterpoint the original outlines
of II and III begin to re-establish themselves more and more
solidly.

Ex.186

But Liszt's ingenuity is by no means exhausted. The music sounds as though it is driven onwards with inhuman energy, yet in fact it is growing increasingly cerebral. The next step is to 'invert' II, turning it upside down.

Ex.187

This is a common enough trick even in the most academic of fugues; what is not so common is to fit a fugue subject against itself in yet another version. It needed genius to spot this opportunity, especially in the heat of such a moment. Here is the newly modified version of II:

Ex.188

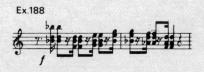

it will be found to fit perfectly against the first two bars of the previous example. This 'battle-in-Looking-Glass-land' is sustained for some time until once again II emerges triumphant (as heroes should); lightning flashes, thunder rolls, and suddenly we are plunged into the recapitulation that I prophesied on p. 424.

It is these classical landmarks within such a novel landscape that make this sonata such an outstanding achievement. However, they bring an interesting comparison to light. Aware as he must have been that he was running the risk of losing control of a work conceived on such a huge scale, Liszt not only felt

the need for some vestiges of classical discipline, but, paradoxically, put music into a far tighter straitjacket than it had been
in for years. The loosening-up process initiated by Beethoven
and continued by Schubert could be said to have been carried
on by Liszt in so far as much of the work is revolutionary in
concept. But just as political revolutions prompted by a desire
for freedom often result in worse tyrannies, so did this musical
revolution result in a tightening of control. The extraordinary
concentration on a very small amount of musical material that
is the hallmark of this sonata is the antithesis of Romanticism.
It is a concentration comparable to that which we find in the
first movement of Beethoven's fifth symphony, even though
the work itself seems to belong to a totally different world of
indulgent excess. An exactly parallel situation is to be found
at the start of the twentieth century—the revolution accomplished by Schoenberg, aiming at a new freedom, resulted in the
most repressive and total discipline ever imposed on music,
serialism.

   Liszt's recapitulation contains a number of new features, as
good recapitulations should; most of them are clearly recognizable,
though one ingenious compression of the octave theme deserves
mention.

Ex.189

This is later developed into a notoriously difficult octave passage in
B major which is a cruel hurdle to place so near to the end of one
of the most daunting technical challenges in the repertoire.
Surprisingly though, the work ends quietly. After the ultimate
supreme climax in terms of volume and physical effort, there is a
long silence, out of which theme V emerges like a benediction.
The final page is an inspiration; eight times we hear the knocking
theme grumbling away in the bass as enigmatic harmonies rise
slowly towards the upper reaches of the keyboard. The quietest
and most contemplative version of II that has appeared so far
gives way to a few solemn chords. We begin to realize that

Liszt is reviewing the material for the last time, in the reverse order to that in which it first appeared (III—II—I). The slow descending scales of I make their way down to the lowest C on the keyboard, the bottom note but one. On this note, so near to the tonic (B), Liszt pauses tantalizingly. It lingers in our minds as he places first a chord of A minor (which is related to C♮) then F major (also related to C) then, three times, the chord of B major, which is totally foreign to C. By now the low C is scarcely audible; but it remains hanging in the air, an infinitely subtle irritant that prevents the three B major chords from giving us a sense of true finality.  At last, after one of the longest pauses in music, the tension is released with a soft touch on the bottom B. It is a marvellous exploitation of the benefits of a tonal system. Yet it was Liszt, more than any other figure in the nineteenth century, who was the first to foresee the possibility of that system breaking down. As an old man, he wrote some remarkably prophetic pieces, anticipating developments in harmony and musical thinking that were to take another thirty years to come to fruition. With the collapse of tonality, the backbone of sonata form was broken; we shall see in the next and last chapter a work which, like this one, strives to bring classical disciplines to revolutionary ideas; unlike this, it stands on the very brink of a period when the entire tonal system was on the point of disintegration.

Liszt never wrote another sonata, but plenty more sonatas were written, mostly for more than one instrument. In some way, composers seem to have felt that the possibilities of dialogue between two players would prove more productive. During the twentieth century, the piano itself has suffered a certain devaluation as a solo instrument;[1] increasingly, composers have come to regard it as a sophisticated member of the family of tuned percussion. Over the whole history of music, its period of supremacy was comparatively short; perhaps the reason for its decline was the extraordinary inventiveness and mastery that Liszt, Chopin, Schumann and Brahms showed in handling an instrument that provided their most personal and satisfying mode of expression.

[1] We are currently witnessing a similar decline in interest in the standard symphony orchestra; composers want to use combinations of sound that are less hallowed by tradition.

## CHAPTER XXXII

# ALBAN BERG
## Sonata Op. 1

Composed 1907–8. Published 1910, but twice revised, in 1920 and 1927. First performance on 24 April 1911, together with the String Quartet Op. 3. Originally planned as three-movement sonata, but Berg found difficulty in composing the other movements. On the advice of his teacher, Schoenberg, he decided to accept that the work was complete as it stood.

WAGNER'S EARLIEST LISTED WORK, written in 1829, was a piano sonata. He was to follow this with two more (one for four hands), but they are student works which reveal nothing of his true musical personality. It is tempting to say that the Sonata Op. I, by Alban Berg, is the sonata Wagner might have written had he lived a few more years, and, in his old age, wished to turn back to a medium he had neglected entirely since his student days in Leipzig. (He took lessons with the cantor of the very church at which J. S. Bach had been organist a century before.) The Berg sonata is enormously influenced by Wagner; but since Wagner and Liszt shared many of the same ideas about music, it seems logical to follow the Liszt sonata with a brief analysis of this work. Three quotations alone should be enough to establish a mutual relationship between the three composers. Here, first, is the main theme of Liszt's Faust symphony, unquestionably his finest orchestral work.

Ex. 190

Lento assai

This remarkable work was composed in 1854: in the same year, Wagner began his opera, Die Walküre, which, not surprisingly, took the best part of two years to compose. In the second act we find this theme:[1]

Ex.191

One of the most important motifs in the Berg sonata, as we shall see, is a very near relative to the last three notes of bars 1 and 2 of Ex. 190. The similarity of style is most easily identified in this passage from the start of the development; compare the left hand with Ex. 190.

Ex.192

Berg
Op.1

The Faust symphony theme, Ex. 190, has been often cited as evidence of the historical inevitability of Schoenberg's method of composing, treating all twelve notes of the chromatic scale as equal. It is perfectly true that bars 1 and 2 of Ex. 190 contain the twelve chromatic notes presented in such a way as to give no definition of key. No harmony made up of any of the three-note patterns is explicable in terms of classical tonality. Of course the textbooks have a name for them (augmented triads) but that does not explain their function, which is to be 'no-man's-land' chords. As has been suggested in the previous chapter, the whole tonal basis of music was beginning to disintegrate around the turn

[1] For other equally intriguing parallels between Liszt and Wagner, see Humphrey Searle: *The Music of Liszt*: Williams & Norgate, 1954.

of the century. If conventional harmonies were used, they were often combined in such a way as to disguise their true nature, as Stravinsky did in Petrushka when he combined the arpeggios of C major and F♯ major, both of them pillars of orthodoxy, but here presented in close juxtaposition.

Ex.193

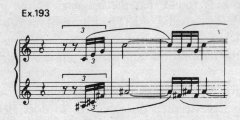

Even such violent oppositions of tonality as this had been anticipated by Liszt in such late piano pieces as Unstern, at whose climax we find chords of astonishing dissonance.

(Although this is a good deal more complex harmonically than the Stravinsky example above, it could be interpreted on rather similar lines if we think of it as a combination of chords of C major and E major, both of them knocked out of shape by the violence of the collision.)

I have no intention of embarking on a long explanation of the conclusions Schoenberg reached after fifteen years of intensive thought, conclusions that led to what might be termed an entirely new grammar and syntax for the expression of musical thought. All I have tried to do in this brief introduction is to establish the situation in which Berg and his contemporaries found themselves in the first decade of the twentieth century. To those who continue to bewail the loss of tonality in music I would just offer one reminder; every one of the great revolutionaries who changed the course of music during this era, Schoenberg, Stravinsky, Bartók, Debussy, Hindemith, started by writing tonal music that acknowledged their inheritance from the great Romantic era that preceded them. Each one came to the same conclusion, not as a result of attending a conference in Margate in 1910 where a resolution was passed saying, 'Let's all write beastly music that nobody will like', but because they found that the language of the post-Wagner era was no longer a valid one. The historical interest of the Berg sonata, which justifies its inclusion here, is that it is a perfect symbol of the state of flux into which music was drifting at the time.

Just as Liszt had to impose severe disciplines on a work that could easily have seemed disorganized, so does Berg fall back on classical procedures. The sonata clearly has an Exposition (repeated in the tradition established so long before), a Development, and a Recapitulation. Instead of two subjects, it has three, which in the original edition he obligingly labelled with their own tempi—tempo I, tempo II, and tempo III. These labels were subsequently dropped, since Berg must have realized the essential contradiction of identifying a theme by its tempo when the tempo itself was subject to continuous change. Admittedly he begins with the instruction 'Mäßig bewegt', or Allegro Moderato in more conventional terms; but as we can see in this next example, there are only two beats before the speed begins to change.

Ex.194

It is interesting to see that although Berg gives the sonata a key-signature of B minor, he seems to have so little faith in the power of tonality that he plasters the score with gratuitous accidentals,[1] in case the performer should be in doubt as to his intentions. Even in the brief extract shown here, there are fourteen accidentals that are not strictly necessary, since they are already covered by the key-signature. It is obvious from this that although Berg acknowledges tonality, he isn't really *thinking* tonally. As to the instruction '*a tempo*' in the fourth full bar, a cynic might be tempted to ask, '*a* what *tempo*?', since so far all we have had has been an accelerando and a ritardando.

This continual fluctuation of speed continues through the next phrase which involves two more bars of getting quicker followed by a long drawn-out retardation, which in turn is replaced by a new tempo, faster than the opening one. Now contrasts of tempo are nothing new; we find them brilliantly exploited in late Beethoven, and in the Liszt sonata we saw him presenting three themes at three different speeds on the very first page. The continuous *variation* of tempo that we find in the Berg sonata is something very different; it injects a feverish quality into the music. One feels that emotion is being conveyed at a very 'physical' level, no longer subject to the controls which are still to be observed in the music of Beethoven, Mozart or Bach, even when they are at their most expressive. The influence of 'Tristan' is very powerful, not only in terms of musical texture, but also in musical purpose— the expression of sensuousness and eroticism in music.

The stage is set for a conflict, then, between the expressive force of the music and the essentially intellectual mould into which the youthful[2] composer has chosen to pour his ideas, rather as if a man had agreed to play three simultaneous games of chess at a championship level while making passionate love to his mistress. Time and again in this sonata one feels that the emotion is overtaxing the structure; the indication of *ffff* is qualified a

---

[1] Accidentals are the signs for natural, sharp, or flat: ♮, ♯, ♭; also double sharp or double flat: 𝄪, ♭♭.

[2] In his early twenties.

bar later by the reservation 'always expressive'. During the course of eight consecutive bars near the end, we find these instructions to the player:

> *ff*. Broader. Quickening again. Broader. Quickening again.
> *fff*. Expressive. Very expressive. Getting quieter and slower.
> Continually expressive. (Getting quieter and slower.)

together with fifteen symbols of ⸏ and ⸎, and sixteen notes specifically marked with accents.

Opposed to this extreme outpouring of emotion is the notable discipline of the structure itself. The music may seem to be built on very shifting ground from the point of view of tonality, but there is hardly a note that cannot be regarded as relevant to one or other of the three subjects. Even the subjects themselves are subtly related. We have already seen the first subject in Ex. 194. A subsidiary version appears as early as the eleventh bar, by which time we have already experienced a substantial climax followed by a dying fall that takes us down to *pp*. It is what I have sometimes called 'a little death', and from it, Berg lifts us up once more.

Ex.195

The essential orchestral and contrapuntal nature of Berg's thought is clearly revealed by the extreme care that has gone into the notation. The left hand chords in bars 3 and 4 are not thought of as chords at all; having devised a canon between the two hands, he continues to think in terms of interweaving lines of melody whose identity must be preserved. This explains the eccentric notation of what a pianist would think of as a perfectly ordinary fifth in the fourth bar.[1]

The rising triplet marked  is enormously important, sprouting persistently through the texture like a fast-growing plant. Berg soon reveals its relationship to the first subject when he replaces the opening three notes of Ex. 194

with this substitute from Ex. 195.

Ingenuities of construction are so frequent that it would be unnecessarily arduous to point them all out; their purpose is to impose unity as much as to develop, and this they succeed in doing admirably. A typical example is the way that Berg arrives at his third subject. A characteristic climax has flared up, sparked off by what seems to be little more than a romantic gesture of the head-tossing kind.

Ex.196

[1] Compare Beethoven, Op. 110, Ex. 124.

(Notice again that there is a canon between the two hands.)

This agitated pattern continues to erupt from time to time in a slightly compressed form:

Ex.196a

gradually dying down until it emerges in a transformation Liszt himself would have been proud to have devised.

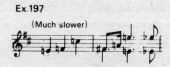

Ex.197

(Much slower)

A quick glance at the second bar will show how easy it is for Berg to find his way back from this theme to the opening subject (Ex. 194).

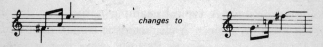

*changes to*

The second subject, which I have so far only mentioned, is also linked to the first, since both themes begin with the same rhythm ♩♪♪. Where one rises, the other falls.

Ex.198

(Slower than Tempo I)

Here, again, we have the contradiction of music of extreme sensuousness wearing academic dress; the fragment 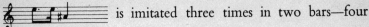 is imitated three times in two bars—four

times, if we include the augmented version 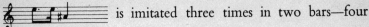.

Although the harmonic texture is almost too rich, Berg is continuing to 'think' entirely in counterpoint; the three-fold repetition of the ♮ symbol on the note A in bar 2 is clear evidence that in his mind, the note is played by a different 'instrument' each time.

The brevity of this sonata, a mere eleven pages, is amply compensated for by the concentration of the material, and the tremendous intensity of emotion. The ending is hauntingly beautiful, a long-drawn-out cadence, intellectually strengthened by the bass (which is an inversion of Ex. 197), while at the same time conveying a sense of exhaustion that is quite proper in a work that has had more than its share of emotional ups-and-downs.

Ex.199

I have often maintained that the history of music shows composers continually having to find new ways of saying things that have already been said by their predecessors. It is obvious that the simple, direct ways are discovered first; therefore, one can argue with some cogency that musical evolution has enforced an ever-growing complexity upon the creative artist. If a path is well-trodden, it is simply because it is the easiest route to take. I am not in any way belittling Berg's achievement when I say that this dying cadence, in which one can discern the twilight of Romanticism, has been expressed before in infinitely simpler

terms by Chopin. Tears are tears, whatever dress the man who
sheds them may wear.

Ex. 200

# INDEXES

# INDEX: PART ONE

# INDEX: PART TWO

# INDEX: PART THREE

Other Pan books that may interest you
are listed on the following pages

## Leslie Ayre
## The Gilbert and Sullivan Companion £1.50

'The complete reference-book for the lover of these immortal operas . . . it will heighten the pleasure, enhance the magic of Gilbert and Sullivan' RT HON HAROLD WILSON, EVENING STANDARD

'Brilliant . . . the story of the explosive partnership, full text of the main songs and ensembles from each of the operas and biographical details of artists who have played leading roles. This Companion should last as long as the operas, of that there is no doubt' MANCHESTER EVENING NEWS

'Numerous quotations and anecdotes make fascinating reading' AMATEUR STAGE

'Monumental . . . a book which sparkles from beginning to end with the lilt of the operas themselves—to be read through with uninterrupted delight and then browsed over for years to come' THE EVENING NEWS

'Bubbles with high-spirited erudition' SUNDAY TELEGRAPH

## Arthur Jacobs and Stanley Sadie
## The Pan Book of Opera £1.25

'Opera is a complex, strange and ever-fascinating art'
*the authors in their Introduction*

This ideal reference book – by two well-known music critics – describes in detail 66 operas by 31 composers, ranging from Purcell to Britten, and mentions many other operas and composers. There is a chapter on early opera and one on the opera today; many musical examples are given and there is an up-to-date Bibliography.

'A potent weapon in the battle for the establishment of opera as an integral part of our musical life' COMPOSER

## Charles Osborne
## The Complete Operas Of Verdi £1.50

From *La traviata* to the vanished *Rocester*, this penetrating and sensitive guide takes us through all of Verdi's operas, introducing them through plot, music and general characteristics and linking them with a fascinating account of his life at the time of composition.

'Mr Osborne gives a true picture of an exceptionally rich nature and of an art which, like Shakespeare's, transcends all petty cavil' GUARDIAN

'An extremely thorough and valuable guide' WORLD OF MUSIC

Richard Capell
**Schubert's Songs** 95p

The music of over six hundred songs is discussed chronologically, with brilliant insight into the evolution of Schubert's genius and power of inventing rhythms, harmony and melody perfectly fitted to the text.

'Everyone will enjoy its splendid treatment of all the great songs, its plea for the many yet practically unknown gems . . . a book that must be on every musician's bookshelf' MUSICAL OPINION

'Whether the reader be singer, accompanist, student or listener, he will find in this wonderful commentary so much of enduring value that it will bid fair to rank in his affections with the songs themselves' MUSIC AND LETTERS

Gervase Hughes
**Fifty Famous Composers** 75p

'It is quite clear that these accounts of composers . . . have been based not only on a reading of the authorities, but also on a first hand acquaintance with the music' THE TIMES LITERARY SUPPLEMENT

'As a cavalcade of musical biographies it is the best of its kind I have ever read' THE MUSIC TEACHER

'The book is admirably cross-referenced, and excellent in its provision of historical and topographical background' MUSIC AND LETTERS

There is much to provoke thought and stimulate interest' MANCHESTER EVENING NEWS